T5-DGW-038

Walking the High-Tech High Wire

Walking the High-Tech High Wire

The Technical Entrepreneur's Guide to Running a Successful Enterprise

David Adamson

McGraw-Hill, Inc.

New York   San Francisco   Washington, D.C.   Auckland   Bogotá
Caracas   Lisbon   London   Madrid   Mexico City   Milan
Montreal   New Delhi   San Juan   Singapore
Sydney   Tokyo   Toronto

HD
62.37
A 33
1994

Library of Congress Cataloging-in-Publication Data

Adamson, David.
   Walking the high-tech high wire : the technical entrepreneur's
guide to running a successful enterprise / David Adamson.
       p.   cm.
   Includes bibliographical references and index.
   ISBN 0-07-000468-4 :
   1. High technology industries—Management.   2. New business
enterprises—Management.   3. Success in business.   I. Title.
HD62.37.A33 1994
620'.0068—dc20   93-24208
                                                                        CIP

1 2 3 4 5 6 7 8 9 0   DOC/DOC   9 9 8 7 6 5 4 3

ISBN 0-07-000468-4

*The sponsoring editor for this book was Caroline Carney, the editing supervi-
sor was Jane Palmieri, and the production supervisor was Donald Schmidt. It
was set in Palatino by McGraw-Hill's Professional Book Group composition
unit.*

Printed and bound by R. R. Donnelley & Sons Company.

This book is printed on recycled, acid-free paper
containing a minimum of 50% recycled de-inked fiber.

*This book is gratefully dedicated to
Col. Kenneth E. Adamson, my father,
and in memory of
Catherine G. Adamson, my mother.*

Contents

Preface

I started writing the notes that evolved into this book in 1990, a few years after I cofounded a small high-tech company. The notes were just a means for me to think through the issues confronting our business. At the time, although we had managed to struggle through the early start-up stage and achieve some initial success, quite abruptly sales started to level off, then decline. With considerable pain and effort, we were able to turn things around and restore modest growth. However, that unexpected change of fortune got me to thinking about the forces, real and imagined, that drive high-tech businesses and make them such a challenge to successfully manage. As the notes piled, it occurred to me that what I discovered might be useful to others, and the notes began to grow into a book. A few years later, I completed the first draft.

The publication of *Walking the High-Tech High Wire* coincides with a time of unprecedented opportunity and growth for small high-tech companies. This will become increasingly obvious as the following factors in the business environment align themselves in favor of small high-tech firms:

1. The growth of high technology is a government priority. Even the President talks about it. "High tech" is synonymous with high-paying jobs and international competitiveness. Trying to give substance to good intentions, the government is taking strides toward the commercialization of advanced technologies, revising tax codes to encourage private-sector investment in high-risk technology ven-

tures, and accelerating the flow of information through the govern-
ment-university-business complex.

2. Right now, the United States has hidden assets, worth more than all
   the gold in Ft. Knox, residing in a priceless inventory of promising
   technologies. These are stockpiled inside a massive public and private R&D infrastructure. All technologies must await just the right
   time for the alchemy of an entrepreneurial culture and free-market
   economy to transform it into economic wealth. For personal computer technology, the right time was in the 1980s. For many other
   new and exciting technologies, the time is now.

3. With the advent of the "virtual corporation" and "outsourcing," as
   large businesses "devertically" integrate themselves to restore profitability and compete globally, they will increasingly rely on their
   smaller brethren for a supply of products and ideas. This trend will
   enhance the prominent role of small, high-tech companies as economic catalysts which connect ideas to a marketplace in much the
   same way that hemoglobin carries life-sustaining oxygen to the rest
   of the body.

4. Finally, and most important, a tremendous number of first-rate scientists, engineers, and technicians are being laid off, literally thrown
   onto the streets to tend for themselves, due to the end of the cold war
   and corporate downsizing. In the long run, this transition, though
   difficult and disruptive for those caught in the middle, will be a boon
   to the U.S. economy. It is as if a million flower seeds are being
   thrown into an open field. As in any natural system, some number
   will perish, that is, quit their professions and become insurance
   salespeople or restauranteurs in the new service economy. Others
   will survive by finding another large company in which to seek
   refuge, if, indeed, there is such a thing as safety anymore. And many,
   by necessity if initially not desire, will become entrepreneurs. For
   them, the opportunities will be almost limitless. By applying their
   ingenuity and technical knowledge, they will unleash an unprecedented number of innovations to everyday life and, in the process,
   generate personal and national wealth as well as more jobs.

Does this bright forecast mean things will get easier for small high-
tech companies? Not necessarily. Business will also get more competitive, from both domestic competitors and new foreign ones going after
the same markets. Success never comes without struggle and some
battle scars. Those who succeed will be lean and mean and mobile.
Their profits will be commensurate with their ability to balance high
risks and scant resources. The relationship of the two never change,

and survival and growth, in spite of these challenges, is the real theme of this book. It's written for those who are already on the high-tech high wire or soon to take the first step as well as those who need to understand more about the chaotic dynamics of high-tech business.

Acknowledgments

I was fortunate, indeed, the day that I sent the manuscript to McGraw-Hill's Professional Book Group on the off-chance that because the company was the leading publisher of technical books, it might also have an interest in technical business. I owe a hugh debt of gratitude to Caroline Carney, my editor at McGraw-Hill, who had faith in *Walking the High-Tech High Wire* and whose expert guidance made it a much better book, from the title to the last chapter, than the first time she saw it.

In addition, my special thanks to:

- Joyce Bowser, Maury Deines, Ed Hoey, and Bear Gebhardt, all of whom directly contributed valuable ideas and insights on the structure and content of this book
- George Krausse and my other colleagues at Directed Energy, Inc., with whom I share the day-to-day experience of competing in high technology
- Cynda, my wife, for her encouragement and patience during my effort to articulate what follows

To my readers, I hope this book helps you get across. See you up there.

David Adamson

1
Competing in High Technology

This book is an insider's view of how to increase the odds for survival and growth in small high-technology companies. I wrote it because I could have used it six years ago when we started a high-tech company, but no book quite like this was to be found in any library or bookstore. If it had been available then, perhaps we would have been able to allocate more of our meager resources, much sooner, toward the problems of growth rather than those of survival.

As it was, sometimes due to our own errors of judgment, we were subjected to our share of trial by fire, and more than once we had to rise like a phoenix from the ashes. Needless to say, the technical problems, marketing failures, and cash crises we experienced were not milestones set forth in the original business plan. To the contrary, the sales growth and profitability forecast in our pro formas followed a smooth, exponential function like an F-15 fighter taking off. Reality turned out to be less smooth and exponential. In fact, our month-to-month sales, when recorded in a simple line graph, more closely resembled the EKG of a heart in morbid fibrillation.

The philosopher Nietzsche said, that which does not destroy us makes us stronger. If this is true, then we are probably much stronger. But character building was not what we had in mind in the summer of 1987 when we founded a company called Directed Energy, Inc. (DEI), to design and market the fastest high-power semiconductor devices in the world. At the time, the idea appeared to be a sure-fire, fast-growth business opportunity. However, growth did not come that easily. It took us six years to scratch and claw to $1 million in annual sales, and, in the process, our business focus changed markedly. Looking back with the wisdom of hindsight, this should have come as no surprise. As will be evident in the chapters that follow, from inception weaknesses in our business plan, management team, and capital structure precluded fast growth. A more objective and knowledgeable outsider would have rated our prospects for survival, much less growth, as marginal. But we sported the full complement of obligatory virtues necessary to be entrepreneurs. Any niggling self-doubts we had when we started were dwarfed by our optimism, ambition, determination, enthusiasm, and, it deserves mention, just plain naiveté. These qualities helped and hurt us at the same time.

High-Technology Industries

High technology, as used here, broadly encompasses computers and software; semiconductors; aerospace; lasers and electro-optics; acoustics; biotechnology; pharmaceuticals; test and measurement; communications; automation and robotics; materials science; and emerging environmental technologies such as bioremediation and renewable energy.

Computers and semiconductors have experienced such meteoric growth, and now have so much glitz and wealth associated with them, that they really belong in a category all their own. Some dilettantes in other technologies would argue that computer products do not rate the "high-tech" designation anymore because they can be built at *maquiladoras* in Mexico, but these people are just envious. Isaac Asimov said that the birth of microelectronics was the most important invention since humanity emerged as a life form. Perhaps that is a slight exaggeration, but certainly the birth of the computer industry will mark the seminal industrial event of the century. In the popular mind, computers *are* high technology. Most of the other promising technologies vying to contribute to the quality of human life are as obscure and ignored by the general public as computers are recognized and revered. As a result, when your neighbor asks what you do for a living and you answer, "I work for a small high-tech company," he will likely respond, "Ah, so you're in computers." Even if you are not, you are inclined to nod in the affirmative rather than try to explain what you really do.

In the emerging global economy, the prospects for high technology are bright because all advanced economies are, to some degree, dependent on it. A high-technology business exemplifies the "high-value enterprise" described by Robert Reich in his provocative book *The Work of Nations:*

In the high-value enterprise, profits derive not from scale and volume but from continuous discovery of new linkages between solutions and needs. The distinction that used to be drawn between "goods" and "services" is meaningless, because so much of the value provided by the successful enterprise—in fact, the only value that cannot easily be replicated worldwide—entails services; the specialized research, engineering, and design services necessary to solve problems; the specialized sales, marketing, and consulting services necessary to identify problems; and the specialized strategic, financial, and management services for brokering the first two.[1]

It is to these kinds of companies that power and wealth will flow in the post–Cold War world. Certainly many well-known high-tech companies—Microsoft, Intel, Motorola, Texas Instruments, Merck, Thermo Electron, and Novell, to name a few—support Reich's contention.

Small High-Tech Companies

Although small high-tech companies appear to fit Reich's definition as well and should, therefore, anticipate an auspicious future, they are also distinctly different from larger high-tech enterprises, so much so that their fortunes are not as certain.

The profile of a typical small high-tech company includes some combination of these traits:

- It was founded by a scientist, engineer, or technician.
- It has been in existence less than 10 years.
- It is undercapitalized.
- It employs fewer than 50 people.
- It has sales less than $5 million per year.
- Its competitive advantage is a technical one such as improved performance rather than a nontechnical one such as such as manufacturing know-how or efficient distribution.
- It lacks in-house expertise in one or more business management functions (e.g., finance, sales, operations)
- Its customers are original equipment manufacturers (OEMs) or research laboratories, rarely consumers.
- It offers a high value-added product or service.

Small high-tech companies number in the tens of thousands. They perform several critical functions in our economy: They are a wellspring of industrial innovation and, hence, one of the best hopes for future industrial competitiveness; a committed ally in the nation's defense; and, most important, a source of gainful employment for the hundreds of thousands of citizens who work for them, and, it goes without saying, a valuable source of revenues for the communities in which they live. Though most small high-tech companies are unknown to the mainstream public, their innovations materially contribute to every facet of industry, medicine, commerce, science, defense, and education. Yet despite their important economic function, by their very nature, not only do they exist in obscurity, but they must, of necessity, constantly struggle to exist at all.

The more Darwinian (and always safely tenured) economists in academia say companies like this do not deserve to exist anyway, that it's better they fail because that's how the economy, in compliance with natural law, winnows out the weaklings and allocates resources to the strong (these economists forget that dinosaurs were strong, too). The vacuity of this view is that it overlooks the fact that all large enterprises start as smaller, weaker ones. Certainly without small companies, human life would be more nasty, brutish, and short. It is well known that 50 percent of the most significant innovations of this century originated in small companies.

But for a small company several significant obstacles loom on the walk across the high-tech high wire. One is that the business environment for high technology is inherently volatile and unpredictable for reasons described in the next chapter. The proliferation of a significant technology is a very inefficient and glacially slow process. Most technologies that make life better take a long time to find their way from the research laboratories to their ultimate markets. The role of linking a new technology to its practical and economic applications usually falls to pioneering, small companies. Once the technology is in widespread use, the small companies either metamorphose into larger entities or, as is more often the case, simply vanish.

Another obstacle to overcome is that high-tech companies tend to be undercapitalized. MIT Professor Edward Roberts published an informative study of high-technology businesses entitled *Entrepreneurs in High Technology*. He discovered that almost half of them start up on less than $10,000 and nearly 80 percent with under $50,000, modest sums indeed with which to capitalize any business.[2] Any high technology in its early stages is costly. The product development requires long periods of time, exotic or expensive materials, and specialized, high-priced human knowledge. Yet, expensive as it is, the product development may be the least costly stage in the company's quest for viability.

The largest cost, which can be many times the cost of the technology development, can be finding a customer to adopt your technology and your company as its supplier. Once a product exists, customers are expensive to find because of the distance that must be travelled to contact them or the amount of advertising media required to attract them. Assuming the customer's interest can be piqued, rounds of evaluation and qualification follow, first of your technology by the customer's technical staff, then of the company's financial strength, ability to deliver, and QA. The time elapsed in overcoming the status quo, bureaucracy, and competing technologies, not to mention intermittent economic perturbations, combine to have profound effects on the ebb and flow of money. Usually the money ebbs out long before it flows in. Worse, it ebbs out faster and in greater volume than it flows in.

Undercapitalization is a debilitating handicap for any business, and it defies any quick and easy cure. The term *undercapitalized* has numerous meanings and manifestations, but its basic import is that a company lacks the capital resources required to get where it is trying to go. The timeless truism in business is that it takes money to make money. Unfortunately, money for high-technology ventures has not been that abundant since the U.S. government destroyed the tax incentives to compensate for the high risk of investing in small companies when it reformed the tax code in 1986, ending favorable tax treatment for R&D and capital gains. Hopefully the Clinton administration will usher in a new era of tax policy to reverse this trend.

In the meantime, a small high-tech company finds itself with an arduous and unenviable task: to make money with little or no money. The undercapitalized company is like a rocket trying make it into orbit with half the fuel it really needs to overcome gravity. The problem is that the rocket has already been launched, so its choices are to find a way to add fuel, to make the fuel go further than expected, or to plummet back to earth. To say that the situation calls for above-average courage and ingenuity is understatement. Undercapitalization places a company at extreme risk because there is absolutely no margin for error. It also places a tremendous emotional strain on the people who work there.

If a company is undercapitalized, there is probably a good reason for it. The company is unable to attract money in the form of investment or as profit because something is missing in the business equation—a certain management skill, a product at the right price, a market with real demand. The bitter paradox is that often the equation could be completed with a single, critical input of money, often a relatively small sum as investments go.

In the final analysis, though, most small high-tech companies end up bootstrapping, that is, relying on their own financial resources, skills, and savvy, undeveloped and limited as these may be, to create an ongoing enterprise. In short, these companies make it on their own with survival being their first and foremost priority, though growth and prosperity is their real goal. To bootstrap successfully, you need to overcome any infatuation with fast growth, a syndrome that afflicts U.S. business in general and plagues high technology in particular. Fast growth blurs the thin line between positive entrepreneurial vision and destructive delusions of grandeur, the latter being deadly for a financially weak company.

Dynamics, Financial Results, Customers: Three Important Themes

Three related themes recur throughout this book. The first is that managers of small high-tech companies must be aware of the special dynamics of high-technology businesses that make them difficult to grow. High tech is glamorous, but that does not make it profitable. Contrary to popular notions, success for most high-tech companies is a long, uphill struggle. Technology businesses are complex and risk-laden even in the best of circumstances. Many high-tech companies aspire to become manufacturers but never get beyond being specialized job shops or technology boutiques. Their founders would make more money working for the *Fortune* 500 companies they abhor. But, alas, money is not what motivates them. They enjoy their work, though, too often, the business is a pretense for them to be able to engage in their hobby for a living. That works fine as long as the hobbyist is lined up opposite another hobbyist. However, if serious business competitors appear, and they always do where there is a real business opportunity, the hobbyist has no chance.

A second theme is that a small company can survive and grow only when it places the appropriate focus on financial results. When a company fails, it fails financially, a point that receives repeated emphasis throughout the pages that follow because it is so often overlooked in the pursuit of technical leadership, market share, and public image. Managers with technical backgrounds, the ones who usually found high-tech companies, can, ironically, predispose their companies to failure. The brilliant technologist and brilliant businessperson are rarely the same person. By their nature, technologists are often intrigued with technology for its own sake, and they do not always respect that the success of a business is measured by cash flow and ROI. This is a perennial problem in high-technology businesses. Thomas Edison, the consummate U.S. technologist, had to be rescued by J. P. Morgan, the financier, because Edison failed to manage the complexities of his business.[3] Therefore, the inevitable strong technology pull in a high-tech company must be counterbalanced by a management team that remains obsessed by business performance.

The third theme is the critical need to identify and acquire customers in markets that will put the company on a growth trajectory which can be sustained within its financial limitations. This may cause priorities, or even the entire direction of the company, to change. However, acquiring these customers may enable the company to finance most of its growth with profits. If not, the company at least will establish a financial track record which elicits the cooperation and interest of the banking or investment community.

Additional Resources

A multitude of thoughtful books on business topics hits the stores each year on every major functional area of business: finance, marketing, operations, and management. However, most of them pertain to large enterprises. Too often the information contained in them is no more germane to the problems of a struggling small company than the mechanistic laws of Newtonian physics are to the unpredictable behavior of subatomic particles. These books assume a plentiful supply of the very resources that are painfully lacking in a small company—time, money, and skilled management. Consequently, the books' broad, sweeping generalities display a distinct lack of authenticity, specificity, and applicability, thus rendering them of limited usefulness.

At the same time, however, many excellent texts and how-to books have messages that are pertinent to the small high-tech company. In fact, throughout this book are references to other books which I have found very helpful. More and more appear each month as industrial and scientific competitiveness become the catchwords of the day. Usually these books treat a topic in greater detail and with more expertise than I could ever pretend to possess. I urge you to find the time to read them because they contain invaluable information. When you are undercapitalized and your management team is incomplete, you are in dire need of advice. Although a book is no substitute for an on-site expert, it is the next best thing. Rarely can you afford consultants. Your circumstances dictate that you leverage every dollar. Most of the books to which I refer can be found in your local library. If not there, they are available in a bookstore. The modest cost of one good piece of advice can give you a percentage return on your investment far surpassing any you may ever see from your technology.

Do not overlook worthwhile periodicals such as the *Harvard Business Review,* MIT's *Sloan Management Review,* and *Inc.* The academic journals always have some gems of wisdom that can be extrapolated into the small business environment. *Inc.* continues to address the problems of small businesses more directly and expertly than any other publication on the market.

Always keep in mind that your business is the beneficiary or victim of your decisions. Exercise your right to be the final judge of the utility of what you read, regardless of who wrote it. Maintain a dose of healthy skepticism. Search, cull, compare, criticize, ponder, talk to everybody you can, then draw your own conclusions.

For every hard and fast rule I cite here, there are one or more exceptions. I make no apologies that as this book freely dispenses advice and dogmatically promulgates certain views, it is riddled with paradoxes, enigmas, unanswered questions, ambiguities, contradictions, and Catch-22s. Some of the advice, particularly on marketing, will seem unorthodox and contrary to conventional business wisdom. It is. That is because many aspects of management in a small high-tech company are unique. Sometimes you do get a profound sense of vertigo, and, indeed, up is down. You might zig when conventional business wisdom tells you to zag. You must devise your own means by which to navigate and trust your own judgment. You have no other choice.

Included in italics in selected chapters are anecdotes collected from the actual experiences of Directed Energy, Inc. These anecdotes offer illuminating examples, ironic juxtapositions, and counterpoints to what is presented in the text. Only the names have been changed to protect the innocent. You may find many of the anecdotes familiar. Treat them as real-life case studies, the empirical data which have taught us everything we have learned thus far. I am confident that the lessons are not over yet, nor will they soon be forgotten.

The poet Thomas Grey wrote these beautiful lines in "The Elegy Written in a Country Churchyard":

Pure many a gem of fullest ray serene

The dark unfathomed caves of oceans bear.

Pure many a flower is born to blush unseen

And waste its sweetness on the desert air.

This poignant quatrain describes the fates of many beautiful objects which will never be discovered and thus never be appreciated or enjoyed. The lines describe the fate of many high-technology companies as well. Hopefully yours will not be one of them. The world needs your great ideas.

2
Uncovering the 10 Technology Traps

High technology does not guarantee profitability. Indeed, many high technology industries are much less profitable than some low-technology industries due to their unfavorable structures.[1]

MICHAEL PORTER

The "unfavorable structures" to which Michael Porter refers are an academic euphemism for deadly traps that make the road to economic success for a high-tech company a difficult and perilous one. These traps afflict companies of all sizes but have even more pronounced effects on a small company because it lacks many of the resources necessary to overcome or escape them. In fact a small company is very likely a small company because it is a victim of one or more of these traps, although not aware of it.

Working in a high-technology business has many advantages. It is intellectually stimulating. In more enlightened companies, managers tend to enjoy a high degree of responsibility, flexibility, and participation in decision making. Such work can even be glamorous if you are in a technology the media and investment communities are excited about at a particular time. Like everyone else, investors are susceptible to fads, whether they be designer blue jeans or biotechnology or Star Wars. But make no mistake about it, there are probably faster ways to get rich. Only a handful of high-technology entrepreneurs become wealthy from their endeavors. The vast majority do not. Worse, because they try to emulate inappropriate business models, they place their middle-class existence at risk.

High technology was the 1980s' analog of the California Gold Rush of the 1800s. The rags-to-riches stories of the likes of Steve Wozniak and Steve Jobs (Apple), Bill Gates (Microsoft), Robert Noyce (Intel), Mitch Kapor (Lotus), and the venture capitalists who bankrolled them are the stuff of legend—inspiring, exciting, and incredible. They are also very atypical. As David Birch, an MIT expert in small business economics, warned: "Don't be fooled by the superstar success stories. Think, instead, about how many times you've heard the same ones (Apple Computer, Compaq Computer, Federal Express). There's a reason for this—there aren't that many stories to go around, and a few get retold often."[2]

The fortunes that were made in the 1980s in microprocessors, computers, and software were staggering. However, do not be deluded by the relatively short time span that these industries showed their phenomenal growth. As Peter Drucker has pointed out, the computer industry began in the late 1940s, but it was not until the 1980s, 30 years later, that the industry as a whole reached a breakeven point.[3]

In fact, most high-technology companies do not spin off large profits in short periods, if ever. Much more typical of high-technology business is the laser industry. Over 30 years have passed since Theodore Maiman, a researcher at Hughes Aircraft Company, used a solid ruby crystal to produce the first coherent laser light. Since then, the worldwide laser market has grown to around $1 billion in sales, which may sound impressive until you realize that McDonald's sold almost $7 billion worth of hamburgers in 1992 with *profits* of nearly $1 billion. This stark contrast is made not to belittle a fledgling industry but to establish a realistic perspective on technology as a business vis-à-vis other businesses. Lasers are not alone. Sales in biotechnology zoomed to almost $6 billion in 1992, yet the industry continues to invest at least that much annually in R&D!

The reasons that the laser and biotechnology industries, like so many other high-tech industries, have not reached their expectations is not that they lack intelligent technologists, or capable business managers, or, for that matter, capital. The dynamics are more complex than that and can be attributed to the effects of the 10 technology traps.

Trap 1: The Deadly
Paradigm Wars

Technology companies are engaged in paradigm wars. By their very nature, wars are wasteful and destructive.

In the 1960s, Thomas Kuhn, an obscure professor of the history of science, wrote a modest volume entitled *The Structure of Scientific Revolutions,* whose subject was how scientific "knowledge" evolves. The development of physics from Ptolemy to Copernicus to Galileo to Newton to Einstein was one of his many examples.

The book had an unexpected, far-reaching impact on numerous disciplines, including business, because Kuhn explained how, at any point in time, there is a prevailing view of things that determines what is accepted as truth. The paradigm has only a partial basis in rational science, whereas the other part is "an apparently arbitrary element, compounded of personal and historical accident" that is "always a formative ingredient of the beliefs espoused by a given scientific community at a given time."[4] Substitute the word *market* for *scientific community* and you can understand why Kuhn is also germane to business.

A new paradigm is born when the prevailing paradigm cannot explain a certain phenomenon and a new one is offered that explains it better, though not necessarily completely. Typically the founding of a new paradigm is attributed to a single individual, but, as Kuhn notes, a paradigm change is "intrinsically a revolutionary process that is seldom completed by a single man and never overnight."[5] As Galileo found out the hard way, new paradigms receive strong resistance from "the specialists on whose area of special competence they impinge," because the new paradigm "implies a change in the rules governing the prior practice" and "reflects on much scientific work they have already successfully completed." Reflects negatively, we can assume. If the new paradigm can muster enough credibility to overcome the skepticism, a new paradigm is established.

The thoughts of the individual founder are recorded for posterity and codified into a body of knowledge. When the founder passes from the scene, what might be termed "normal puzzle solvers" follow. These people basically repeat the fundamental work of the innovator over and over again, making small iterative improvements to, not significant demarcations from, the conventional paradigm by which manner it becomes a credible, established discipline.

Kuhn's thesis applies to almost every human endeavor (although he would surely deny he intended such universality), and the paradigm wars he describes prevail in industry as well. In the 1940s the economist Joseph Schumpeter, a seminal thinker on capitalism and entrepreneurship, coined the oxymoron "creative destruction" to describe the chaotic process of industrial change.

Paradigms make or break technologies and the companies that champion them. The prevailing paradigm creates an organized resistance to change. Kuhn notes that the ongoing refinement of the accepted paradigm leads to "professionalization" among the normal puzzle solvers and "an immense restriction of the scientist's vision and to a considerable resistance to paradigm change."[6] Applying this to business, the normal puzzle solvers, often at a middle-level management and higher inside large companies, defend the prevailing paradigm either through direct hostility or lethargy. This should come as no surprise, because their power, influence, and incomes are derived from their knowledge of, and loyalty to, the prevailing paradigm.

Industrial history is the history of paradigm wars won and lost. Thomas Edison, advocating direct current for power transmission, lost the broad paradigm conflict to George Westinghouse, who advocated alternating current. In another paradigm conflict in electronics, germanium, a rare metallic element, defeated vacuum tubes. Within industries, smaller paradigm conflicts are constant. Silicon replaced germanium. Now silicon is under attack from gallium arsenide, which appears to move electrons more efficiently. On the horizon lurks another paradigm war when photon-based optic devices exist that can replace electron-based devices like transistors; beyond those waits superconductivity.

You must understand where your company fits in the paradigm wars. You are fighting whether you know it or not. Your company is a rebel army. The only reason you exist is to promote a new way of doing things: a new process, technique, form factor, material, architecture. If you offered nothing new, you would not exist. Larger companies do the old things.

Paradigm wars cost time and money, the most limited resources in a small high-tech company. It takes money to develop the product, educate and persuade potential buyers, and gear up for production. The more entrenched is the prevailing paradigm, the more time and money it will take to defeat it. Frequently fighting the paradigm war will cost more in marketing expenditures than developing the technology itself. The companies who espouse the prevailing paradigm will always be bigger and better financed. For them, too, the stakes are high: careers, profitability, and image. A small company with a product that will change an industry should anticipate a protracted and expensive struggle. The cost will be directly proportional to the size of the opportunity.

The good news is that a competitor may be too entrenched in the old paradigm to change. The bad news is that so may be potential customers. Many times the paradigm has been institutionalized, in which case suppliers and customers collaborate to protect the old paradigm as an industry standard.

The Six-Legged Monster

Our power transistor, the DE-Series MOSFET, had advantages over conventional devices in almost every parameter. It was smaller, lighter, faster, and provided improved thermal and mechanical performance. Physically, it was different from any power transistor package most design engineers had ever seen.

The traditional transistor that our device was designed to replace was originally designed in the 1950s to mimic the octal pin pattern of a tube. The overriding design criterion used when this device was engineered was that it have the same form and fit factor as the tube it replaced. No consideration was given to the electrical performance and only marginal attention to thermal performance. But this became the prevailing paradigm.

In the first days after our product was introduced, a typical reaction was, "That's a great device. Why don't you put it in a TO-3 package?" That was a difficult question to answer because our device was designed to replace the TO-3 package. The paradigm was so strong that they did not even realize that, and when they did, their interest waned. Once in a while, there was outright hostility.

We made a sobering realization: We had a nonstandard part in a standardized industry. This was nested in larger issues of how to dual-source, the cost to the customer to lay out new boards, and our small size. Being nonstandard was one strike against our device. The other was price, the one they fell back on the most to shun it because it was easier to cite economic reasons than scientific ones.

Paradigm conflicts do not always express themselves as resistance to change from Luddite managers inside stodgy, big companies. The conflicts also arise from end users. Sectors of agribusiness eagerly anticipated the approval of bovine somatotropin (BST), a hormone that increases milk production in cows by 20 percent. But the hormone has been rejected by its potential beneficiaries. Consumers worry it will cause mutations in children. Animal-rights activists think the cows are being abused. Farmers worry the increased production will disrupt the market equilibrium and send numerous farmers to bankruptcy. BST is the product of an industry which has expended $1 billion since 1980 to support over 5000 researchers. Thus far this effort has produced no net return on investment.[7]

Trap 2: New Technology Is Adopted Slowly

The popular press gives the impression that new technologies are appearing faster and faster, but that is because it is ignorant as to the actual development history behind the latest miracle. Most technologies are the result of a long, protracted development cycle, often spanning generations. Indeed, technology developments that seem to arise from a revolutionary breakthrough are the culmination of innumerable, complex multidiscipline endeavors that have occurred over a period of 20 or more years. The success of today's high-flying companies was built on the pioneering efforts of innumerable individuals, companies, and institutions, many of whom are long gone (i.e., dead, retired, broke, dissolved, bought out) by the time a technology sees any commercial success.

This is true for the computer industry as well. John Mauchly and Presper Ekert are credited with the development of the first digital computer when they made the ENIAC for the Army, but as early as 1937 John V. Atanasoff, an Iowa State University professor, had already developed the prototype from which the Army design would be derived. In the popular mind Apple invented the personal computer, but it already existed in the late 1960s as the Digital Equipment PDP-8/L. It took 10 years for IBM to adopt the RISC microprocessor, IBM's own invention, despite the advantages which were so obvious to IBM's competitors. As described in George Gilder's excellent book *Microcosm*, the success of companies like Intel, Apple Computer, Sun Microsystems, and AMD have their roots back in the early part of the century, when odd-ball, underpaid scientists such as Bohr, Einstein, Heisenberg, and others were unraveling the mysteries of quantum physics. Their ideas were followed by painstaking and expensive research and development efforts in solid state physics, metallurgy, thin-film processes, vacuum technology, and lithography that allowed abstruse theories to become reality in useful, economically accessible products. Millions upon millions of dollars, careers, aspirations, and companies were lost in the long development cycle.

Theodore Levitt, a marketing professor at Harvard, once quipped that the problem with being a pioneer is that you get killed by the Indians. That is true, but surviving even long enough to fight the Indians might be described as a high-class problem. Closer to the truth is that many more pioneers perished from the mundane problems of starvation, illness, and freezing to death than were ever killed by Indians. This is true for the small companies as well. The Oregon Trail that leads to any technology company's success story is strewn with the bones of legions of long forgotten innovators who preceded it and made its success possible. Most of these companies disappeared before they ever had the opportunity to compete, to do battle with the Indians, much less make any money. Their slow and painful advances along the trail made it possible for the money-making merchant class, today's high-flying entrepreneurs, to follow and set up shop in relative safety.

There are many small companies in the ranks of the pioneers. Often they arrive with the technology before the market is prepared to receive it. In technology, timing is everything.

Trap 3: The Best Uses of a New Technology Are Unknown

It is impossible to predict where technologies will be best applied or which will succeed commercially. Many great innovators and innovative companies have lacked the vision and understanding to take advantage of the technology they have developed or could have easy access to. Technical understanding is rarely complemented by an equal proportion of marketing insight. A few revealing examples will suffice:

- Dr. Robert Milliken, a Nobel prize winner in physics, said man would never tap the power of the atom.
- Thomas Watson, founder of IBM, resisted computers in favor of punch cards.
- William Schockley, one of the inventors of the transistor, thought the big opportunity for the transistor was in replacing high-power tubes, which to date has not been the case.

- Gordon Moore, a cofounder of Intel, saw the immediate application of the microprocessor as something to be used to run the appliances in a house, the one application for the technology that has remained insignificant.

- RCA failed to see that the real application for video recording was not in a handful of TV studios but, as several Japanese companies proved, in millions of homes. RCA was not alone. Such august companies as CBS, Avco, Magnavox, Motorola, Kodak, Bell & Howell, Fairchild, Zenith, MCA, and Polaroid failed also.

- UNIVAC believed that by the year 2000 the world demand for computers would be about 1000 units. They were off by orders of magnitude.

- When Sony's Morita went to AT&T to request a license for the former's transistor technology for the paltry sum of $25,000, AT&T advised him he should use them to make hearing aids, rather than proceed with his idea to make portable radios.

- George Gilder notes that "Like many epochal inventions, the microprocessor was greeted without enthusiasm even within the company that produced it."[8]

- Chester Carlson, the inventor of the xerography machine, approached 21 major U.S. companies trying to find someone interested in his technology. In retrospect, it appears sheer stupidity that astute managers could not see the possibilities inherent in this technology, but they did not. In fact, it took a faltering small company called Haloid to change the office world with copiers.[9]

As was the case with the microprocessor, often a technology flourishes when it is so widely diffused that it is accessible to numerous creative designers, most of whom will be outside the companies where the technology was developed and most of whom are from very diverse industries, but who, due to their intimate understanding and experience, are better able to apply the benefits of the technology to their particular applications.

Uneducated Guesses

At a symposium, an employee of our company ran into a former colleague from Los Alamos National Laboratory. The former colleague held a doctorate in electrical engineering and was considered a guru in his specialty. When he asked our employee what he was up to professionally, the employee told him that we had started a company whose first product was a high-speed MOSFET transistor, a device whose potential the professor was in a good position to assess.

The professor said summarily, "I bet you can't sell one of them. Who'd use it?"

We guessed in the millions, though at the time we had not even sold one. We have sold many thousands since.

He had a Ph.D. and forecasted wrong. None of us had Ph.D.s, and we forecasted wrong, too.

Trap 4: New Technology Is White-Collar-Labor-Intensive

New technology products have high-cost human inputs in the early stages of development and production. Typically technology is developed by people with advanced degrees. Indeed, doctorate level "workers" are quite common. Furthermore, technology development may require special equipment or exotic materials, and by the time a development is completed, many hundreds of thousands or even millions of dollars may be sunk into the development alone. Then, due to the small volume requirements for most new technologies, especially in the early stages of introduction, the products are virtually handmade. The businesses which supply these products resemble boutiques that practice an art or craft such as weaving, pottery, or glass blowing. But unlike the arts and crafts shop, where the employees are low-paid artisans who are satisfied with low wages because they get to do what they like to do best, the employees of the technology companies are highly trained, well-compensated knowledge workers. Many products routinely require the continuous, hands-on involvement of physicists, engineers, and technicians. Kenichi Ohmae described the phenomenon succinctly:

> People used to think that high value added meant high profits. The information industries in particular are characterized by high value added in terms of systems know-how, integrated circuits, and so on. Has that fact led to high profits? Not noticeably. The reason is simple. In these industries top management is replacing its assembly-line workers with knowledge workers. In a sense they are simply exchanging blue-collar for white-collar jobs, bleaching out the color of the blue collar, so to speak. The point is that the number of white collars or engineers employed is roughly proportional to sales....In these industries, at least, high value added cer-

tainly does not equal high profit. There are hardly any economies of scale to begin with, and these dedicated white-collar workers behave like a variable cost.[10]

Again, looking at the laser market for an example, many lasers require a device called a Pockels cell, which modulates the laser much like the shutter in a camera controls the light. A Pockels cell is a special glass crystal, polished to exacting specifications. A Pockels cell that can rest in the palm of your hand may cost only $300 to $400 but may require a doctorate to use.

Trap 5: Mature Technology Is Capital-Intensive

Once a technology has volume demand, it switches from being very labor-intensive to very capital-intensive. The test instruments and manufacturing equipment can be as exotic as the product being manufactured.

The miracle of the microprocessor is that it no longer requires the direct participation of solid-state physicists to make them. The various sputtering, etching, lithographic, diffusion, and doping processes are now rationalized into machinery that ordinary, high-school-educated employees can run under the supervision of college-educated process engineers and statisticians.

However, the machinery that the high-school-educated employees operate is very expensive. In fact, an average fabrication facility to manufacture a $10 microprocessor requires a capital investment in equipment of hundreds of millions of dollars. Charles Ferguson, writing in the *Harvard Business Review*, assigned even more startling numbers to semiconductor manufacture: "Current technology requires, on average, $200 million to $1 billion for each generation of process development, $250 million to $400 million for each factory, and $10 million to $100 million for each major device design."[11] It's ironic that the information revolution that was spawned by small companies has become the battleground of the giant Japanese conglomerates.

Trap 6: Stealing Technology Is Accepted Business Practice

Once a technology succeeds, it is easy to steal because it is based primarily on intellectual property that is almost impossible to protect.

Ideas are totally mobile and easily modifiable. Information moves around fast because so do people, between companies, conferences and trade shows, venture capitalists and bankers, universities and research centers. Therefore a competitive advantage can be like a car stolen off the streets of New York in the morning, taken to a garage for a paint job to disguise it, then sold again in the afternoon.

Not only is theft easy, it is condoned. In the old days, if you wanted to steal the car industry, you would be hard pressed to move the massive industrial apparatus that is Detroit somewhere else. It took Japan decades to obtain the know-how to duplicate it. It's not that way in high technology. It walks out the door in the cerebral cortex of a single individual.

In a sense, Silicon Valley owes its existence to theft, beginning with Fairchild. Professors Charles Ferguson and Robert Reich have been correct in carping about this issue. Undeniably most of the Valley's celebrated start-ups are founded by individuals who learned about a technology, its markets, and the economics of the industry into which the technology fits, from the company they left. All the information they learned, including the time they spent learning it, was paid for by that company. Unwittingly, it created its own competitors.

In high technology, competitive advantage frequently equates to proprietary information and know-how, not just marketing clout or manufacturing efficiencies. The U.S. government ostensibly wishes to protect the intellectual property rights of companies through legislation, as evinced by 14 laws passed since 1983 especially directed against foreign competitors. However, the government means to see to it that the public (i.e., voters') interest is ultimately best served, not individual companies, no matter how great the risk and cost associated with the latter's achievements in technology. The protection offered by airtight, enforceable patents can slow the process, but not stop it, if indeed the technology is judged by the market to have real value. The wider and faster that information is diffused, the lower are costs to the consumer and the less likely that a company can gain a monopoly or sustain a long-term competitive advantage. That is an unstated government objective.

It is also a condoned business practice. Copying, me-too products, and reverse engineering all mean the same thing: stealing another company's innovation. This is epidemic in the software business where larger companies, with armies of code crunchers at their service, quickly replicate the efforts of smaller ones who have invested thousands of worker-days to write an imaginative product.

For these reasons, pioneering small companies rarely reap the financial returns of their innovations. Studies have confirmed that small pioneering firms do not enjoy the more attractive financial returns that larger companies do who later take advantage of the technology. Recall the case of Bowmar Instrument Company, a supplier of mechanical counters and other electromechanical systems to the military. Ed White, Bowmar's opportunistic president, realized that with the development of the integrated circuit and light-emitting diode, it would be possible to make a handheld calculator. He tried to convince other companies in the calculator business at the time that his idea was a money maker, but he received a cold shoulder. So Bowmar went into the business on its own in 1971. Its product, called the Bowmar Brain, doubled the company's sales from $13 million to $26 million in one year, with after-tax earnings of $2 million, a stunning performance—and too good to last. The dramatic success of the product and the profits it earned attracted Texas Instruments and the Japanese. Bowmar tried to compete and ended up in Chapter 11 bankruptcy (from which it was able to eventually emerge, but no longer as a force in the calculator business).[12]

Trap 7: Economics Always Prevails over Technology

Technology products succeed primarily for economic reasons rather than technical ones. Years ago the management expert Peter Drucker said that a technology has to have a 10 to 1 cost advantage for it to have a chance to alter the existing structure of an industry. Only a ratio of that magnitude can justify the switching costs for a customer to adopt a new technology. These switching costs, which are explored extensively in Michael Porter's *Competitive Advantage,* include retooling to use the new technology, retraining personnel, and reselling the existing customer base that may be quite content with the old technology.

A good example of this is Du Pont's Kevlar, a material that is superior to nylon in strength. Du Pont hoped it would find its way into every tire on every car in the world. Instead it has found little niche markets for products such as skis and bulletproof vests.[13]

There are also many examples in the more obscure technologies such as machine vision. In the early 1980s there was dreamy talk of every boring task at home, the factory, and the office being performed by personable Star Wars–type robots. Over 200 companies jumped into the industry. The technology was sophisticated but difficult to build and operate and expensive to purchase and maintain. Economics shook out the industry, so now only a handful remains.

A variation of this trap allowed IBM's entry into the personal computer market. Among computer afficionados, it was widely recognized that many smaller companies offered technology that was demonstrably superior to IBM's, yet within a few months of the introduction of the PC, IBM dominated the market. The perception was that with IBM, you got much more for the money in service and distribution, which more than compensated for only average technology.

Trap 8: Prices Fall Faster Than Sales and Margins Rise

Morgan Stanley's Andy Kessler said it very well: "Don't you find it fascinating that a TV set, available in the 1950s for $200, costs about the same price today—only it comes with color, remote control, automatic fine tuning and is cable ready? Or that an IBM 360/158 mainframe originally priced at $2 million in 1975 now sells as a PS/2 Model 80 for $3,500? Or that a $100 calculator of 15 years ago is now given away free in a box of Cheerios?"[14]

The conventional rule of thumb in electronics is that a memory component will drop approximately 10 to 20 percent a year in price. The economic assumption is that the manufacturing learning curve will drive down the cost, the volume will go up, and so will profits. The tepid financial performance and shake-outs of many large companies do not lend credence to this assumption.

Combine this fact with the extremely short product life cycles of many technology products, and it can be difficult to ever get a respectable return on investment. In the computer disk drive business, a product that lasts five years is a cash cow; usually the cycles are much shorter. Because of this, expensive research and development is never-ending, employees must be constantly retrained, production equipment must be scrapped, marketing efforts redirected, sales forces retrained, and customers resold.

Trap 9: Technologies Get Blindsided by Other Technologies

With global competition and a rising rate of education throughout the world, new technologies are born every year, and they compete for the same applications. A salient contemporary example is the collapsing market for mainframes and supercomputers caused by cheap, high-performance microprocessors in personal computers. Other, as yet unresolved, conflicts are:

- Lasers versus microwaves for treating nearsightedness

- X-ray versus e-beam versus optical lithography in semiconductor production

- Shock wave lithotripsy versus chemicals versus lasers in treating kidney stones

- Acoustic versus laser angioplasty for treatment of vascular disease

Competing technologies make for a precarious business environment. A company in one technology may find itself competing against a company from a completely different technology. For instance, a laser company's most dangerous competitor in a market to test materials in airframes may not be another laser company but an acoustics company. If yours is the laser company and the acoustic approach is winning the customer base, you are in an untenable situation. No laser company has the expertise to migrate quickly into a technology that relies on ceramic transducers, so it will lose the chance to be even a secondary player in the market.

These conflicting technologies also confuse the marketplace. End users have difficulty deciding which technology is superior. As a result, purchasing decisions are delayed, and already small markets are fragmented into even smaller ones. This trap plagues manufacturers of medical equipment.

Even IBM with its financial and marketing strength fell prey. With its expensive mainframes and powerful sales force, IBM was able to dominate the industry for decades. But then along came inexpensive distributed processing to change everything. IBM may or may not be able to adjust. If not, it will be like a fly stuck in a spider web, resisting valiantly but growing steadily weaker, a victim of unexpected change.

Trap 10: The Government

The government, directly or indirectly, controls technology. *Control* may seem too strong a word, but the government's role in technology extends well beyond just benign influence. It exerts control through its funding mechanisms and regulatory policies. To be sure, by law the government's intentions are always the best, i.e., to protect the national security, health, or environment, as the case may be. However, it is a clumsy and inefficient substitute for Adam Smith's "invisible hand." The government is high technology's largest customer as well as its most unreliable and unpredictable one.

The federal government spent approximately $73 billion on research and development in 1991, of which over half was allocated to the Department of Defense (DOD). In fact, as of 1992, DOD research employed one in four U.S. scientists and funded almost 50 percent of university research in computer science and electrical engineering. Although the government consciously avoids having an explicit industrial policy, the funding is sufficiently large to influence the viability of numerous technologies. By default, the nation's technology future is determined by the direction of the prevailing political winds. Political fads are a flimsy foundation on which to base a business, as scores of electrooptic companies, formed to support the Strategic Defense Initiative, discovered. This is no less true of computer and software manufacturers selling to various government agencies which go in and out of favor from administration to administration.

Indubitably, the DOD plays the central role in determining what technology can and cannot be sold in the global marketplace and thereby determines the size of a technology's potential market. A U.S. company with a promising technology can find itself limited, through export licensing requirements, to a market consisting of the U.S. government and a few select allies. This has had a devastating effect on semiconductor equipment manufacturers and other capital goods suppliers.

The Food and Drug Administration, the watchdog of U.S. health, is notoriously slow in approving new drugs. According to the Pharmaceutical Manufacturers Association, as of 1991, the FDA had approved only 14 drugs in the last nine years. In 1992 the FDA approved only two biotech drugs! There are now over 1100 companies involved in biotech research and development in the United States. What does this statistic bode for their growth prospects, especially small companies?

Even in the smallest paradigm wars, such as that between the

Ti:sapphire laser and the dye laser, the outcome may be settled ultimately by the government, not on technical grounds, but on purely environmental ones. The dye laser uses solvents with carcinogenic properties. The Environmental Protection Agency will no longer allow such solvents to be flushed down the drain, so the cost of disposing of the solvent, in combination with Trap 7, may doom the technology and cripple the companies that sell them.

The effects of government policy are, for better or worse, reflected on the income statements of every high-technology company in the United States. Thus trends in government spending and policy must be monitored as vigilantly as competitors.

In summary, you must recognize and carefully analyze which composite of the 10 technology traps are ensnaring your company. No high-tech company is immune to these traps because they are inherent to high-technology business. Your ultimate challenge is to organize and lead the business to survive and thrive in spite of them.

3

Overcoming Undercapitalization

The image of the entrepreneur as a great inventor and great promoter or the great and daring risk-taker simply doesn't square with the facts. Reality is far less spectacular than this. In fact, the beginning entrepreneurship turns out to be a mundane affair and not at all heroic. There is the entrepreneur without capital resource, without apparent social skills, and without even a good idea. No respectable element in the community is even aware of him, let alone ready to help him.

ORIVIS COLLINS, DAVID MOORE, AND DARAB UNWALLA[1]

Most small high-tech companies are undercapitalized. Very likely, yours is too. By definition, your company lacks the resources to be in business even though it already is in business. Specifically, it lacks sufficient assets—cash, inventory, and equipment—to properly support its business activities. As if the 10 technology traps weren't handicap enough, undercapitalization places a small high-tech company at a further disadvantage. Although undercapitalization does not predestine a company to failure, it makes achieving any semblance of business stability, much less profitable growth, more difficult, improbable, and haphazard. Overcoming the condition requires a unique set of management skills.

You will search in vain through the indexes of most books on corporate finance for even a passing reference to undercapitalization. Though widespread in the small business world, it is rarely addressed by the business pundits. One reason is that it is a seemingly simple problem with an obvious solution—the company needs to obtain more capital. But it is right here that the standard bromides fail. Your company is undercapitalized because, for a host of reasons, it is not able to attract capital. Not surprisingly, undercapitalization is endemic among companies that are unprofitable or marginally profitable. And it is also possible for a company to be undercapitalized and making a profit, though genuinely profitable companies do not remain undercapitalized for very long.

Undercapitalization is a relative term. A company with $2 million in the bank is undercapitalized to launch communications satellites into orbit or to carry an HIV/AIDS vaccine from the laboratory through FDA approval—the approval process for a drug can take 10 years and cost $250 million.[2] However, this company may be well capitalized to introduce a new software for a niche market. A company may be adequately capitalized to grow 25 percent from one year to the next but would self-destruct if forced to grow 100 percent.

Your company may not be undercapitalized at all. You may only think that it is because you are trying to get the business to be something that it cannot be. Your business may be adequately capitalized for what it is but not for what you wish it were. Factors beyond your control, such as the size of a market niche, the limits of your technology, and the means by which your product must be manufactured, may predispose your company to be a certain size. Consider if this may be a possibility, and then heed the advice of Bill Gates from an interview in *Business Week:*

> The way I see it, some product areas, if you have a passion for them, that's great. And if it turns out that you can build a huge business around it, that's a lucky thing—like what happened in the case of Microsoft. But whatever the size is, the things you really know and love and see opportunities in—you ought to pick your business based on that. And then let it have its natural size.[3]

Warning Signs

Undercapitalization can often be detected by a trained financial eye studying a sequence of income statements and balance sheets. For instance, most manufacturing companies, in terms of annual sales dollars, are able to turn their total assets only two or three times. If a company is generating $1 million in sales on $50,000 of assets, it is surely overtrading. A sequence of growing order backlogs may reveal that a company cannot afford the human resources or inventory to supply its demand. Or income statements may show marketing expenses fluctuating wildly from month to month, not because of seasonal business cycles but because the cash is not there to support a consistent marketing effort.

Examining the company from the inside, the major telltale sign of undercapitalization is that every business decision is determined by its short-term impact on cash flow. You will find yourself preoccupied by immediate issues such as the timing of disbursements for basic expenses like the rent and payroll, whereas important long-term issues such as strengthening the management team or new product development are set aside. This will not necessarily be due to your myopia. There is no other choice. The plain fact is that undercapitalized companies which do not operate this way quickly go bankrupt, so long-term strategic thinking is completely precluded.

Sometimes undercapitalization remains concealed until an abrupt perturbation in business conditions, down or up, precipitates a crisis. In a recession orders can slow down so much that there is inadequate demand for the company's products, making the company unable to generate enough cash to stay solvent. In the case of upward conditions, a customer may place a large order for shipment in a few months, but your company cannot make the forward cash investment in people or materials to meet the order. The resource requirement is simply too large.

But, just as frequently, the condition remains concealed because the symptoms are less apparent. Like the flu, undercapitalization is evidenced by the presence of one or more nagging symptoms, all of which may appear at first to be unrelated but which all share the same origin and are mutually reinforcing. These symptoms will be chronic until you can accumulate some capital. They manifest themselves, not in the extremes of a crisis, but in the day-to-day activities of the company as it attempts to operate like a normal business. For instance:

- *Your company is not able to tolerate losses for more than a few months, even weeks, or it will be out of business.* Few businesses, particularly in their early stages, are profitable month in and month out, or from quarter to quarter, particularly if their industry has a cyclic function, as in the case of many high-tech businesses which ride the federal fiscal year acquisition cycle. There must be adequate cash reserves to buffer the cash flow from a delayed product release or an unexpected expense (ideally no expenses should be unexpected, but, for instance, a customer might request on short notice that you appear at the firm's facility for an important meeting).

- *Products are given totally unrealistic time frames for acceptance because they must generate cash immediately after introduction.* Very few products are overnight sensations. It takes time for a market to learn about them, ascertain if they meet a need, get them into its purchasing cycles, test them, and order more of them. Driven by a need for cash, the company will be forced to ship products before they are actually completed and properly tested. So-called production units are really one-of-a-kind prototypes whose real operating parameters have not been fully characterized and whose failure modes have not been exhaustively identified and corrected.

- *Your company must seek small, marginally profitable and/or technically risky business opportunities because it cannot afford to address larger, more profitable ones.* Perhaps a large OEM has a special requirement for which your company has the expertise to offer an excellent solution, and your company could end up in the enviable situation of being virtually a sole source. However, the product development and system integration at the OEM will follow a two-year development schedule. When you are in business, the OEM expects you to have the staying power to work along side it, at your expense, for the large payoff later. In products destined for a defense acquisition, this process can easily take 5 years. If the company cannot get by in the interim, it must find other business perhaps not really in the long-term interests of the company. Or, in other instances, the company may be able to survive the development cycle, but the follow-on business is so large that you cannot afford the investment in inventory and receivables over the period necessary to complete the order.

Dancing Close to the Fire

Two months after going into business, we were delighted to receive a call from a physicist at a national laboratory. He was doing an exotic experiment involving "space painting" and needed a pulse generator. He had seen the ads for our MOSFET and figured we might be able to build what he needed if we could make MOSFETs go that fast.

Several parameters of what he wanted were right at the limits of any available technology, and he knew it.

We were desperate for business and optimistic concerning the technical challenge, so we quoted it at the low end, fully understanding the risk. We had no idea who else might quote (none did—other companies had better sense), so we priced it low. We got the contract.

We hit most, but not all, the parameters. What we did accomplish was worth twice what we charged. But because we barely missed in two parameters, the customer withheld a portion of the payment. We were never paid for something that was grossly underbid in the first place.

■ *The company lacks the proper equipment it needs for development or production.* High tech invariably means specialized, sometimes exotic, equipment for even the routine tasks. Your company may possess the technical expertise required to operate the equipment but not the equipment itself. The engineering and manufacturing groups may be compelled to share equipment, so neither is efficient.

The Kitchen Laboratory

To complete the data sheet on our high-speed device, we had to measure its thermal impedance. We had very little lab equipment beyond an oscilloscope and ohm meter, so we lacked the proper equipment with which to make the measurement.

With no other alternatives, we took a crockpot and filled it with oil. After it got hot, we sat on the floor for several hours and took measurements, alternately putting in and removing the device from the hot oil, and then recording the data.

Shortly thereafter, a large power semiconductor company was trying to replicate our data and they asked us about our test set up. We gave them an accurate description of the procedures but did not mention the exact test apparatus we used.

They got the similar results. We never asked them if they, too, used a crockpot. They would not have found it very funny.

■ *To increase sales, the company needs to market harder, but it cannot afford the cash outlays that precede the cash income from sales.* Your company simply cannot execute a marketing plan. It cannot advertise or promote consistently. It cannot buy the space, size, quality, or repetition of ads that it needs to secure the market's attention. It cannot afford either the space or a professional presentation at trade shows. It cannot afford products for free evaluation. It cannot afford the plane fare for a salesperson to travel to visit a customer with excellent long-term potential. The company will attempt to sell expensive, capital equipment off of second rate, photocopied specification sheets.

■ *Employees perform tasks for which they have neither the experience nor the training.* This may be true from the president on down.

Consequently a technician is expected to perform the work of an engineer, or inexperienced assemblers find themselves acting as production managers, or an engineer doubles as an in-house ad agency by writing ad copy, or a founder's spouse, who once had high school bookkeeping, is acting as a CFO. In the long run, everything actually ends up costing far more than it would if your company could have access to the appropriate skills, but because it does not, whatever is done will not be accomplished as professionally or as efficiently as desired.

Time Bomb

A complex pulse generator for which we had an order required an internal switch-mode power supply. It was not a particularly difficult task for an engineer familiar with switch-mode design, but our lone engineer was totally preoccupied with a more critical portion of the design.

The best solution would have been to have an outside consultant do the design for us, but, lacking the money, we decided it was best to let a part-time technician, with some experience gathered from working at a switch-mode power supply house, do the design.

When it came time for system integration, the power supply functioned, but it was far from optimum. However, we were under the pressure of a tight delivery schedule. The system worked, so it was shipped.

During the next year, the power supply failed several times before we replaced it. Because it was under warranty, it was expensive to the company. Worse, the customer was not happy.

- *Payments to vendors are always late.* This is the beginning of a self-reinforcing problem because the vendor will terminate conventional trade credit terms and ship only on a COD basis, which in turn places a more severe financial burden on the company and can prevent delivery of materials, thereby delaying delivery of a product that generates cash flow. Inevitably there will come a time when you need the cooperation of a vendor to ensure that an important shipment goes out on schedule, but you will have no leverage with the vendor.

- *The company does not make the engineering changes to a product that has demand, though so doing would make the product more manufacturable and profitable or enable the price to come down to make it more attractive to customers.* Product development is an iterative process. Rarely is any product perfect upon introduction, not to the customer and not to those inside the company who have to build or support it. The activity of building the first few of a product always reveals ways to produce it faster or with improved reliability. If a product cannot be modified to be manufacturable by assemblers of average skill, then it will have to be hand-built by engineering personnel, thereby restricting the potential volume and profitability. Improvements always require changes in documentation, testing, or tooling—in other words, additional investment. Not making the changes demoralizes those who suggested the improvements, slows production, and lowers margins. Ultimately it loses customers.

■ *The company cannot hire competent professional services.* Any high-tech business has a plethora of needs for professional services in every aspect of the business. In a young technology business there is a need for legal counsel to protect intellectual property, to write employee agreements, to review contracts, to establish warranty policies, to distribute stock, and so on. Good accounting advice is an absolute necessity (as discussed in Chapters 6 and 7) because it helps guide the company financially and placate the fears of bankers and stockholders. The company needs the most effective advertising and promotional pieces it can devise and could use the services of a marketing consultant. Yet these services are expensive and tend to be seen as feasible only when discretionary funds are available, which, of course, they never are.

Dangerous Precedents

At six months old, our company was almost broke. We had $5000 in the bank, more in payables than we had in receivables. The good news was that we were receiving some orders for evaluation quantities of MOSFETs and had a small inventory so we could ship immediately. But it was clear we were only a few weeks away from a major cash crisis. To make things worse, a development contract we had expected to contribute in the next two months fell through. The clock was ticking.

We came up with an idea we thought no one had ever thought of before (someone had). We would sell ownership shares in the MOSFET sales. The investors would be guaranteed to receive 10 percent of the gross sales until they received three times their investment back. We would raise $100,000, enough (it wasn't) to get us going.

We went to a local securities attorney to discuss details. Amidst photos hanging from his sumptuous paneled walls taken during his recent photo safari to Africa, he explained it would cost between

$5000 and $10,000 to do the offering memorandum, including an up-front retainer of $2500. Of course filing in other states to comply with their "blue sky" laws would be extra. Plus there would be some accounting expenses, printing expenses, etc., and three months would be required to get everything together and perform "due diligence."

We concluded that in three months we would be out of business, and, besides, he would cost half our remaining cash. The next day we went to the university library and found racks of law books with sample forms. We copied a limited partnership agreement, probably similar to the boilerplate that the peripatetic attorney had on his word processor. We made sure to include plenty of language stating, in essence, that the investment was risky and anyone would have to be out of their minds to invest. We went to a copier shop and had 20 copies made and nicely bound.

Within three weeks we had sold $95,000 worth of $2500 units to friends and relatives, who, for the record, received a good return. (Don't ever do this—go to an attorney.)

Changing for the Better

The presence of any of these or similar symptoms dictates that you must face several business realities and alter your management perspective accordingly.

First, your financial status is precarious. Each of the symptoms will have a cumulative negative financial effect on your company, and, if they appear in the right combination or sequence, they can put it out of business. In turn, your ability to compete will be compromised. In a capitalist system, demand creates supply. If there is demand for a product, ultimately, no matter how proprietary or exotic the technology, there will be a supplier. If you are unable to get the job done, then a competitor will. Despite this, you must ignore feelings of desperation which can lure you into taking unnecessary risks; instead, concentrate on cash flow.

Second, undercapitalization can disguise very serious marketing and management problems, thus making it difficult to isolate and solve them. For example, a new product doing poorly on the market may appear to lack a needed feature or a consistent advertising campaign because the company cannot make the necessary investment. However, it may be just as likely that marketing has not defined a product to meet a real need, so the real problem is that there is no demand. Similarly, a product may meet a real need, but it cannot be manufactured cost-effectively. Is it because production lacks a drill press, or is it because the product was poorly engineered in the first place to require a process that needs a drill press? Or take the case where shipments are delayed due to parts shortages. Is it because the purchasing manager was instructed to minimize the investment in inventory so he or she cannot hold safety stock, or is the purchasing manager simply not developing reliable vendors? You will have to be constantly probing for the real causes of problems.

Third, the working environment of your company will be very stressful. The company may not be able to pay its employees what they are really worth in terms of their credentials, contribution, or actual work load. Many times employees must work extra hard without additional compensation, which is bad for morale and an unethical business practice if it becomes the day-to-day mode of operation, as happens all too often in small high-tech companies. In addition, employees may lack all the tools or equipment they need to perform their jobs correctly, whether it be a CAD system for a drafter, a market study for a salesperson, or software for a book-keeper. It is as if they must perform to their maximum while simultaneously playing Russian roulette with a loaded gun because there is little margin for error.

Invariably, the level of interdepartmental tensions will fluctuate with the bank balance. In the typical scenario, finance drives production to ship to a schedule based on what the cash disbursements schedule indicates is required to meet payments, not on a realistic production schedule maximized for quality and efficiency. Marketing must sell unreliable products, which decreases the probability of long-term acceptance, because engineering does not have the time to perform adequate testing and complete manufacturing documentation. Accounting discovers that a product is not achieving the target gross margins forecast by marketing and engineering, but the latter claim that is not because the product is not priced or engineered well but because purchasing is not buying effectively. But purchasing counters that the company will not allocate the funds to order at quantities adequate to command discounts. Parts get purchased in small amounts at retail prices because management has directed that investment in inventory be held down.

When managing employees under these circumstances, remember that is does no good to browbeat an anemic marathoner to run faster. If you forget and set unrealistic expectations for employees, this, combined with other demotivating factors like low wages and inadequate support, will induce employees to find other jobs. With them departs proprietary technology and know-how that frequently migrate directly to competitors.

Last, you and your management team, having high expectations for yourselves and the company, will be the victim of the most pernicious effects of undercapitalization: constant frustration and humiliation. Without doubt the deadliest threat to the existence of an undercapitalized company is not financial ruin but the sense of defeatism that comes to plague the company after years of effort. As David Birch of Cognetics has pointed out, most entrepreneurs do not go out of business because they go bankrupt; they go out of business because they just get tired of the fight and quit.[4] Surely many former small high-tech companies are buried in his statistics. To avoid this, you must learn to become energized by the battle rather than embittered.

Cash Bar

The summer we started up, we were invited to a weekly meeting of a venture club where investors came to hear entrepreneurs tell their stories and to scout for investment opportunities. The evening included a cocktail hour for everyone to circulate and "network."

When we went to get drinks, we realized it was a cash bar. Each of us looked in our wallets and neither of us even had a dollar.

We circulated anyway, without drinks. Because social drinking is so commonplace, several people were curious as to why we did not have any drinks. We avoided answering directly. We must have left them with the impression that drinking was contrary to our religious beliefs. It had to be obvious that we were not athletes in training.

Diagnosing undercapitalization is easier than curing it. The symptoms are chronic and do not just go away over time. It would be foolish to ignore this fact. But there are reasons for hope. Many companies do overcome undercapitalization. It is within your power to change the odds so that your company is one of those. To do so will require that you understand exactly why your company is undercapitalized in the first place. Once you do, your priorities will change. So will the way you do business.

4

Finding the Missing Ingredients

If you had the chance to ask one year's worth of guys who come meet with us to ask for investments the question, What do you think in terms of your net worth when you succeed? most would say, A million dollars. I'm not interested in guys that want to make $1 million. I want the guy who says, I want to make $100 million.

DON VALENTINE[1]

Most small high-tech companies are undercapitalized for a good reason—they deserve to be. This may sound like a summary judgment, but it is not meant to be. It is true. Lack of capital has identifiable causes which reside both internally and externally to the company, both within and outside of management's control. It is very important to understand which factor is limiting your company so you can act to remedy it or, if it is beyond your control, find a means to compensate for it.

Investment capital is a scarce resource, but what is available gets invested in companies that have a good story containing all the key ingredients for success. If you cannot find capital, chances are good that your company is missing one or more of these key ingredients.

Big Deals

Before proceeding to explore in more detail why your company is undercapitalized, compare your business's story to that of another high-technology company that is not undercapitalized. The differences may be revealing.

First, the properly capitalized high-tech company probably has a management team with extensive experience in the industry into which it will sell a product. The team knows the industry's leading players, established channels of distribution, prevailing technology base, economic dynamics, geographical patterns, seasonal business cycles, and overall growth trends. Management can tell you who buys what, when, and why, and for how much and how well it performed. In short, the management team knows the business.

Second, the management team is strong in every key functional area necessary to operate the business: engineering, sales and marketing, manufacturing, purchasing, human resources, and finance. A complete, well-rounded team is in place almost as soon as the company starts up or, at least, has been identified and is committed to join as growth dictates.

Third, the company has a manufacturable, proprietary product (sometimes stolen from the previous employer along with key members of the management team) that is the same form, fit, and function as the products against which it competes but with the addition of a demonstrable and obvious performance advantage plus a substantial cost advantage over the market leader.

Fourth, the product is targeted toward a multimillion-, preferably billion-, dollar industry that is growing at a double-digit rate and seems immune to any market or macroeconomic upheavals.

Such a story may sound too good to be true, but there are companies that meet many of these criteria. They become the "big deals" that attract millions in investment, such as Steve Jobs's *next* computer company. The big deals appear to investors to have a high probability of success. The reasoning that investors use in the big deals is the same that leads you to think that a batter who has hit a home run before is more likely to hit another than a batter who has never hit one. In your career have you ever hit a home run?

To a small company manager, hearing about the big deals is as frustrating and painful as it is for a penniless child to gaze longingly through the window of a candy store. The founders of the big deals are already personally well off; they already own their Rolex watches, and they will not have to mortgage their homes to finance their start-up, nor do they have to personally guarantee the credit lines of the new company. The first offices they occupy will be in an opulent high rise with rosewood furniture and plush pastel carpets.

Of course, even the founders in the big deals have to endure a high level of stress and hubbub because they have so much to do and so little time. (Truly, the bigger the investment, the louder the performance/expectation clock ticks.) But the founders have plenty of money to hire office help, advertise wherever and as often as necessary, rent attorneys and accountants, build production lines, install a first-class management information system, dispatch a field sales force. The managers in the big deals receive generous salaries so they can afford a winning image, replete with monogrammed shirts with gold Cross pens clipped in their pockets and imported company cars. If something does not work out as anticipated and they find themselves at odds with the money interests, they have golden parachutes to give them soft landings, so, if they fail, primarily their egos suffer, not their net worths.

However, do not think for a moment that the big deals are not fraught with risk. They are, very big risks, risks measured in millions and millions of dollars wagered by insurance companies, trusts, and wealthy individuals who entrust their funds to venture capitalists to make "prudent" investments. If big deals fail, and they do in a surprising number of cases, the money is lost. The reputations of the venture capitalists and founders are tarnished, but financially all it usually means is that they might have to drive their year-old Porsches for at least another two years before they can purchase their new ones.

Those that do make it, make it very big indeed. If you want to get the flavor of what it's like, read Michael Malone's book about MIPS Computer entitled *Going Public*.

Look in the Mirror: What Do You See?

Without a doubt, internal factors are a primary cause of undercapitalization, though, ironically, they are the very ones within your control. When trying to analyze why you are undercapitalized, start first by taking an objective look at yourself.

The Right Set of Passions

Many technology companies are managed by engineers or scientists who simply do not know anything about money—what it represents, how or where to go to find it, and what people who have money want (almost always more money) in return for the use of it. Money does not intrinsically interest them. Consequently they do not possess the humility or sales skills required to convince someone who has money to give it up. In fact, these managers are almost phobic about selling, for the reasons explored in Chapter 10.

Technophiles can be very one-dimensional in this regard. Deep in their souls they equate financial success with the crass materialism of, say, Rodney Dangerfield in *Back to School* or Richard Dreyfus in *Tin Men*. They suffer from a bona fide approach-avoidance conflict similar to the Victorian attitude toward sex. They think money is impure because it does not always belong to people who, in these managers' judgment, deserve it, worked for it, or need it. Many technophiles just do not have the appropriate lust for money necessary to succeed in business. Rather, their driving passions are for the praise and recognition of their peers, the pursuit of Knowledge (yes, with a capital K), the Progress (of course, with a capital P) of Western civilization, or some similar, vague intangibles. Whatever their passion, it is not money. When Edward Roberts conducted research for *Entrepreneurs in High Technology,* he found that making a profit was rarely a focus in the original business plan of many high-tech companies.[2]

This attitude creates an obvious and immediate problem for a potential investor. Not surprisingly, potential investors can sense this lack of interest in money, and it scares them off. They know that too many technophiles try to use a business as a vehicle to subsidize their hobby or personal technical interests, a sure path to failure.

It is difficult to trace the origin of this misguided thinking. One possibility is that most technophiles have spent considerable time in academic institutions. Their mentors have been professors who are ambivalent toward money, who have made a career of avoiding concrete measures of performance, and who believe there is something ennobling about being underpaid and underresourced.

Do you fit this profile of a technophile? If so, you would do well to recognize that a fundamental fact of capitalism is that it is extremely democratic. People vote with dollars. Money flows where people perceive value. If it does not flow, it is because people do not see value. This is true in the technology arena as well, where typically your customers are your peers. If they do not perceive value in your technology, they will not vote for it with their purchases.

Some technophiles avoid this simple truth by rationalizing that the market, their peers, is not smart enough or is too short-sighted to see the brilliance of their technology. It can be humbling and very beneficial to your business to acknowledge that if your technology is not selling, you have not created something of perceived value. According to Gerald Gunderson in *The Wealth Creators: An Entrepreneurial History*

of the United States, Thomas Edison learned this lesson the hard way.
His first product, a mechanical punch card system to tally votes for
state legislatures, was a dismal failure because he overlooked a very
basic fact: Politicians really did not want their constituents to know
how they voted. Then, Gunderson writes, Edison realized that:

> The obvious implication was that inventions must meet a genuine
> demand in order to be worthwhile. A professional inventor, depen-
> dent on earnings, must contribute toward ends that users value
> enough to purchase. Inventions created primarily to satisfy the
> inventor's curiosity are properly understood as recreation.[3]

Edison also discovered that "he could keep his innovative curiosity
fully engaged while pursuing applications with commercial returns."[4]
To be sure, trying to achieve economic success provides ample mental
stimulation for anyone.

Another internal factor to consider is that you are finding capital
hard to acquire because you will not accept the performance expectations and management control from investors that rightfully accompany the investment. One frequently cited trait of entrepreneurs is that
they go into business on their own to escape the control of others.
Whether this is a personality strength or weakness is a moot point.
But you must ask if the reason you cannot ever come to terms with
potential investors is that you cannot compromise on the issue of control. If so, do not be surprised if you are undercapitalized. An obses-
sion with independence makes for wonderful characters in Clint
Eastwood movies, but you must surrender this romantic notion when
you ask to use other people's money.

Potential investors may be suspicious of your ability to run your
business. It is irrelevant that most venture capitalists are ill-suited to
run your business either because mastering multiple industries, multiple markets, and multiple technologies is a Herculean task in this era
of innovation and specialization. However, somebody who gives you
money has every right to expect that you will do what you said you
would do, when you said you would do it. Surprisingly, technophiles,
schooled in advanced mathematics, often seem to have a learning dis-
ability when it comes to the comparatively simple concepts of the time
value of money and return on investment. In fairness, if you said that
the demand would be X and the return would be Y in Z time, and
things turn out differently (usually worse), you should not be surprised that investors expect that you should suffer direct and tangible
repercussions. They do; it is anguishing to someone who understands
money to hold an investment that is not performing. One means

investors use to correct the situation is to adjust the equity distribution to ensure the promised return. That is how business must operate, a painful reminder that a business is distinctly different from an academic or research institution, where results are a goal rather than an absolute necessity.

Venture capitalists do not always understand the technology side of a technology business, but they always understand the business side. Technical successes are not enough.

The Right Management Mix

Most small high-tech companies have engineering talent but lack marketing; have a significant technology but are unable to manufacture it efficiently or with consistent quality; or are strong in R&D but weak in developing the commercially viable products. In other words, the companies are lacking in one or more human resource in the skill matrix that is critical to their success. Any weakness in human capital makes a risky venture even riskier.

In *Financing and Investing in Private Companies,* Arthur Lipper observes:

> Many of the entrepreneurs an investor meets have neither the background nor particular talent for managing a company. They will only rarely have experience as a chief executive officer and commonly will have never had the responsibility of personnel management. Being a good scientist, engineer, or marketing person is not the same as being a good chief executive officer of an entrepreneurial and developing company.[5]

Many investors evaluate a company's investment potential soley on the management team. Any weakness is a problem that must be solved as a precondition of the investment. The larger the opportunity, the more uneasy will be the investor because big opportunities require perfect execution. Any large opportunity draws immediate competition. Investors know that the battle is ultimately won or lost by management skill, not technology.

Learning Experience

For a while our "insurmountable opportunities" made us look like a possible candidate for venture capital. Through contacts in another fast-growing company, we were introduced to a venture firm in Denver.

The venture firm evaluated the business plan, then, piqued with interest, moved on to evaluate us personally. Its custom was to use a group of industrial psychologists to interview the entrepreneurs and construct profiles of the various individuals. The profiles appraised the suitability of the entrepreneurs' business background, emotional traits, etc. for the jobs slotted for them in the company.

However, the less obvious purpose was to assess the degree of match between the venture firm and the company's management, because the venture firm took a very direct hands-on approach to working with its investments. It was important to ensure that the investors would be comfortable and effective in guiding the entrepreneurial team.

The shrinks visited the company and spent an hour conversing with the key management in a loose question-answer format, and then went back to Denver to write their reports.

Copies were returned to us a few weeks later. Each report was a few pages long, with a nice heavy stock cover, a statement of confidentiality, and in clear print. The report on the president of the company concluded, "It is our experience that (venture firm) will typically require more from a person in (entrepreneur's name) position than his background suggests he is prepared to provide."

We both learned a great deal from that report and wasted no more of each other's time.

Miniscule Markets

Your technology may be exciting, but the market may be too small. Most markets in high technology are small. This makes for very attractive, defensible niches but will not attract investment.

As a general rule, if a market is under $50 million, you will have a hard time attracting a venture capital investment because of simple arithmetic. First of all, it is unrealistic to expect that you will get all 100 percent of that market. Let us assume you are a huge success and get 30 percent of it. That means that your annual sales are $15 million per year. You run a tight, productive company, so let us also say your net profit is 10 percent after taxes, so your net income is $1.5 million per year. For a $1 million investment, you gave up 49 percent of the company, so your investors are entitled to $750,000 of the income. There are numerous ways to value a company, but let's use a simple technique. For a small company, you would do very well to sell your company at a price five times your annual earnings after taxes or $3.75 million. So the investors' share entitles them to $1.875 million. A venture capitalist must usually get at least a fivefold return on an investment (for reasons explained later in this chapter), and in most cases would like as much as tenfold. Clearly $1.875 million is a long way from $5 million and a very long way from $10 million. To achieve its target return, the venture group could only invest $750,000 and would have to own 100 percent of your company!

Many high-tech companies are started as consulting or contract development companies. They deliver high value-added hardware that incorporates a special expertise. Although they might use the vernacular of a manufacturing company and hope to eventually have a manufactured product, these companies more closely resemble a professional practice such as that of an attorney or a surgeon. The hourly rates for the professional may be very high, but there is no way to create financial leverage. According to Stanley Rich and David Gumpert's *Business Plans That Win $$$*, derived from their work with the MIT Enterprise Forum, investors are not attracted to custom product or applications engineering companies because, "When a company's basic product or service needs to be altered or specially designed for each customer, potential investors see high costs and low profits."[6] The reason is that the real product of these companies is engineering time, a finite quantity that cannot be extended beyond the number of hours in a week.

The Mythical Venture Capitalist

The definitive guide to venture capital is *Pratt's Guide to Venture Capital Sources,* updated and published annually by Venture Economics, Inc. It tells you how and where to search for venture capital. It is comprehensive, reliable, and informative.

However, do not expect much help from venture capitalists, because there are fewer of them than in the 1980s, they have less money, and they are rarely interested in the vast majority of small high-tech companies. The fact is that there are many more promising ideas on which to attempt to build businesses than there is venture capital available to pursue these ideas. For every 2000 business plans submitted to venture firms, they invest in only 4 or 5.

The confident prose and ascending graphs of the best researched business plan cannot conceal that the viability of any new-technology product is a crap shoot. There is no assurance that: (1) the technology will perform as intended, then, (2) if it does, that it can be manufactured economically, and (3) if it can be, that anybody will buy it. Entire growth markets can be obliterated by a cut in the federal budget or the emergence of another technology.

In fact, venture capital has never have been a good source of capital for small businesses. According to David Birch, venture capitalists "represent an insignificant source of capital for start up and growth companies—investing $3 billion in a good year for a class of businesses that requires roughly $70 billion or $80 billion."[7]

By the 1990s, the venture capitalist industry was undergoing profound change. Inspired by the stunning growth of Silicon Valley and the incredible returns earned by those who first invested in Intel and Apple Computer, capitalists poured fortunes into technology, mainly computer and semiconductor companies, between 1983 and 1985. Like many of the start-ups they financed, things went pretty well for the first couple of years. Arthur Rock, for instance, parlayed a $57,600 investment into $21.8 million. But then venture investments began to falter. Returns on venture capital partnerships dropped from the range of 40 to 50 percent in the mid-1970s to 15 percent by the mid-1980s (remember that back then you could get double-digit interest on a risk free T-bill). By 1990 returns from funds started after 1985 were averaging a paltry 5 to 6 percent.[8]

The funds' declining performance was due to a fact that the magic formula they used in the past to cash out of their investments was not, as most things are not, eternal and immutable. The way it always worked in the halcyon days was that the venture capitalists would inject a large amount of capital into a privately held company that fit the profile, as closely as possible, of the perfect company. The company's management would drive the company hard, push up sales at a precipitous angle for five, at most, seven years, then take the company public and sell out its position in the company. Of course, the stock would sell at a price based solely on future expectations of growth. The eyeball can see a growth trend in a graph and easily extrapolate right on off the paper and conclude that a $200 million company will easily be, presto, a $1 billion company only three years later. So a company that, in many cases, had never shown a real profit (a syndrome where the company is always reinvesting in growth) sold for an amount that was not rooted in any rational system of valuation, just a stockbroker's breathless excitement. Investors grabbed up this superstock at ever escalating prices with the exuberance of sharks in a feeding frenzy.

Of course, this could not go on forever. Soon the buying public got wise. Fortunes were being made, but many more fortunes were being lost. The companies attracting so much investment couldn't maintain the torrid pace and collapsed, went bankrupt, were acquired, or slowed down to a more modest growth rate, one at which the stock might be worth the price the investors paid by the year 2025. Venture capitalists got stuck in investments they could not get out of. They, just like everybody else, ride the fear-greed cycle, and the downside can be breathtaking.

By the latter part of the 1980s, venture capitalists were nicknamed "vulture capitalists" because they demanded such obscene returns on their investments. What is usually forgotten by those critical of them is that on most of their investments the venture capitalists made mediocre to terrible returns. On average, two out of five investments were dismal failures, two performed nonspectacularly, and one was a home run. They subscribed to the Reggie Jackson School of Investment where you hit it over the fence or you strike out. Very risky business.

Predictably, during the boom, the government jumped on the bandwagon. Through the SBIC (Small Business Investment Company) program, the government pumped $1.2 billion to seed small growth companies in the form of government-backed loans. The companies had some success, too—Cray Research, Federal Express, and Apple Computer. However, the number of loans in default has doubled since 1986.

So the venture community has been experiencing painful change. Unfortunately none of it bodes well for small, early-stage companies. Whereas in the 1980s, 48 percent of the venture groups invested in start-up companies, by the beginning of the 1990s the number had dropped to 25 percent. The gross amount of venture disbursements, even in the big deals, has been going down steadily, as well. Consider these figures from Kathleen Devlin, managing editor of the *Venture Capital Journal*:

1987: $4.0 billion
1988: $3.8 billion
1989: $3.4 billion
1990: $2.3 billion
1991: $1.4 billion
1992: $2.5 billion

The encouraging increase in 1992 was due to a record year of initial public offerings (IPOs) and renewed hope for software, medical, and biotechnology companies that resulted in a new flow of funds to venture funds. According to Robert Pavey, the president of the National Venture Capital Association, professional venture capitalists finance about 1500 companies per year with an average investment of $2 million per company.[9] However, this average is misleading because two-thirds of the dollars invested are going toward later-stage investments (smaller risk, smaller return) in expansions of established companies, acquisitions, and leveraged buyouts. Only about 10 percent of these new investments were made to seed and start up stage companies.

The venture capital industry is getting conservative in its middle age. There are two good reasons for this. The first is that the industry is becoming increasingly dominated by megafunds which manage billions of dollars, so much, in fact, that it is unable to economically select and manage small (less than $5 million) speculative investments in early-stage companies.

The other reason is that venture capitalists answer to a very impatient constituency, typically institutional investors and wealthy individuals. Institutional investors have a high anxiety level because they are responsible for people's life savings and retirement funds. As a result, they are white-knuckle investors with high expectations. They think very short term because time represents risk. Early-stage investments can take 7 to 10 years to get a payback. Ironically, though they are also very risk-aversive, institutional investors cannot resist the lure of the spectacular returns possible in high technology. So they make comparatively modest investments in high-risk enterprises through venture funds with the expectation that their speculative investments will pull up the mediocre returns they make from their dull, safe (once upon a time), and sizable real estate portfolios. Wealthy individuals are wealthy because they are careful with money. Because the government offers them no tax incentives to assume risks, when they do, their expectations are astronomically high as well.

Black Bunting

We had an appointment with two partners in a venture capital firm. Upon arrival we were ushered to a waiting area because they were both tied up.

Looking for the restroom, I came to an area where pictures were displayed of the products produced by the various companies they had invested in. The products served a range of markets. Each was nicely designed and gave a positive impression.

Then I noticed something odd. A few of the pictures had stick-on labels with a smiley face on them. Most had nothing at all. And a few had black bunting draped over them. One of the products with nothing on it was manufactured by a company we were quite familiar with because they were from the same city in which we were located.

When the venture partners came out to greet us, I asked about the pictures. The venture capitalist smiled wryly and said that the happy faces were for the big winners, no label meant they were only doing so-so to disappointing, and the black bunting labeled investments that were outright failures.

The company that was doing so-so by his estimation was on the *Inc* 500 list of fastest growing small companies. We knew the people there and admired what they had achieved. But for the venture capitalists it was not good enough.

The real financial risk to a technology investor is not that most companies go broke but that they do not provide a rate of return commensurate with the risk they represent. This is particularly true of investment in companies which do the pioneering work in a new technology. Pioneers usually do not reap the financial windfalls of their technology breakthroughs as often as other, larger companies do. The laws of economics dictate that money will find its highest and best uses. There are many, easier ways to get rich without having to figure out a novel way to rearrange the atoms inside a semiconductor. Just look at the Wendy's hamburger chain—all it took was a square hamburger.

Can venture capitalists still make breathtaking returns in high technology? Of course. When Exabyte, a manufacturer of a high-capacity tape drive, went public in October of 1989, right at the height of the venture industry's funk, Institutional Venture Partners (IVP) made a $60 million profit on its $2.5 million investment. Very impressive indeed.

But consider a more mundane company called Allied Capital Corporation. It deliberately invests in low-technology enterprises such as muffler shops, discount toy stores, and auto scrap dealers. The company produced a 36 percent average annual return through the 1980s and a 19 percent average annual return over its 30-year history. One could safely bet all his or her stock in Stardent, Miniscribe, and Prarie Tek that none of the high-technology venture capital companies will remotely approach this record over the same time period.

Real Competition

Six months into the company, we were invited to give a presentation to a venture capital club in Denver. We were invited by a venture capitalist to whom we had sent a business plan. Although our plan did not fit his objectives, he thought somebody else might be interested. (Plus he was in charge of filling the schedule with presenters.)

We went to the Brown Palace Hotel in Denver. Milling about were many smartly dressed men and women. There was a surprising number of young people, especially very attractive college coeds. On the agenda, in addition to our company, were a computer mapping company, a clothing manufacturer, another electronics company doing power of some kind, and a divorce kit company. We were fourth on the agenda, after the clothing company.

The first two presentations went just as we expected—stories of good ideas, a technology angle, projections of fast growth. When the third came, a dynamic young man in coat and tie went to the podium. The lights dimmed, rock music burst forth from giant speakers on either side of the speakers' platform, and the main doors to the ballroom flung open. In came the young people dressed in hats, T-shirts, turtlenecks, and shorts, in every imaginable neon color. (The coeds in shorts or spandex pants were, as intended, especially eye catching.) As the performers skated, jogged, and bicycled around the tables, the president told about how these clothes were for people on the go, the hip, the young at heart. The company was located in Boulder, a city known for being a little out of the mainstream. The visual presentation was synchronized with the music. The forecast showed growth as steep as the Matterhorn. The president said this bold look was on the way in. It was a once-in-a-lifetime opportunity to ride a fad to fat city. The company needed $2 million to go after the world. The president invited everybody to a party the company was having afterward at its table to present its wares. He received a resounding ovation, and, as our representative made his way to the podium, all eyes followed the coeds out of the room.

Our speaker had to wait until the applause subsided before he was able to start. He talked about how our technology was used in extracorporeal shock wave lithotripsy, atherosclerotic plaque erosion, RF pumped lasers, switch-mode power conversion, and ion implantation. We showed projections that were modest when compared to the neon clothing business. The audience listened and clapped politely when it was over.

Afterward, we went to our respective tables to chat with prospective investors. The neon clothing table, where the wine and champagne were flowing freely, was jammed.

Ours was deserted.

J. P. Morgan, Where Are You?

The small high-tech company cannot expect much help from banks. The banking industry is unstable due to a complex set of factors ranging from deregulation to unexpected deflation in real estate to gross mismanagement. But the truth is that banks have never been eager to loan money to small businesses which is why the government had to establish the SBA and other loan guarantee programs.

Banks have been willing to loan even less to high-technology companies because the banks do not understand these businesses nor do they make much of an effort. Banks are chartered to avoid risk. Dating back to ancient times, the only way to ensure against the risk of a bad debt was to have the debtor provide collateral. If the debtor did not pay, then the bank would liquidate the collateral and replace its loss. The problem for the small high-tech company is that it has very little collateral in the form of pledgeable assets, nor do the company's principals have very high net worths. Unfortunately, in the event of a disaster, the bank does not know what to do with what little collateral you may own. Where does the bank go to sell a spectrum analyzer or an ion source? A few banks located where there are high concentrations of high technology have learned how to liquidate technical assets, but these banks are few and far between.

The best you can expect from a bank is a loan against 75 to 80 percent of your receivables. This form of financing can be very useful. Also banks will sometimes finance facilities construction and equipment. They do understand bricks and mortar, though, ironically, a major cause of their problems has been bad real estate loans.

What high-tech companies usually need money for is people to design, make, or sell products. Banks will not loan on people because they are lousy collateral. They can get sick, die, or quit, and they have no salvage value.

Relatives, Friends, and Associates as Investors

The largest source of capital for small companies is called "informal" venture capital, in other words, relatives, friends, and neighbors. Understandably, the pool of available capital is small because most founders do not have wealthy relatives, friends, and neighbors. If you do, your relatives, etc., will probably be illiterate in technology and in no position to make an assessment of your company's prospects.

High What?

Two weeks into the company, we were seeking customers and investors. One of us happened to know a local real estate syndicator who put partnerships together for the local medical community so the doctors could shelter their money from taxes. With changes in the tax laws and a soft real estate market, I thought he might be interested in having his people look at a technology investment. I figured he, being a former IBM employee, might have some inkling of what a technology business was all about.

His office was in a well-appointed new complex by a lake in the fashionable part of town. He was always dressed like he was going out to play golf. To keep dapper, he even had an automatic shoe shine wheel in his office.

Even though he had no understanding of what we were saying, he could sense our excitement and became excited himself. Our forecasts showed meteoric growth and margins the likes of which were never seen in real estate. Yet he was still wary enough that he did not think it a very good idea to put us in front of the doctors until every aspect of our business plan was clear and accurate. He advised us to work on a list of milestones, which could be integrated into a set of goals and objectives, utilizing management by objectives (MBO) like he used at IBM.

So we made some goals and objectives.

He said he needed to make some more checks. He needed our complete résumés, which we supplied. It was early July.

Then he needed a technical assessment of our technology. He would show a neighbor who was an engineer for Hewlett-Packard designing computers. It was early August.

Then he said he wanted to involve another possible investor and his group would coinvest. The coinvestor was an independently wealthy accounting professor from the local university. He drove a new Mercedes convertible. We had a meeting, and he patiently listened to our spiel about volts and amps, then politely excused himself because he had to get to a tennis match. It was early September.

We scheduled another meeting a week later, supposedly to get down to the nitty-gritty.

As soon as we got there, the real estate syndicator informed us that the other investor had decided to put his money on a unique and exciting high-tech idea he himself had come up with. His unique idea was to develop a database that contained all the workman's compensation claims filed in the past so potential employers could do a background check on prospective employees and see if they were bad apples who really earned a living by filing bogus claims. He said the target market was big companies, and he could save them literally millions with this service. The real estate syndicator thought that was a great idea, and that's where he put his money also.

Significantly, this group invests eight times as much in small companies as venture capitalists. A recent SBA study cites that small investors funnel as much as $55 billion into small businesses. That is a large aggregate sum, but do not forget that this money is divided among 445,000 companies annually, which translates into a modest investment of $125,000 per company, a marginal amount with which to fund a high-tech company.

Further, gaining access to this capital is not easy because ownership in corporations and certain types of partnerships are security transactions that fall under the aegis of the Securities and Exchange Commission. The SEC is rightfully protective of little old ladies in tennis shoes, like your aunt, who might fall prey to a fast-talking technologist with a bright idea for a new laser flyswatter. Many (obviously the SEC) share the view promulgated by Peter Drucker, the professor of business management, who said that "most entrepreneurs don't know what they're doing."[10] It is true that friends and neighbors are likely to invest more because they like or trust you and overlook the missing ingredients in marketing or management which a professional investor would never tolerate.

Therefore, in order to legally gain access to this capital, the company may have to spend $5000 to $10,000 in legal and accounting fees to draw up an offering memorandum. Then, once the legal paperwork is in place, the individual investors must be sold. Herein lies a Catch-22. Most quality brokerage houses are not interested in raising money for small deals, a small deal being $2 million or less, or, if they are, they require a fee amounting to 10 to 15 percent of the offering, with some of it as cash paid up front. If a brokerage is not used, then the small company must go out and sell the deal itself, which is easier said than done. The average $125,000 investment described in the SBA report is probably comprised of investments between $2500 and $5000. That represents lots of time-consuming, one-on-one selling.

Then, if the entrepreneur is successful selling the new company to relatives, she or he can look forward to giving an annual report at every birthday, national holiday, and anniversary, assuming, of course, that everything is going well. If not, the founder may feel like being out of town on business for most of those occasions.

Other Companies: Licensing and Strategic Alliances

The amount of capital you need is driven by the scale of the organization you are trying to build in order to address a business opportunity. If your company chooses to limit the business functions it performs, then your capital needs can be reduced by sharing or selling those value-creating activities to another company. This is, in essence, what occurs if you elect to enter into a licensing agreement or some other form of strategic partnership.

Consider the chart below. As shown, in a fully self-contained (vertically integrated) business all the various functions exist within the company. Each function spontaneously generates a requirement for additional capital on the balance sheet. However, through licensing or strategic alliances, these capital requirements are transferred to other companies.

	Self-Contained	Licensing	Strategic Alliance
Administration	X	X	X
Research	X	X	X
Development	X	X	X
Production	X		X
Marketing	X		
Sales	X		
Distribution	X		

In the above scenarios, although the amount of capital you need rises in direct proportion to the functions you will perform, it is possible, in some circumstances, for the profits of your company to rise if you do less! In the right circumstances, collaboration with a larger business can generate profits in excess of what you can achieve on your own due to the other company's substantial capitalization, well-developed distribution channels, or high-efficiency manufacturing operations.

The relative attractiveness of the various partnering scenarios open to you really depends on two factors: (1) the size and characteristics of the industry you are addressing and (2) the goals of the company's ownership and the experience, abilities, and ambitions of the company's management.

Some industries, like pharmaceuticals, have an incredibly high cost of entry because of the lengthy and expensive government approval process. The legal and regulatory barriers in biotechnology are enormous because the inventions are pushing the limits of legal frontiers; indeed, the products being invented defy conventional legal understanding, i.e., "designer" research rats and human organ replacements obtained from animals. For this reason, many small biotech companies elect to license or jointly research and develop new products for the industry leaders. Taking a product all the way to market is simply out of the question. In computer software, where competition is intense and brief windows of opportunity open and close in a matter of months, many times the only way for a small company to catch some profits is to license to a company with a strong sales force that can guarantee instant market penetration.

The issues of goals of ownership and management are equally important. Like an individual, a company must know itself, where it is trying to go, what it wants to do, and what it is willing to sacrifice in order to get there. Collaboration with other companies represents risks as well as potential rewards. In order for the prospective collaborator to evaluate your technology, you will have to disclose sensitive information that can be abused. Also, each business function you transfer to another company is one you will not develop. How will you ever learn how to manufacture if you never do it? You can limit your growth potential because your partner may not share your zeal and determination to sell. You must weigh if your ally is better suited by virtue of management skills and market presence to generate the return on investment that your ownership needs. However, a collaborative model might enable your company to do what it does best and the people inside it enjoy doing the most and still obtain good financial returns. These must be considered as a whole because all forms of partnering can, to some degree or another, dilute the control of ownership and management over a company's destiny, shift the balance of power within it, and limit the company's earning and learning capacity.

In licensing arrangements, you authorize another company to make and sell your product in exchange for payments in the form of royalties, which typically range between 1 and 10 percent with the majority falling between 3 and 5 percent. The amounts and timing of those payments will be determined by competitive factors and conventions in the industry, the degree of exclusivity you grant, the quality of the legal protection of your intellectual property, and a number of other factors. Sometimes you read about licensing deals between large companies, usually one U.S.-based and the other foreign, in which massive amounts of money exchange hands. However, seldom does a small-company licensor receive a windfall down payment or one-time fee and then retire to the Bahamas. Rather it will share the risk with the larger licensor and share in the income flow as (and if) it occurs. Moreover, at least six months, and sometimes more, will pass from the time of the signed agreement before you see royalties.

Licensing agreements are complex. If you decide to seek a licensee, contact an attorney experienced in licensing technology similar to your own because terms and conditions vary by industry. This is no place to skimp on professional services. You will need assistance immediately to prepare a nondisclosure agreement that enables you to reveal enough information so that prospects can assess your product. An attorney can also help you consider and define your positions on a multitude of issues such as:

Scope of the license: Is it exclusive? Limited by geographical territory or application? Can the licensee modify or improve the product? Can the technology be used by another subsidiary or affiliate of the licensee?

Technology transfer: What is being licensed? What documentation and training is part of the deal? Who is responsible for technical support?

Royalties and payments: Are royalties determined by percent of net sales or a fixed amount per sale? Is there a sliding schedule for higher volumes (i.e., 5 percent on first $5 million, 4.5 percent on next $5 million, etc.). Are promotional units excluded? Are there minimum guaranteed royalties?

Marketing responsibilities: Does the licensee need to commit specific resources (e.g., $XX for advertising per year)? Does the licensor's name need to appear on the product?

Product liability and warranty: Who's responsible if the product hurts someone or someone's business? Who supports warranty repairs?

Term limits: How long does the agreement last? How can it be terminated? What constitutes default?

Other forms of common strategic alliances include R&D partnerships, marketing or manufacturing agreements, and the classic joint venture.

R&D partnerships are very common in high technology because they enable larger enterprises to tap the innovations of smaller, more agile companies with creative scientists and engineers. In these partnerships, the smaller company is reimbursed for contract research plus shares in the income stream resulting from successfully commercialized developments. In addition to funding, a small company can gain access to better equipment and synergistic technical know-how residing in the larger company's staff.

Marketing and manufacturing alliances are appealing when your company prefers to specialize in high-value-added engineering and product development. Or perhaps your product will quickly have high demand, as is the case with many computer and telecommunications products, but you cannot afford the capital investment or time to go through the learning curve to become a high-quality, high-volume manufacturer.

In the classic joint venture a small company will combine with a larger company to form a third company that is jointly owned and operated. Usually the larger company brings most of the resources and gets most of the equity. When entering these agreements, smaller companies must ensure that they are truly entering a joint venture and not, in fact, in the first stage of being acquired by the larger company. The termination clauses should be closely scrutinized. Anecdotal evidence from various joint ventures to date indicate that many do not work out, mainly because the corporate cultures of the small and large companies tend to clash. For this reason, for most small companies the other forms of strategic alliance are probably preferred.

One fact you must grasp in any collaborative scenario is that you will have to "sell" your product to the prospective licensee or strategic ally. He or she becomes your customer. Very rarely are small companies and their products serendipitously discovered. Quite the contrary, you must work hard and smart to draw the attention of larger companies, and, when you do, they are likely to assess what you bring to the market with the same skepticism or indifference as venture capitalists. Large companies do not buy technology, they buy business opportunities. Being risk-aversive, they will prefer to see you prove there is a market for your product by your having found some customers for it yourself.

No matter which form you might decide may be appropriate for your company, the most important thing is to identify the right ally. You are trying to find the missing ingredients. You are seeking market access, financial clout, or manufacturing expertise. Your ally's strengths must match your weaknesses, and, to an extent, vice versa. Observe the same rules used to find the right customer (described in Chapter 11). As you search for an ally, take your time and be discerning. The stakes are high, and you only have a few cards to play.

Despite what your formal business plan reads, it's wise be open to collaboration with other companies. They can lead you to new markets. You need them and they need you.

SBIR—The U.S. Government as Venture Capitalist

A major source of venture capital for small high-technology companies is the U.S. government through the Small Business Innovation Research (SBIR) grant program. You should investigate this program if you have product idea that requires additional research and development. A unique aspect of the SBIR program is that, unlike most other government-funded research, a primary goal is the commercialization of your technology.

The SBIR was created by an act of Congress in 1982, and the act mandated that federal agencies with extramural R&D budgets of $100 million award 1.25 percent of their funds to small businesses. Eleven government agencies support the program, with the largest five being the Department of Defense, Department of Energy, Department of Health and Human Services, NASA, and the National Science Foundation. The program has grown very rapidly. In fiscal 1983, a total of $44.5 million—686 grants—was awarded. By fiscal 1991, a total of $483 million, or 3341 grants, awarded. A few months prior to Bill Clinton coming into office, the Congress passed the Small Business Innovation Development Amendment Act of 1992, which increased SBIR funding to $1.4 billion by 1996 and the size of the maximum grants for both phases I and II. Phase I provides up to $100,000 for six months of research to explore the feasibility of an idea. The real object of phase I is to qualify for phase II awards, which provide up to $750,000 to develop a prototype over a 24-month period. By phase III the government wants the recipient to find outside financing from venture capitalists, banks, or other sources to carry the product to market.

The program is extremely competitive. To date, records show that about 12 percent of the applicants receive phase I funding. Of those who complete their phase I projects, fewer than half are selected for a phase II. These percentages may improve as the program is expanded in the coming years.

The allocation of the funds among the agencies is determined mainly by politics rather than a clear, rational industrial policy. The trend in the Reagan/Bush years was toward defense, reflected by the fact that the DOD consumed 60 percent of the SBIR allocations. Very likely these funds will be slightly redirected to reflect the Clinton administration's interest in manufacturing processes, information technology, and the environment.

To pursue an SBIR grant follow these steps:

1. Contact the Office of Innovation, Research and Technology, U.S. Small Business Administration, 409 Third Street, Southwest (8th floor), Washington, D.C. 20416 (phone: 202-205-7777) to get on the mailing list for the solicitations from the participating federal agencies.

2. Once a year the various federal agencies send out a presolicitation announcement, highlighting research topics in which they are interested and providing a release schedule for the official solicitation announcements and the closing dates for proposals. The dates for the releases of the solicitations vary by agency but are spread over six or more months.

3. The presolicitation announcements are followed by the actual agency solicitations, which include detailed descriptions of the topics for which the agencies are inviting proposals, as well as information pertaining to proposal format, deadlines, and selection and evaluation criteria. On average, there are three months between the release date and the deadline for proposals.

4. Read the solicitation to see if you can find a government R&D topic that matches what your company needs to research. If so, you send a 25-page-or-less proposal for a phase I grant. Instructions for the proposal format are explicit, and you must follow them to the letter. Any deviation from the format and your proposal will be considered unresponsive. Also, your proposal must be in the agency's hands by the deadline. A few hours late is too late.

5. Your proposal is evaluated by scientists or engineers specializing in the area of your proposal. Awards are then made on the basis of technical merit. You will be notified of acceptance or rejection of your proposal within about six months of submission.

6. If you are rewarded a grant, some time between two and six months after notification of award you will receive a call from a government procurement officer to negotiate the terms of the research contract and to discuss when you can begin work. Prior to commencing work, your company may have to be audited by the government, which can delay the project by weeks or even months.

A positive feature of the SBIR program is that it may be the only source of funds available to small companies with promising but unproven product ideas that need a high degree of R&D. The SBIR program is not really designed for a company to make money, although some companies earn a living doing nothing more than developing products for SBIR grants. SBIR is intended to subsidize the development of an ongoing commercial enterprise which sustains itself with private investment. According to an SBA study, approximately one in four grant recipients has achieved some commercial success.

In the early years there was some concern that the intellectual property of small companies was not afforded adequate intellectual property protection in the binding language of SBIR contracts, especially given that the government, by virtue of supporting the research, is thereby granted a royalty-free license to the technology if the government chooses to exercise it. Since then, however, additional protection has been provided. Though the government still maintains special rights, these are rarely exercised. The odds that a small company will make a discovery that is so momentous that the government will transfer it immediately to a larger enterprise for its own purposes or place it in absolute secrecy are extremely remote.

Admittedly, the SBIR program has drawbacks, the obvious ones being that the process is competitive, slow, and paperwork-intensive. Also, your research needs must coincide with those of the government. Nonetheless, there are many positive benefits as well. The government awards these grants with the full understanding that the company is going to make a best effort to succeed but with no guarantees. If the project doesn't succeed, the government doesn't ask for the money back or fire the management. There is no doubt that the SBIR program underwrites high-risk ventures that would have no chance with private funding sources. And, in the long run, only a few have to pay off in significant innovations to give the U.S. people a good return on their investment.

Business Incubators

Another alternative for a new high-tech company to compensate for missing ingredients is to locate a business incubator. As implied in the name, business incubators, which number over 500 in the United States, exist to help fragile early-stage businesses survive and grow during the first few years of the start-up phase.

Incubators, many of which specialize in high-tech businesses, are operated by economic development agencies, private investment groups, universities and colleges, and combinations thereof.

In their most basic form, incubators provide affordable rental space and business services. Several companies share the costs of basic administrative and secretarial services, conference rooms, and photo-copying, and, by so doing, substantially reduce each company's fixed overhead, an important factor in increasing the company's odds for survival. Some incubators offer an even wider scope of services, including legal and business counseling, extensive networking with other entrepreneurs, and assistance in finding capital.

Further information is available from the National Business Incubation Association (NBIA) at 614-593-4331.

Coming to Terms with Reality

The hardest realization to make is that the major cause of your undercapitalization is, one way or another, attributable to you—your management limitations, the small or obscure market you have chosen, or your unwillingness to sell more of the company to compensate investors for risk. True, the general scarcity of capital contributes to your condition, but investments still get made in the leanest of times.

Once you clearly identify the causes of your undercapitalization, two courses of action are open to you. One is to make the radical changes necessary to attract larger investments. These may include identifying newer and larger markets, bringing in more skilled management, or giving up more control to outside investors.

However, changes of this magnitude are easier to imagine than to implement. Larger markets may not be that easy to find. An aerospace engineer with an idea for a special component based on a new material for a limited application does not have the option to build an airplane. No amount of equity may attract skilled management into a small company because of the perceived risk or downward change in lifestyle that will be entailed. It may not be possible to attract investors despite your willingness to accept any of and all their conditions. Indeed, it is not unusual for the small company to be willing to sell its soul to the devil in exchange for some capital, but, alas, he has no interest in buying it.

The other option, which you may have to choose by default or go out of business, is to recognize your condition for what it is. The reality is that nobody will save you but yourself. If you can learn to compensate for the missing ingredients by utilizing the information in the chapters that follow, you will be well on the way to creating the capital that you seek.

5
Planning for Survival, Then Growth

> Thrown up against things, or into new arenas, we confront new possibilities and discover bits of ourselves we never knew were there. Discontinuity is a great learning experience, but only if we survive it.
>
> CHARLES HANDY[1]

Your company should have many lofty goals for itself, but the first priority must be to survive. Survival may not sound like a lofty goal, but all else—growth, innovations, market leadership, profits—is predicated on it. A definite occupational hazard of managing a small high-tech company is that there are too many decisions to make and too few resources (time, capital, or knowledge) with which to act on them. The wrong decisions can threaten your survival and rob you of your opportunity to grow. Fortunately, the quality of your decisions can be greatly improved by a plan and, ironic as it sounds, by understanding why you may be inclined to resist what the plan is telling you to do.

Strategic planning has been a sacrosanct topic in business for the past 30 years. Recent events in the world economy have raised serious doubts about the value of planning beyond very short time horizons. Many *Fortune* 500 companies such as IBM and GM, veritable masters of planning, have steadily declined in performance. Their bureaucratic planning resulted in corporate atrophy rather than excellence. But the futility of their planning is an expression of the obsolescence of their management methods, which are poorly matched to the chaotic contemporary business environment so accurately described by Tom Peters in his book *Liberation Management: Necessary Disorganization in the Nanosecond Nineties.*

Your main purpose in developing a business plan is not to mimic the antiquated habits of the ailing giants but to use a plan as a means to think creatively and systematically about how you will grow your business despite your limited resources and missing ingredients. A good model by which to accomplish this is found not in the usual business lore but in a well-known theory from behavioral psychology.

Maslow's Hierarchy

In the 1950s Abraham Maslow offered a theory of human motivation which became known as Maslow's hierarchy of needs.[2] He identified five distinct levels of human need, from the most basic physical needs, such as food and sex, to the more abstract and spiritual ones, such as the contemplation of beauty (as shown in the Individual column of Figure 5-1).

Level of need	Individual	Business
5	Self-actualization	Cashing out
4	Status and prestige	Market leadership
3	Acceptance	Market penetration and growth
2	Safety and order	Profitability
1	Physiological needs	Positive cash flow

Figure 5-1. Maslow's hierarchy of needs.

Maslow's basic idea was that the various needs must be satisfied in a fixed sequence; that is, lower-level needs of the individual must be satisfied before the higher ones can be attained. For instance, a person who is unconscious from hunger is effectively precluded from running for President of the United States. Similarly, a person with a knife to his throat is incapable of appreciating the beauty of a Renoir. Of course Maslow understood that the human personality is very complex, and, therefore, in reality, satisfaction of several levels of need is always pursued simultaneously. Not surprisingly, behavioral problems arise when individuals seek to fulfill the needs out of sequence.

Maslow's hierarchy became part of academic orthodoxy, not only in psychology but also in the marketing curricula of business schools. Marketers, naturally eclectic and hungry for insights into human behavior, seized the concept to explain the subtleties of consumer decision making (i.e., the boy buys the red car because it will attract the girl, or one just like her, who is leaning sensuously against the car in the magazine ad).

However, Maslow's ideas have much broader relevance to business than just how to sell products. The sequence of need fulfillment for an individual and a company is similar, if not identical, because a company, just like an individual, is in a dynamic process of development. A good business plan is really nothing more than a description of the means by which a company will fulfill each level of the hierarchy. Needless to say, a company that satisfies the various needs in sequence will be more successful.

The key lesson for you to grasp from Maslow's theory is that *the level at which your company is seeking to fulfill its needs should dictate how resources are allocated.* Once this principle is understood, it can be used to establish criteria for day-to-day operating decisions as well as long-term strategic ones.

Physiological Needs = Cash Flow

Early stage high-tech companies exist on the most basic level of needs. Your company's need for positive cash flow is exactly analogous to the individual's physiological need for food, as shown in the Business column of Figure 5-1. Your company's very survival depends on generating cash. Without cash, the existence of the enterprise is in jeopardy, no matter how impressive the technology, no matter how foolproof the long-term strategy, no matter how large sales are projected to be in year five. The business must pay its creditors and employees with cash in the near term, real time.

Cash flow results only from sales, and, therefore, your company's resources should be directed first toward the fastest and least expensive development of a product or service to sell and, second, toward finding customers who might want to buy it. Finding a customer takes time and money—advertising, travel, brochures, samples, phones, and faxes. Logically, expenditures not tied to product development and sales and/or marketing should be held to a bare minimum.

To generate cash flow off a limited capital base, it may be necessary to sell a product with less sophistication or at a lower level of integration than you might prefer or be capable of, but at least you will have a product that can get to market fast. If worse comes to worse, it might be necessary to sell a high-tech company's most precious resource—its knowledge. A viable survival strategy for your company is to begin as primarily a consulting or contract R&D company and metamorphose over time into a manufacturing enterprise. This type of intermediate business, or "bridge business," is a workable concept that no small company should overlook if it needs to buy time to develop a product. The technical know-how already exists. A minimum of materials or special equipment is required. But be aware that once you gain momentum as a custom/consulting company, it can be difficult to change your direction. Some do, however, succeed with the metamorphosis from consultant to manufacturer. Hauser Chemical Research, a biotech company founded in 1983, started as a contract research company and turned $50 tests into a multimillion-dollar business. When Hauser went public, a share of its stock skyrocketed from $0.05 a share to over $20.[3]

Two Pearls

With only $18,000 in the bank, we had to take on any business we could find, or the money would have vanished within the short span of three or four months because device sales were growing more slowly than hoped. We decided we had to take on almost anything that came our way to make that money go further. By supplementing the bank balance with long hours and one-of-a-kind "specials," we could buy time for our power device to capture the attention of the electrical engineering community and turn into some evaluation sales.

We went back and forth regarding whether to accept specials, because they took away our exclusive attention from getting the device accepted faster, which was absolutely true. But we were also convinced that had we focused on it, our cash would have been gone sooner than the MOSFET would have been able to generate a compensating income. Though we'll never know for sure, it was probably a good guess. What was difficult is that doing these specials sometimes entailed proliferating technology that might be very valuable in the future and that by so doing, we were depleting our bag of technology tricks, our true assets, and the future of the company. But then we began to think about it in a different light.

Our company was very much like a man crossing the desert without food and water. He is fortunate enough, however, to have two pearls. If he can get to his destination, each of the two pearls will be worth a fortune.

Just when he is about to succumb to hunger and thirst because he has under estimated how long it would take to get across the desert, he comes to an oasis. The oasis has food and water, but like Bartertown in "Mad Max Beyond Thunderdome," you have to have something to trade for it. All the man has to trade is the two pearls.

When asked what he has to trade by the shrewd trader who runs the oasis, the man replies reluctantly he has a pearl and shows it to him.

The trader looks at it carefully, then offers a piece of cheese and one goatskin of water.

At first the traveller is offended at the offer. "That's ridiculous," he complains. "It's worth a million times that."

"You have my offer," says the trader. He knows how large the desert is.

"I will need least four goat bladders to finish my journey," says the traveller.

The trader sighs and looks again at the lustrous pearl. "Three is the best I will offer," says the trader.

"We have a deal," said the traveler, who knows he really needs only two, and hands over the pearl.

The traveler made a good decision. The remaining pearl would buy all the food he could want for the rest of his life. The pearl he traded, he traded for his life. Both pearls would have been worthless if he had died in the desert.

While your company is focusing on market development, of necessity, it will sacrifice in other areas. Most functional areas will be weak. There may be no resources for a full-time accountant, purchasing agent, or manufacturing manager. When a business has few transactions, how can it justify the presence of a full-time accountant? Having specialized personnel may look good on an organization chart and, admittedly, help the company operate more professionally, but these personnel may represent an enormous, unjustifiable cost. The company is better served to have generalists on the business side who can multitask: be part-time marketers, accountants, operations managers, and human resource managers. Generalists will occasionally make errors that increase costs, but those kinds of costly errors are rarely as expensive as increasing fixed costs. Outside services, if required, can be contracted for specialized business needs on an interim basis. Increased staffing should be postponed until the work load is overwhelming, and even then staffing should be added mostly in areas that produce and sell more products; in other words, hire technicians and salespeople before secretaries and janitors. The wrong people at the wrong time are a drain on cash and management time. By contrast, the right people at the right time will increase cash and free management time to begin to address higher-level needs.

Latex Gloves

DEI started as a consulting company. To set up an electronic lab, we had to finance the purchase of equipment and supplies, so we drew down a line of credit, at a high interest rate, from a credit union.

We purchased a very expensive, top-of-the-line solid oak lab table, a Mercedes of lab equipment. Because sometimes the work required contact with harmful chemicals, some latex gloves were required, too. Intending to use good business judgment and get the best value for the dollar by buying at wholesale, we bought one gross of latex gloves.

Four years later there were still enough gloves for the next four years. With the interest cost included, the company really ended up spending as much as if it had bought one gross at retail—at Neiman-Marcus.

Next to people, the area where it is tempting to squander valuable resources is in physical facilities. Plush offices at a prestigious address are a reward for a job well done, appropriate for a company with excess cash and in need of tax deductions, much further up Maslow's hierarchy. An old bit of folk wisdom says that, "You can't eat your pride." Remember that both Apple Computer and Hewlett-Packard started in garages. Texas Instruments started in a converted bowling alley.

The Doll Fair

We started in the basement of a house. It was not uncomfortable because it was finished, and it was cool in the summer. There was ample space for two or three people.

It did have drawbacks. For one thing, we had a small development contract that required us to build a piece of equipment. Soon UPS trucks were stopping throughout the day. The property was not zoned commercially, and the neighbors no doubt wondered what was going on.

By the second month we had circulated press releases about our new MOSFET. The editor of an influential power electronics publication called and said he was travelling through Denver and would like to take time to come up and see us, if that was okay.

Of course, we agreed.

The house where the business was located also housed a three-year-old child. To get to our "facility," you had to walk through the family room. While we were working, the three-year-old got out every toy she had, and they were scattered across the floor from wall to wall.

We discovered this too late, when the journalist already showed up at the door. Carefully he picked his way through the obstacles and almost tripped over a teddy bear at the head of the stairs.

He commented that he could tell we were in an early stage of development.

Things improved very slightly at our first real upscale address. It was upstairs in a shopping strip across from a mall. Our office was located over a doll store. Across the hall was a group of insurance adjusters. Further down the hall was a guy who made his living going into companies where people were going to be layed off to help them see the humor of their situation. He would dress up in a clown suit and tell jokes. Of course, his fees were paid by management. To prove he was his own man, he brought his dog to work with him every day. Adjacent to us was a group of bank examiners. We worried that the noise injected onto the power lines by high-voltage equipment we were fabricating would wipe out all the data on their computer in the blink of an eye. Just in case, we did most of the testing at night.

Once the reality of your delicate position on the hierarchy is recognized, your decisions will follow a natural logic:

- If you travel, it does not have to be first class.

- If you need stationery, it does not have to be the most expensive linen featuring the company's logo as a watermark

- If you need a phone system, it does not have to the most sophisticated, fastest system able to accommodate a company of 200 employees.

- If you need furniture, it does not have to be the latest designer ensemble.

- If you need lab equipment, it does not have to be brand new.

- If you need to advertise, it may not have to be four-color.

In the early days of Sony, Akio Morita loaded his products into a dilapidated pick-up truck and hauled them around Japan. He intuitively understood the role Maslow's hierarchy plays in developing a successful company.

Safety = Profits

Safety is realized when the company is a going enterprise, able to make a profit month after month. When the company makes a profit, the first impulse will be to spend it—hire more "assistant"-level people and acquire more office furniture or equipment; in other words, to make life easier. Although it may seem reasonable to reward the company by spending money to make life easier, it can also have unintended consequences. It increases fixed overhead, often more than is necessary, keeping the company on a constant treadmill and unnecessarily exposing the company to cash flow risks. Spend money to make the company stronger, not just make life easier. Profits can be used to strengthen management, market more effectively, or improve products.

It is important for you to show an ability to earn and hold onto money because doing so builds credibility with the banks and potential investors. A business that has customers, cash flow, and, better yet, profits is not in the same risk category as a business that has prospects, but no customers, and a negative cash flow. The more you do not need capital from banks and investors the more they will want to give it to you.

The biggest reward that can be given to the company is to make it less of a gamble for those who work in it by building a cash reserve. Money in the bank is the ultimate safety net. Risk goes down as the bank balance goes up. A capital reserve enables the company to plan, take a rational look at real staffing needs, identify equipment that is critical to its mission and products that need to be developed, and implement a practical marketing plan it can afford to execute.

Conspicuous consumption should wait until much, much later, when the company can afford to pay for it out of excess earnings, rather than its capital. You will desperately need the cash when you ascend to the next level of the hierarchy.

Acceptance = Market Penetration and Growth

When the need for acceptance is fulfilled, you will realize market penetration and strong growth, proving your products are judged to have value. A rounded and competent management team will be in place. Your capital will be consumed by working capital requirements. You will book more than you can ship. The early stages of fulfilling this need is an optimum time to seek venture capital (banks will still be concerned about your ability to manage growth). You will be recognized as an emerging "player" and will have access to the infrastructure of influencers (i.e., major companies, journalists, and consultants) in the industry.

Status and Prestige = Market Leadership

Nearing the top of the hierarchy, your company achieves market leadership. You have managed, to use marketing expert Regis

McKenna's words from *The Regis Touch: New Marketing Strategies for Uncertain Times,* to "build relationships with members of the infrastructure who will support and establish your products."[4] At this stage your company is tough to compete against because it is the benchmark against which all others are measured. Your company's employees will participate as keynote speakers at trade shows and on the industry committees which determine standards. The finances of the company are strong. There is a surplus of capital that creates a broad range of choices for diversification into other industries or internal investment in higher productivity. It will also be appropriate, only then, to partake of the perquisites of success, however you imagine or define these.

Self-Actualization = The Option to Cash Out

The pinnacle of the business hierarchy is realized when the company becomes a stable entity that generates excess profits and constant innovation. The company will be a vehicle for the fulfillment of its employees' needs by providing them financial security and opportunities for personal development. You will be able to invest heavily in R&D to ensure long-term growth and to contribute to the advancement of your industry. Finally, you will have the option to cash out, rewarding yourself and those who endured with you the hard climb up the hierarchy with wealth and the choices that go along with it.

A Conflict of Needs

Although the pragmatic logic of Maslow's hierarchy is obvious, you may have difficulty adhering to it for two basic reasons. One is that to survive the inevitable setbacks of building a company, entrepreneurs must possess, among many diverse attributes, irrepressible optimism and dogged determination. You must be possessed by a vision that your company is large, strong, and successful—sometimes larger, stronger, and more successful than it really is. Consequently, the natural urge can be to project the image of a mature business when it is still in early adolescence.

The other reason is more compelling and more prevalent: The needs of the business are in direct conflict with your own needs. Basically, you and the business are striving to fulfill different levels of the hierarchy. As a result, the personal level of need for the entrepreneur is much higher than the business can afford.

Many entrepreneurs are middle-aged. Years earlier in their business careers they personally climbed Maslow's ladder. They rose from lowly, entry-level management positions in other companies to higher and higher levels of responsibility, rewarded at each stage with additional compensation and staff support. Prior to founding or joining the small company, these entrepreneurs may have enjoyed business perks that are customary in the larger enterprise but absent in a well-run small company. Perhaps the entrepreneurs became accustomed to having access to state-of-the-art equipment, travelling first class to trade shows and conferences, having a secretary type letters, and being able to vacation on national holidays. But as entrepreneurs, they find themselves performing routine lab tasks, licking envelopes, and emptying the trash.

Also, while fulfilling their personal higher-level needs for status and prestige, they may have embraced a more opulent lifestyle and accumulated the burdensome personal financial obligations that accompany it. However, in order to contribute to the success of an early-stage company, entrepreneurs must literally postpone their personal gratification. The tough reality for small-business managers is that their previous personal and professional lifestyles rarely are supported, either in or out of the office, at the level to which they became accustomed. They may indeed have to work on vacations, use second-hand equipment, and have less disposable income.

This readjustment of personal needs can be hard to make because entrepreneurs are products of their times. Like so many others, they may be afflicted with the notion that to have the trappings of wealth is the same thing as being wealthy. Having watched too many episodes of *Lifestyles of the Rich and Famous*, they become inclined to drive Mercedes when their net worths are better matched to Ford Escorts. Similarly, it also bewitches the companies they manage, whose balance sheets should locate them in the barest, functional offices, to lease space in architectural wonders with reflective glass and plush mauve carpeting at an appropriately high cost per square foot. It is fatal to copy the behavior of *Fortune* 500 managers. Managers of undercapitalized companies who stay in five-star hotels on business trips or insist on walnut-paneled conference rooms jeopardize their enterprises.

The hard truth of Maslow's hierarchy dictates that you must be willing to direct the company's scarce resources toward the satisfaction of the company's lowest-level needs first rather than your own higher-level needs. To be sure, attempting to fulfill the need for status and prestige before the business has actually earned them will squander the very resources that, if properly managed, will enable you to succeed.

The Internal Plan versus the External Plan

You need two plans, one external and one internal. Both describe how you will allocate resources at a particular time to achieve desired results. But that is their only similarity. They serve distinctly different purposes. The external strategic plan exists for constituencies outside the company, whereas the internal tactical plan guides the operation of the business. Remember, planning should never become an end in itself; planning can never become a substitute for doing.

The external strategic plan is a written statement of your company's mission and best intentions, given a certain set of assumptions. Its main purpose is to attract money from venture capitalists or obtain bank loans. Numerous books, seminars, and software are available that explain the standard format and mechanics of preparing a written business plan. For a high-tech business, one of the best resources is *Business Plans That Win $$$: Lessons from the MIT Enterprise Forum* by Stanley Rich and David Gumpert because it discusses the structure and content of plans that were successful in attracting capital and those that were not. It has especially valid insights on the plans of high-tech companies.

In the external plan, you are trying to write an enticing story, one that convinces investors that you are a risk worth taking and bankers that you are no risk at all. Thus the external plan contains only positive scenarios, preferably only one because a focused plan is easier to comprehend, and statistics indicate it has a better chance of acceptance by outsiders. The plan should be written in a tone that is authoritative and confident, with declarative sentences that carry the same force of conviction with which Winston Churchill assured the English people that they could defeat the Germans. There will be a noticeable lack of equivocal words such as "maybe," "approximately," "hopefully," or "perhaps"; in short, absent are any words that denote uncertainty. The external plan will extend out to five years. It will contain estimates of market size which are pure conjecture but which, nonetheless, must be presented with an unwavering air of confidence. In truth, as William Davidow wrote, "If a company knows the size of a total market, it can probably estimate the size of its market segment within a factor of two. I know that sounds very imprecise, but with a new technology it's about as close as you are going to get."[5] Remember that market sizes are only known after the fact, when they are already established and have leaders.

The external plan should minimize technical details and focus on business issues. There should be a clear emphasis on selling, pricing, competition, markets, financial performance, and management. Very few people who read an external plan will be capable of assessing the technology. In the rare cases that they are, application notes and articles can be included in an appendix. Special attention should be paid to making sure that the company addresses how it intends to fill in the missing ingredients from Chapter 3.

In contrast, the internal plan is focused on what the company will attempt to do in the next three to six months. Its overriding purpose is to ensure that your company maintains adequate cash flow. Unlike the external plan that shows that in year 2 you will ship "300 units" to a "market," the internal plan will say that sales will receive an order from a specific company in a specific time frame for a specific number of a specific product and that production will make the products at a specific cost and ship in a specific time frame and that finance will deposit a check for a specific amount in a specific time frame.

The internal plan may or may not be written. (Writing business plans is not as important as business planning. Sometimes the two get confused.) The "plan" may consist of several documents such as a shipping schedule, forecast, and cash flow projection. If written as a single document, the plan should be maintained on a word processor because it will be subject to constant modification. It is a dynamic document that bears no resemblance to the Ten Commandments. The internal plan is always in a state of flux, more like a screenplay that is altered as the best story line is developed during shooting.

The internal plan must be made very visible and accessible to everyone in your company and very explicit as to what everybody should be doing and when. Acting as a common springboard for discussion among departments, the plan becomes the basis of a budget process that determines the type and timing of expenditures. In arriving at the specifics of the plan, the departments will negotiate for resources and trade-offs necessary to achieve the company's cash goals. Because there will be business uncertainties (e.g., an order comes in later than anticipated, a product in development encounters a technical problem) within the time frame of the internal plan, it may describe several if-then scenarios that may require rapid changes and diversion of financial resources, so employees who are affected can get prepared and be able to minimize response time. For example, a project schedule may have to be accelerated to compensate for the delay of another one, triggering a chain of internal events. Engineering personnel may be assigned to the new project and be forced to set aside the one they are on before it is complete; purchasing will expedite different parts and cancel purchase orders on others; travel reservations may have to be altered; certain discretionary spending may have to be suspended.

The internal plan is short-term thinking par excellence. But, as Peter Drucker has said, "There is this need for constant reappraisal and redirection; the need is greatest where it is least expected: in making the present business effective. It is the present in which a business first has to perform with effectiveness. It is in the present where both the keenest analysis and greatest energy are required."[6] Sage advice, indeed. Only if your company is effective in the present is there a future.

6

Averting
Financial Failure

I think a business is very simple. Profit, loss. Take the sales, subtract
the costs, you get this big positive number. The math is quite straight-
forward, but a lot of people don't have this fundamental business
understanding.

BILL GATES[1]

Technology companies flourish, languish, or perish because of numbers measured in dollars, not angstroms, nanometers, decibels,
amperes, roentgens, MIPS, hertz, or other arcane units. It comes as a
cold, painful reality to many high-tech entrepreneurs that the success
of their endeavors is measured in the same prosaic monetary units as
pizza parlors, dry cleaners, beauty shops, funeral homes, muffler
shops, liquor stores, and used car lots. Technology is a business, and,
in the final analysis, business comes down to dollars and, all too often,
too few of them. Remember: When a company fails, it fails financially.
For this reason, the small company must become as strong in financial
management as it is in technology.

Management Science

Throughout the second half of this century, business has been the subject of clinical scrutiny by academics, consultants, think tanks, economists, large corporations, and governments. Every imaginable quasi-
scientific and statistical method has been utilized to analyze, describe,

predict, understand, guide, control, and shape business behavior, organizations, and outcomes. The urgent motive behind these efforts is to increase economic prosperity. Only businesses create wealth. Therefore if one can truly understand how to create successful businesses, individuals and societies should be able to create wealth at will, much like the baker stamps out cookies with a cookie cutter.

Though this aspiration has remained unrealized, a useful result of this voluminous research over the decades is that a body of knowledge has been distilled as management "science." By no means as reliable and foolproof as one of the hard sciences, management science can predict certain outcomes with a high degree of certainty. One certainty is that if a business does not place a conscious emphasis on the measurement and control of financial events, the business will fail.

Why Businesses Fail

The fundamental cause-and-effect relationships that lead to business failure are no mystery. They have been empirically verified. In 1974 the Englishman John Argenti conducted a detailed study, which he published under the title *Corporate Collapse: The Causes and Symptoms.*[2] Argenti analyzed the failures of companies of all sizes and in a variety of industries. This narrowly distributed book, whose findings are as pertinent today as they were 20 years ago, should be mandatory reading for every aspiring entrepreneur. It is as useful to a businessperson as a pathology text is to a medical student. Although the book does not directly address the major cause of failure for the innovative-technology companies, which is lack of demand, the work does methodically examine the subtle and universal web of financially destructive cause-and-effect relationships of which every small-company manager should be very aware.

Argenti identifies three characteristic profiles of companies that fail. Type 1 companies include small high-tech companies. As Argenti describes them, type 1 companies are young, the "general health of the company probably never rises above `poor,'" and "it probably fails within five years," a statistic very consistent with reality. These companies are characterized by a familiar catchall phrase as those which "never got off the ground." Type 1 companies are plainly of little interest to the author because their failures do not have the profound social impacts of the colossal failures such as Penn Central, where thousands of jobs and millions upon millions of dollars vanished into oblivion.

Type 2 companies include the fast-growth big deals and former high fliers like Stardent or Prarie Tek, which had one or more dynamic (maybe *too* dynamic) managers, adequate capital, great prospects, and some success in their markets before suddenly stalling and crashing.

Type 3 companies are the large companies that operate profitably for a long period in developed markets, then begin a seemingly inexplicable, inexorable, and protracted decline. Argenti, more familiar with the English business scene, cites Rolls-Royce as one of his examples. IBM and DEC may turn out to be future examples.

Argenti established that, regardless of type, all failing companies share a deadly etiology, or "story line," of twelve causes and symptoms. These inevitably occur, in sundry combinations and degrees, at one or more intervals along every failing company's morbid trajectory. What is most significant is that eight of the twelve of them pertain to lack of financial management.

It comes as no surprise that a company's death spiral begins with bad management, of which a major component is a *weak finance function*. By this Argenti does not mean the lack of only good accounting information, which is a cause unto itself that is addressed shortly, but also of proper emphasis on, or perhaps even grasp of, financial issues such as the difference between cash flow and profit, the use of credit and bankers, the dynamic relationship of current assets and current liabilities, and budgeting. In his words:

> There will be no budget, no cash flow plans, no costing system. The proprietor will almost certainly not have included loan interest, depreciation, and so on, in the few calculations he has made. He will not have allowed for losses in the early years. He will not know the marginal cost of his product. He may never have heard of "contribution."

Accountants, if involved at all, are used solely to generate obligatory statements, not for analysis, insights, and, most important, guidance.

Understanding this, you should take deliberate action to develop a strong finance function. It is easy to fall prey to the illusion that outstanding technology will, of itself, generate outstanding financial returns. But this is patently false. The two are in not necessarily connected and may actually have an inverse relationship. A focus on technology not counterbalanced by an equal concern for financial results can lead to decisions with disastrous financial implications. Small companies with a weak financial function will not even be aware that they are already in danger because of a condition Argenti fails to mention explicitly—undercapitalization, a condition that makes them even more vulnerable to the other financial causes of failure Argenti describes.

Hand in hand with a weak financial function arises another major cause of failure—a *lack of accountancy information.* Typical of the quote at the beginning of this chapter, many small companies do not really know if they are making money or not, when their bills are due, when they can expect payment for products delivered, where the largest percentage of their capital is being consumed, and what the real burdened cost of products is. In other words, the company is not controlled financially.

In an era of inexpensive personal computers and spreadsheet software this is inexcusable. One of the most odious results of lack of accurate accounting information is that it precludes competent management. There is no business management without accurate financial information. No company can function for long without a detailed cash flow forecast, income statement, and balance sheet. The company is in no position to offer quotations, to plan and schedule product developments, to plan staffing and equipment expenditures, to seek bank loans or venture capital, or to present itself as a trustworthy vendor to a potential customer. A small company without accurate financial information is in the unenviable position of a brain surgeon who must diagnose and operate on a life-threatening brain tumor without the benefit of an X ray or brain scan. If a small company is financially weak, accurate financial information is more important than trade secrets or patents, because the latter are worthless if the company is bankrupt.

Another financial cause Argenti describes is *overtrading,* that is, attempting to generate excessive sales on limited invested capital. This problem will appear for any undercapitalized company that experiences some growth. The rate of growth a company can sustain is directly tied to its asset base and profit rate. In a simple example, assume a company has $200,000 invested in inventory, receivables, and fixed assets, and annual sales are $600,000. If sales increase 50 percent to $900,000, so will inventory and receivables and fixed assets, in roughly the same percentage, from $200,000 to $300,000.

If the profit margin after taxes is 10 percent, which is not that easy to achieve, believe it or not, then there will be $90,000 with which to finance the $100,000 increase in assets, for a $10,000 shortage. However, if the profit margin is only 5 percent, there will only be $45,000, for a shortfall in assets of $55,000. If the asset base does not go up, it is doubtful the company can maintain the sales because, for instance, the parts or machinery necessary to make the product will not be available. In both profit scenarios difference must be made up either by additional outside investment or debt, both of which may be difficult to acquire. Disaster can strike when the company discovers it cannot get a bank loan and it owes cash on the additional inventory or new piece of equipment already ordered to support the sales.

Overtrading combined with a penetration strategy of low profit margins to stimulate sales is a certain recipe for disaster. Few small companies can ignore profit margins on the dubious logic that the company must first get market share, then find a way to drive down cost to get the profit back on sales sometime in the future. This is a game reserved for Japanese conglomerates.

Too often small companies are enticed to offer a bargain price on a small first order by savvy buyers promising volume business in the future. However, the more your company's profit margin goes down, the more the pressure on its feeble financial structure goes up. This strategy is particularly dangerous in high technology because about the time the volume is attained, outside competition will force price down right along with cost. It can be difficult, if not impossible, to even recapture the original investment.

Chasing Imaginary Carrots

A German company, a world leader in a rapidly growing medical technology called "extracorporeal shock wave lithotripsy," contacted us through a distributor to see if we would build a pulse generator to drive large acoustic transducers.

As we were working up a quote, we rationalized that there would be huge follow-on because of the enthusiasm of the German distributor and a forecast we read of the technology's business potential: 200 systems per year the first three years, growing to 500 systems in year five—let's see at an average price of $11,000 that would mean $XX millions over five years.

We quoted the system at a little over $18,000. They accepted after nudging the specification slightly. "Could we have a little flatter pulse?" they asked. "Sure," we said. "And maybe a slightly higher burst frequency?" "Sure," we said. We knew the bid was very aggressive, in fact we were absorbing all the development costs, but we would get back anything we might lose plus more in all the follow-on units.

A few months later, we shipped it. The cost to us was $40,000.

It worked and they liked it, but over three years have passed and we have never seen another order.

Argenti also warns about *gearing,* the British word for what Americans call "debt leverage." Leverage enables companies to buy assets, for which they do not have the cash themselves, by borrowing money from the bank. The word *leverage* implies that one can control a large, producing asset with very little cash out. For example, the company figures that a $100,000 piece of equipment will enable it to produce an additional $500,000 on which the company keeps 10 percent in profit, or $50,000. The company can make a down payment of $10,000 and the bank will loan $90,000 on a four-year note at 12 percent, so the annual payments amount to $28,000. If everything goes according to plan and sales stay strong, the first year out-of-pocket cash cost is $38,000. If sales increase $500,000, the $50,000 profit pays back all this cost and leaves $12,000. After the first year, the machine will net $22,000 per year. Not a bad financial move at all! That's an example of leverage working at its best.

But leverage has a downside, too. What happens if sales don't go up as much as planned? For example, what if Congress cuts the defense budget and sales only increase by $100,000, producing $10,000 in profit? Whether sales go up or down, whether the administration in Washington is Democrat or Republican, the company still owes $28,000 in cash per year to the bank. It is obvious what happens if sales do not increase at all, or worse, go down.

Recall that Argenti's book was written in 1974. Soon thereafter, high interest rates caused leverage to go out of style. Then, in the second Reagan term, interest rates came down again. The 1980s saw an explosion of leveraged buyouts, where financiers borrowed money to buy companies on the assumption that cash flow from the purchased company would service the debt. But a slowing economy belied the assumption, and banks were left sitting on a lot of bad debt. There is a lesson in this for the small company. Leverage works both ways— when it's good it's really good, but when it's bad, it's really bad. Leverage only works in a stable and improving business environment, at best a questionable scenario in the 1990s.

Leverage is rarely a big problem for the small company, because banks are not anxious to loan them money. In the few cases that small companies are highly leveraged, the assets of the owners or major stockholders, serving as collateral, are in jeopardy.

On first consideration, the *big project* Argenti cites as another cause of failure might not seem to be a financial cause, but ultimately it is. The big project can be a new product development or large contract. As Argenti says, the big project may even be "the very product or service that the company was formed to launch." But if you are not very cautious and know your costs exactly, you can go broke on what seems to be a good opportunity. How, you might ask, can that happen? Easy. You estimate that you can manufacture the product for $500, including parts and labor, and sell it for $1500, for a handsome gross margin of 67 percent. The key word in the previous sentence is *estimate.*

Argenti observed that typically the costs and development/production times are always grossly underestimated and the revenues similarly overestimated. If you are working with new technology, his observation is especially true. If you have not built the product before for $500 and sold it for $1500, do not assume that you will. Here is why: The parts will cost more than you guess because you did not factor in breakage and scrap; a primary vendor will fail to supply you parts on time, and you will have to pay a higher price from another supplier; and you will also forget to include the higher freight cost on the expedited shipment. Then labor will be higher, too, because your employees have not been through a learning curve. An assembly you estimate will take only one-half hour to build, which on a perfect assembly line would be the case, will take one hour because you forgot the test time required after the assembly is built and the rework time when it has to be fixed because of a quality problem. And it will be a higher-dollar-per-hour employee because the repair will be made by a technician, not an assembler. So now the product that should cost $500 actually costs $850. If you can still sell it for $1500, your gross margin has now dropped from 67 to 43 percent. However, the deterioration of the gross margin is not over yet. It is true that you can retail your product for $1500, but your "big project" is an OEM order for 200 pieces for delivery over a 12-month period. The OEM will expect a volume discount, say 20 percent off the list price, so the selling price is $1200. Now the gross profit margin has gone down from 67 to 29 percent. In some businesses, a 29 percent gross margin would be tolerable, but not in high technology. What about customer service? What happens if there is a reliability problem, and the first 30 units are returned for rework? Or worse, you have to send an engineer to work at the customer's site for a week until the problem is resolved? And the above degradation of the gross margin does not even consider the cost of capital for carrying the inventory and receivables. If you miss the pricing on a big project, your loss will be equally big, big enough that the company is unable to recover.

Symptoms of Failure

Once a company falls victim to the causes of failure Argenti described, two financial symptoms appear. The first is *deteriorating financial ratios*. Of course, lacking a well-developed finance function, management will not even be aware that the ratios are deteriorating, but they are nonetheless. A business, like the human body, has vital signs that should fall within a normal range. A current ratio heading below unity is as alarming as a human's temperature climbing above 98.6°F.

The last finance-based symptom identified by Argenti is the appearance of *creative accounting*, a polite choice of words for deception and outright fraud. When a company is in trouble, it has a natural impulse to conceal its situation to bankers, vendors, or investors. One way to do this is to distort or even falsify financial records. For example, the failing company may understate real cost of goods sold, overvalue a worthless inventory of finished goods that will never sell, create phony invoices for products that have never been shipped, or hide the real balances owing on payables. As if this in itself were not bad enough, the company can fool itself into believing its own deceptions. Not surprisingly, Argenti says this symptom appears when failure is imminent and irreversible.

Financial Management for Survival

Some small-company managers are hostile to the administrative aspects of finance because they claim the mundane mechanics of financial control, such as budgets, create bureaucracy. This is just a self-serving rationalization. What they are actually trying to avoid is reality and the painful choices that come with it. All companies operate on finite resources, never as much as they need or would like. No measure of performance is as revealing as the raw numbers in a financial statement. Accurate numbers are natural enemies of hype and wishful thinking.

The conclusions to draw from Argenti's study are plainly evident. A small high-tech company, by its very nature, is financially weak. It cannot afford to be weak in financial management as well. If the goal of your company is financial success, as it should be, the first step toward achieving this goal is to comprehend and recognize the causes of failure so your company consciously avoids them.

7

Understanding Financial Dynamics

As an accountant by profession and an old-fashioned bookkeeper at heart, I had always believed that the numbers were the bare bones of a corporation. The numbers, coming from units of the company all over the world, identified the assets of ITT, the sources of its income, the cash flow, where the money was going. More than that, the relationship among the numbers was for me like reading between the lines of a book. I could visualize the operations from unit to unit, the thrust or lack of thrust of the divisions. In my mind's eye, I could see the men writing the reports I read. I got a sense of the general health of the company, the performers and non-performers, the problem areas. Then I started asking questions.

HAROLD GENEEN[1]

When sailors navigate by dead reckoning, they have to rely on their instincts and knowledge to steer the ship because they lacking the certainty provided by astronomical measurements and sophisticated instrumentation. They estimate their ship's position from the distance run by the log and courses steered by the compass, making corrections for current and leeway. Make no mistake, dead reckoning is not the same as being adrift; the ship has a definite destination. The crew is just without resources that would make the journey easier and safer.

Finance in a small company is managed by dead reckoning as well. You are left largely to your own devices to set a financial course. Going into business requires no license, no proof of competence in financial matters. However, the financial obstacles are real and lethal, as Argenti proved, and somebody in the your company better know how to navigate through them. Your company, too, has a destination, and it must alter its course constantly in order to reach it.

Finance is more than a high-brow discipline reserved for the pin-striped Gucci set. Finance—making, measuring, and controlling money—is the heart of business.

All Decisions Are Financial

People, products, inventory levels, advertising, credit policies, pricing, contracts, insurance, equipment—these all have significant financial impacts to the your company because it is financially fragile.

Every company needs a scaled-down version of Harold Geneen, the former ITT chairman who is quoted at the beginning of this chapter. Admittedly, the breadth of Geneen's financial talents are overkill for a small company. Over a 20-year period he built ITT from $766 million to $22 billion in sales, with 250 profit centers on four continents, and recorded 58 consecutive quarters of uninterrupted growth of more than 10 percent per year, truly a phenomenal achievement. The point is that inside the company someone must supply the financial insight that Geneen provided for ITT. He or she must have the ability to assemble, analyze, and interpret financial records to "see" the state of the company in the numbers. Furthermore, the person must possess the requisite authority and influence to alter the direction of the company based on his or her insights.

Needless to say, the financial numbers in a small company are orders of magnitude smaller than those which Geneen managed in his career, but they are no less gravid with meaning. Certainly the core issues at the heart of the questions Geneen posed to his managers are universal for all companies, regardless of size: What happens to cash flow if this product is two months late? Why is the gross margin for another product so low? Why is marketing 30 percent over budget for the quarter? Why are the receivables getting so high? Who is not paying and why? Why have administrative costs doubled the past year? Why are the returns against gross sales so high? Why has inventory increased 20 percent when sales have only increased 12 percent? Why purchase a computer for $10,000 that will be obsolete in three years when it can be leased with no effect on the debt to worth that the bank is so worried about?

Geneen had the luxury to extract answers to these kinds of questions from an army of managers, who in turn were supplied data from an army of accountants. You do not have this luxury, but you must be able to pose the same questions and come up with credible answers. Therefore it is critically important to develop a strong financial capability in the company as soon as possible. Your success depends on it.

Financial capability means more than just being able to balance a checkbook. You do not have to become an accountant, but you must have a good understanding of financial statements, how they are constructed and how to use them as management tools. The academic aspects of finance can be learned through books or classes at a local college. The practical aspects of finance are learned in the heat of battle, making financial decisions and enjoying or suffering from the results. By careful attention to the movement of money in and out of your company, you begin to develop financial instincts that will enable you to make money.

Your objective must be to develop a complete understanding of the dynamic interplay between the balance sheet, income statement, budgets, and cash flow.

Profit Is a Necessity, Not an Option

Getting to profitability is not an option for a small company, it is an absolute necessity. You read frequently about well financed big deals that are not concerned about profitability because they are after market share or fast sales growth. These companies consistently lose money, but, by keeping their story full of promise, they can go back again and again to suck capital out of the equity markets before their credibility bubble bursts. But your situation is completely different because you do not have ready access to capital.

Profitability means more than just a profitable month every now and then. It means profit month in and month out. Consistent profitability can be an elusive goal. Profit is not easy to make for any business, whether high or low tech. In the *Inc.* 500 fastest growing private companies in 1992, 44 percent of the list had profits of 5 percent or less, and over 10 percent either broke even or operated at a loss.

Profitability must become a passion in your company to which all other goals, including technical innovation, must be secondary. The goal of the business must be to take $1.00 of investment and earn at least $0.20 or more every year on it. The only way this can be achieved is by a disciplined mode of thinking that makes the company constantly mindful of the two factors that combine to create profitability: cost and price.

Selling High

Buy low, sell high. This truism is the essence of a successful business, yet it is often ignored. Price poses a dilemma in high-tech business because a primary cause of lack of demand for innovative technology products is that the economic benefits derived from the product do not warrant the cost in the eyes of the customer, whose judgment is the only one that matters.

Pricing is a decision that is usually relegated to marketing because conventional wisdom says marketing is responsible for price, product, promotion, and distribution. However, in actuality, pricing is a key financial decision, perhaps the most important one a company will make, and it should therefore accommodate inputs from all functional areas of the company.

Too often prices are established on the basis of some rule-of-thumb multiple based solely on cost, such as the price will be 3 times or 5 times parts plus labor. But this is a misguided approach to pricing. Pricing for a product should be determined by two factors: how much a customer is willing to pay for the product and how many customers are willing to pay for it at that price. As Richard White says so well in *The Entrepreneur's Manual,* "Your sales price is totally a function of your product's value as seen by your customers. In no way is your sales price a function of your costs to produce your product."[2]

Your price reflects your cost plus value added. It is the job of engineering, finance, and production to control the cost. It is the job of sales and marketing to create the perception of value added.

Under no circumstances should your company sell below cost. Not selling below cost may appear to be simple enough to achieve, but many times you may not know the real costs, especially if you have more than one product line. Accurate cost accounting is a tough task. Most small companies know the direct inputs into a product such as materials and labor. What they don't know is the amount of the actual overhead on top of those direct costs and how to allocate it. One product line may be very profitable and others only marginal or losers, yet the company may be inadvertently directing more resources toward the losers. Overhead must be allocated on the basis of what it costs for the company to engineer, produce, and sell a product. When the numbers are closely tracked, it is not unusual to discover that a product really represents a very high cost to the company because, for example, the amount of engineering sales support, number of purchasing transactions, special equipment, or facilities space it requires. A product's price must carry its share of the costs. If it cannot, the price must be changed or the product discontinued. Every cost to the company must eventually be recaptured in a product's price. Where else can it come from?

Upon Closer Examination

Going into our third year, sales were composed of three product classes: MOSFET devices, standard lab instruments, and custom development.

The defense cuts were reducing the number of programs in which our MOSFET device might be used. Selling $500 worth of devices, the average sale at the time, required lots of phone conversations with design engineers struggling with a problem. The phone seemed to be always ringing with somebody needing help. It just seemed too difficult to get a design in and to take too much time. So we reduced advertising and other marketing efforts.

The lab instrument products were growing OK, though they, too, were being impacted by cutbacks in defense-related optics research. The average sale would be $1500 and require one or two phone conversations. One problem with this business is that customers buy one instrument at a time and you may not hear from them again until years later when they have a different requirement. But we had no high expectations that the instrument business would take off, so we made only modest advertising or product development investments in it.

What had been growing fast in the past year was the demand for custom development. These were bigger-ticket items that ran between $15,000 and $75,000. To meet the demand, we had hired an additional engineer, technician, and assembly worker. Also we made modest additions to our in-house mechanical capabilities by adding a drill press and other sheet metal tools.

At year's end, we sat down with our financial statements. Of our $900,000 in sales that year, roughly one-third came from each area. Our profit had been $50,000, which some would say is acceptable, but that represented lots of long hours and scratching and clawing for every dime. It seemed like an awful lot of work for the return. What was not making money?

We decided to examine each product area as if it were a separate business. We carefully allocated the amount of time consumed by everybody, whether in engineering, production, purchasing, or sales and marketing, in support of each product area. We apportioned the floor space required to support these activities, phone bills, advertising, etc.

The results were surprising. All the company's profit was due to the MOSFET devices. The lab instruments at best broke even. The big ticket custom developments had lost almost $100,000, and their losses had been covered by profits from the MOSFET devices.

There's no substitute for a complete understanding of a company's overhead structure, that is, each element that contributes to overhead. The company needs to know why it spends money on every person, desk, square foot, and piece of equipment. It becomes obvious that fixed overhead—the amount in dollars that goes out every month for expenses such as rent and insurance—should be held to an absolute minimum. Fixed overhead restricts a company's flexibility and lowers its margins, while forcing prices higher. When pricing, be careful of the mistaken idea that what you lose in margin you will make up in volume. Higher and higher volume will not ensure that the cost will go down. Cost can go down if carefully managed so that materials can be bought at advantageous wholesale prices and assembly becomes more efficient. However, just as often, as sales rise, overhead goes up disproportionately because increased sales increases the number of administrative transactions, i.e., more parts for purchasing to expedite, more receivables to collect, more inventory to track, more documentation to maintain. Unless costs are closely controlled, the increase in sales never translates into an increase in profitability.

Remember, if you sell a complex product, you must have enough margin in the price to cover the cost of service such as installation support or warranty repairs. Put in enough margin to feel good toward customers when they are expecting this service. As Theodore Levitt has pointed out, "The seller has made a sale, which he expects directly to yield a profit. The buyer has bought a tool with which to produce things to yield a profit. For the seller it is the end of the process; for the buyer the beginning."[3]

If you are in a highly competitive market, the market itself determines the range of the price at which you must sell. But many times with new technology, in the early stages of market development, there is little competition. During this stage you will have to combine your best financial and marketing intuition to maximize profits while not inviting competition. If you take too much advantage of your technology with your customers through usurious pricing, they will literally find ways to get competitors in your business.

Profit Funds Growth

Typically, the only way your company can grow is by cash generated internally from profits, supplemented by a line of credit against receivables from a bank. In this scenario profit margins become critically important, and the higher the better.

Strange though it seems, fast growth is as problematic as no growth. Fast growth can destroy a company because of the stress it places on the company's entire financial structure. The reason this happens is that when sales go up, so do assets on the balance sheet. When you have a receivable on a net-30-day basis, you are acting as a bank for your customer just like a vendor is acting as a bank for you when you get credit in the form of your payables. In most cases when you ship a product, you will already have paid the wages and materials well before you receive payment. Your company's cash is literally locked into the receivable showing on the balance sheet. If your sales increase 50 percent, so will your cash, receivables, inventory, and payables. If you do not have excellent profit margins and banking support, after paying not only the labor and materials but also the overhead, the faster you grow, the faster you will run out of cash with which to pay your bills.

Consider the hypothetical case of High Tech, Inc. (HTI) shown below. HTI has been averaging $100,000 a month in sales and has the opportunity to increase its sales in the coming year because demand is growing fast. HTI is trying to determine just how fast it can afford to grow. First, it analyzes how much additional funds will be required for the additional growth, given various growth rates and these assets and liabilities from the current balance sheet:

Cash	$ 25,000
Receivables	150,000
Inventory	75,000
Total	$250,000
Payables	$ 50,000

In the spreadsheet HTI's management sets up, assets will grow in direct proportion to the increase in sales. Likewise, payables will increase in the same proportion. Payables will be deducted from the additional funds required because the payables represent the credit extended by suppliers. Suppliers help fund your growth, as the following figures illustrate:

Growth rate	10%	20%	30%	40%	50%
Increase in assets	$25,000	$50,000	$75,000	$100,000	$125,000
Decrease from payables	− 5,000	− 10,000	− 15,000	− 20,000	− 25,000
Additional funds required	20,000	40,000	60,000	80,000	100,000

These additional funds must come from profit, debt, or the customer. Receiving funding from the customer is discussed in the next chapter. Debt will be hard to get. Banks will loan against receivables, but they do not like to loan on work in process. Therefore, the profit margins of your products, your ability to earn as much profit as possible, are of paramount importance. The chart below shows the amount of external funding that is required for HTI, given various profit margins. The negative signs indicate a short fall, and figures without indicate a surplus. The chart illustrates both how critical profit margins are and how difficult it is to entirely fund growth on profits.

	Sales (thousands)				
Profit margin	$110	$120	$130	$140	$150
1%	$ − 19	$ − 39	$ − 59	$ − 79	$ − 99
5	− 15	− 34	− 54	− 73	− 93
10	− 9	− 28	− 47	− 66	− 85
15	− 4	− 22	− 41	− 59	− 78
20	2	− 16	− 34	− 52	− 70
25	8	− 10	− 28	− 45	− 63

If HTI's profit margins are 20 percent, the company can support sales growth of 10 percent on internally generated funds. However, if HTI chooses to grow 30 percent, it will have to find $34,000 of additional funding.

Getting Financial Aid

According to *Inc.'s Guide to Business Strategy*, most small companies have limited in-house accounting staffs. The majority of those with sales of less than $1 million employ only one person in a bookkeeping or accounting function.[4] *Inc.* further found that in two out of three companies surveyed the CEO doubles as the CFO. That is great as long as the CEO truly understands finance, which is not often the case.

If your company does not have a financial capability fully developed, avail yourself of outside assistance by retaining the services of an accounting firm. These services can be relatively inexpensive if you do the rudimentary bookkeeping in-house. Bookkeeping in a small company is simple because the actual number of transactions is small. You do not have to make the entries yourself, though there are learning benefits to doing it yourself for a while. It puts you in direct touch with the vital ebb and flow of money in the business. You can always find a retired or part-time bookkeeper to perform the mechanical tasks like posting and check writing. Payroll is best handled by a computerized service center because they will do this faster and cheaper than you because they know the state and federal tax laws, and they provide you accurate, detailed payroll reports that will keep you from getting entangled with the federal bureaucracy.

At the end of each month it is easy and relatively inexpensive to give these records to the accounting firm to produce the income statement and balance sheet. When you get them back, don't be shy about asking what they mean.

Third-Party Scrutiny

Three months after opening our doors, we retained the services of a CPA firm. The firm was not ideal because it had little experience with high-technology companies or manufacturing. However, it was competent in closely held companies and personal taxes. In addition, it was willing to work with us on payment terms because our cash flow was irregular.

Each month we kept close track of the receivables, payables, and checkbook. At the end of the month we would give the accounting firm our check stubs. With this information they would take our cash-based system, convert it to a more accurate and conventional accrual method, make the final adjustments on a trial balance, then generate the monthly statements. They also advised us on inventory tracking and similar issues. When we went to the bank to inquire about a line of credit, the bank officer was delighted that an accountant was watching over our shoulder.

Of course, at that time, the financial statements were only a "compilation," which means that the accounting firm was not staking its good reputation on the information because it really originates from the company's management, not from an audit. But just seeing the accountant's signature on his letterhead (even though the statement contained a caveat emptor that the numbers could be worthless) and bound with a cover gave the bank a wonderful feeling of security.

The cash flow, however, was always kept inside the company, from the very first week of operation, because that is too important to trust to any outsider.

Income statements and balance sheets warrant the review of a professional to ensure that they conform to accepted business standards. These financial records, certainly important to the company, are more important to parties external to the company, such as bankers, creditors, and investors.

Also seek out the advice of people who have been financially successful, especially if they were successful in high technology with all its unique problems. Usually their opinions are free, unlike your accountant and other professionals. You should be willing to share your real thinking, naive and uninformed as it might seem, and solicit their most candid reactions. Listen attentively to their thoughts. They will teach you the thinking processes necessary to make money.

God's Gift to Electronics

A local real estate developer who was sitting on a lot of cash was looking around for an investment. He had been quite successful over the past 20 years, but he did not like the changes he saw in the real estate business, i.e., tight money, foreigners bidding up land prices, and decreasing tax benefits. So he was looking to diversify his portfolio and maybe put a small amount in a high-tech, high-risk venture.

He visited and was given a tour of our facility. He saw a pulse generator being built for a very special application in a semiconductor test, one for a high-reliability radar application, and another for testing laser diodes in a manufacturing facility. He took all this in with little comment. Repeatedly we emphasized how we provided very advanced products and recited specs that were meaningless to him.

He asked who our competitors were.

We said we really did not have any direct competitors. We did things nobody else could do.

He said that must be nice not to have any competitors because in real estate he always had competitors.

After the tour, we went to our upstairs offices and pulled out the financials. He got a cup of coffee and sat there for a long time quietly looking them over.

Finally, he looked up.

We asked if he had any questions.

"Well, hell, I don't know a damn thing about electronics. I'm not sure I know what to ask." He paused and frowned slightly. "But one thing really bothers me," he said.

"What's that?"

"Well, you say you're God's gift to electronics. OK, I'll believe you. But if you are, you should be making a hell of a lot of money. But you're not. Jeez, last year your sales were nine hundred grand and the only profit you show is a little over $50,000. A guy could do that well with a CD at the bank." He paused again, then smiled as if he remembered something. "Of course, I bet if I look into the expenses a little I'll find guys are paying for a couple of nice cars and a condo in Steamboat, huh? There's nothing wrong with hiding things from Uncle Sam, that's for damn sure."

"We're not hiding anything. Those numbers are real. There are no trips to the Bahamas in there or anything like that."

"There aren't?"

"No."

Then he stopped smiling and turned serious. "Hell, I wish there were."

"Why?"

"Because that means you're not charging enough. Hell, if you're gonna work your ass off and you're the only show in town, they ought to be willing to pay for that. They have to, right? You said nobody else can do half this stuff. Look at the numbers. You guys are giving everything away. You don't have to start a business to do that! Hell, all you have to do is call the Salvation Army."

Comparing Comparables

Naturally you often wonder how you are doing. You look around for another company to compare yourself to. You know you are not IBM or Sun or Ciba Geigy or 3M, the caliber of companies you read about in *Business Week*. Unfortunately, there is a dearth of reliable financial data available on small, privately held companies against which to calibrate the performance of a small company.

Financial professionals such as bankers typically assess a company's financial performance by taking its balance sheet and income statement and comparing them to the data on similar companies compiled by service firms such as Robert Morris Associates. But these are of limited value for several reasons. The service firms poll a small number of companies, so it is questionable if they are really representative. The data are arranged by standard industrial codes and thus represent a broad spectrum of companies that may or may not be similar to your company. Although information on manufacturers of electronic instruments is better than nothing, it is not as useful to a manufacturer of laser diodes as knowing the financial ratios for other manufacturers of laser diodes. Data that niche-specific simply are not available. Many of the companies from which data are collected are mom-and-pop operations with no aspirations to grow. There is no assurance the accounting information provided is accurate. No information is available on growth rates, the ages of the companies, or trends. To make matters worse, in many closely held companies the numbers are deceiving because personal expenditures are hidden in income statements as bona fide business expenses. Further, privately held companies are rarely eager to reveal key financial information because it can be used by competitors.

Some information can be obtained from Dun and Bradstreet's credit reports on individual companies, though sometimes the information is not as current as one would like. Publicly traded companies must reveal financial details to comply with SEC regulations, but because of their ages and sizes, these details have little utility for the small company seeking a benchmark.

Trade publications often contain useful financial data. For example, each year *Electronic Business* publishes the financial results of the top companies and ranks them by market segment, profitability, sales growth, and return on investment. Again, this information has limited direct value to the small company because it shares only remote similarities to its much larger counterparts.

The financial statements of a 3-year-old high-technology company that has been engaged in heavy product development and marketing will bear no resemblance to a 20-year-old manufacturer of power systems for charging car batteries which spends 0 percent of its revenues on R&D. So the information available by the financial services and trade publications cannot be used as more than very general guidelines.

Vital Signs

Conventional financial ratio analysis, too, has definite, but limited, usefulness to a small company. The income statements of a small high-tech company often show bloody losses, severe revenue gyrations, and a balance sheet with a disturbing retained deficit. You have to know what you are looking at to see positive signs of life, if indeed there are any. Maybe it's sales growth, a product line with good profit, or an improving current ratio.

A small company will find little guidance from banks. If the company (the officers, actually) is able to obtain bank loans, certain financial guidelines will be imposed in the form of current ratios or debt-to-net-worth ratios that must be maintained. If these ratios are not met, the bank can, and will, call the loan. The ratios are based on the law of averages and should be respected. The averages simply show that those who meet or exceed the ratios are safe risks and those who do not are not because, typically, they do not repay loans. With the ratios, banks are able to compare any two businesses within an industry to each other. Though you feel your company is an exceptional case, to the bank you will be no better than average.

In truth, maintaining these ratios may or may not be in the best interest of the long-term financial health of your company. The problem with relying solely on ratios is that although they are good for setting limits, they may not take into consideration a goal you are attempting to achieve. There may be periods of time where you must take risks and degrade these ratios to dangerous levels. It is not because you are cavalier with the company's future. To the contrary, you have no choice but to take financial risks. For example, when you launch a new product, you may expend cash and operate deeply in the red to advertise and build up some inventory to create sales that will be quickly converted to cash. During these periods, you may enter a danger zone that would frighten a banker or outside investor who does not share your faith that the money will come back in.

In conventional accounting, a picture of the company in the form of financial statements is taken at regular intervals, usually monthly. When you understand finance and accounting, you can time certain financial events to make sure you protect your ratios. For example, knowing your payables will be up because you have been building inventory on a long-range project, you can request a customer to provide progress payments so that more cash shows on the balance sheet to preserve the current ratio to the satisfaction of your debt holders. Or if you have a line of credit against your receivables, you can time shipments so that you can keep your access to the line at a maximum.

You should fully understand the implications of the various financial ratios before you wantonly violate them. They will tell you if your company would appear to the outsider to be in danger. The ability to look at the company like an outsider is important because the small company is very much like the frog in the famous boiling water experiment. If you throw a frog in a pan of boiling water, it will jump out immediately and survive. However, if you place the frog in a pan and slowly bring up the heat, the frog will not perceive the change and boil to death. Likewise for your company, in the day to day battle of financial survival you may become so steadily inured to the wild fluctuations in business conditions and comfortable with extreme financial situations that, unless you are trained to recognize the signs, you may not even be aware that you are in extreme danger.

What is important is that you know if you are in danger, have a clear understanding of how and when you will emerge from the danger, and have a plan for what you will do immediately if something unpredicted and bad happens, e.g., the order you planned on is delayed or you encounter a technical problem. You must have an inti mate understanding of the financial condition of the company.

ROI

The ultimate measure of success is amount of dollar output a business is able to generate from dollar input. The most widely accepted measure of this relationship is called return on investment (ROI). An ability to articulate goals in terms of ROI is evidence of business acumen. ROI is what people who understand money, like bankers and investors, are looking for more than anything else.

ROI is a term that is used loosely, but which has a very specific meaning. The simplest expression of the ROI equation is

$$ROI = \frac{Net\ income}{Investment}$$

Note that the numerator originates on the income statement and the denominator on the balance sheet. These two financial statements, combined in this fashion, are the final judgment on the ability of the company's management. ROI reflects the quality of every decision that is made.

The individual components of the income statement and balance sheet, and their interrelationships, are important to master because every technical, marketing, production, and financial facet of the company are linked, as is evident from even a partial list of methods that can be used to improve ROI:

- Faster collection of receivables
- Higher prices
- Lower inventory
- Lower payroll
- Higher productivity
- Lower operating costs
- Lower cash balances
- Increased volume
- Lower investment in fixed assets
- Faster product development

- Higher or lower debt
- Higher margins

Each of these, in itself, represents a substantial task that will test management's best thinking and ability to get things done.

A technology company, like any other business, is expected to generate a positive ROI. For the risk an investor (even a sole proprietor is an investor in her or his own company) assumes in a small company, the ROI should be at least 20 percent or better. And, in the case of your company, it is not enough to show a good ROI in the form of paper profits on the income statement. The ROI must be realized as hard cash.

8

Maintaining Positive Cash Flow

Entrepreneurs starting new ventures are rarely unmindful of money; on the contrary, they tend to be greedy. They therefore focus on profits. But this is the wrong focus for a new venture, or rather, it comes last rather than first. Cash flow, capital, and controls come much earlier. Without them, the profit figures are fiction....

PETER DRUCKER[1]

The scarcest resource is cash. Cash comes into a company by only three ways: through investment, debt, or payments from customers. A small company may not have the option of the first two, so *it must generate cash from its customers.*

In a small company you can never forget that the only event that can put you out of business is running out of cash. It is your most precious asset. As long as you pay the bills, you will be allowed to exist. There is no substitute for cash, unlike the other resources you manage. Maybe when you lack engineering design time, you can work evenings and weekends. Or when you lack marketing resources, you can get free product announcements. But when you lack cash, there is no way to take what you have and make more. It is the most finite of resources, and it must be aggressively protected and nurtured.

In the discussion that follows, considerable attention is given to *controlling cash flow* because the availability of cash is always the most pressing financial issue for a small high-tech company.

In the end, all management problems manifest themselves as cash flow problems. Products that are delayed because of a technical oversight or because of an inefficient manufacturing process cause the period of time between cash going out for the engineering development or direct costs of manufacture and cash coming in from the sale of the product to be extended. Nonetheless, operating costs will be incurred at each interval during that time. Cash for rent, salaries, taxes, phones, insurance, etc. go out with absolute regularity. Even direct labor costs can be very deceptive because they may look like a variable expense, when in fact they are not. If you have test technicians you pay $3000 per month and they work on a project for two weeks then wait two weeks for the next one, the project may only be allocated $1500 of a technician's cost, but the company still pays him or her $3000. This interval between cash going out and cash coming in, if long enough, translates into a negative cash flow.

Squeeze Cash out of Profits by Treating Them as an Expense

Cash can be squeezed out of operations by treating profit as an expense. This is not a financial sleight of hand. It is a valid financial strategy for a small company. A cash reserve is necessary to insulate the company from a unforeseen events (e.g., a large payment is delayed), to create financial leverage (e.g., collateral for a bank loan), or to seize a business opportunity (e.g., a product for an emerging market).

Unless measures are taken to ensure otherwise, profit has a way of never showing up as cash. What typically happens is that operating expenses, if not closely controlled, are allowed to absorb the profit. Quite simply, the profit gets spent because the *profit is not planned for and protected.*

A conventional income statement looks like this:

Sales

— Cost of goods
Gross profit

— Fixed expenses

— Operating expenses
Net profit

Note in the above that profit is what is left after all expenses are paid. However, examine the modified income statement shown below:

Sales

$$\frac{-\text{ Cost of goods}}{\text{Gross profit}}$$

− Fixed expenses

$$\frac{-\text{ Profit}}{\text{Operating expenses}}$$

In this format, profit is treated as a fixed expense. It has been budgeted. A certain amount of profit has been targeted to be set aside every month. The amount of profit should be enough to ensure a decent, minimum return on the invested capital. If you have $250,000 of paid-in capital, an appropriate interest rate, with a modest risk premium, might be 10 percent over prime. So if the prime is 7.5 percent, the lowest return you will tolerate is 17.5 percent, which amounts to $18,750 per year or $1562 per month. Your hope is for a higher rate, perhaps 25 percent, but, through this technique, you will ensure at least a minimum return.

Now operating expenses are treated as discretionary expenditures. Using zero-based budgeting, the money available for operating expenses is variable. Management must figure out how to fairly apportion the remaining balance to the various departments, without compromising the company's goals more than necessary. The minimum profit is not available to cover these expenses.

In fact, the profit will be turned into cash by treating it as a cash expense that is accounted for on the cash flow statement as cash out. In any month immediately following a month that shows a profit on the income statement, as receivables are collected, cash in the amount of $1562 will be transferred into a separate cash account. In months that show losses this amount will accrue; for example, if June and July show losses but September shows a healthy profit, then in October $4686 will be transferred to this account.

The beauty of this method is that profit is realized as cash, set aside, and protected. The transfer of cash in no way affects the balance sheet, and, of course, the cash is always available for dire emergencies. As a budgeting technique, management is forced to find a way to make the company operate profitably, and nothing, including salaries, is sacred.

Hands-On Cash Flow

The cash flow concept is simple, but maintaining a positive cash flow is hard work and demands constant attention. Cash flow is the ebb and flow of cash as it occurs over a standard time period such as a week or a month. It is a real time process. Real money goes in and out on real calendar dates. Net cash flow is the difference between the cash in versus the cash out in that period. A positive cash flow means more cash came in, in the period of interest, than went out. Conversely, a negative cash flow means more cash went out than came in. In the case of a negative cash flow, that cash can only come from the company's own reserves or its access to bank credit.

Management of cash flow should rest with and have the undivided attention of the highest-level management in the company. You cannot be too preoccupied with it. You should know your cash flow situation in great detail over a moving 30- to 60-day window. There is no room for complacency or error when it comes to the ebb and flow of cash dollars from week to week and month to month.

Positive cash flow is related to, but different from, profit. It is important to understand that you can have a profitable business and still have a dangerous cash flow problem. Indeed, as discussed in Chapter 7, if your business grows too rapidly, you will inevitably have a cash flow problem because cash always goes out long before it comes in. You pay employees, rent, materials to a schedule, i.e., paydays on the first and fifteenth, rent is due on the first, payments are net 30 on invoices to vendors. Usually by the time you ship a product you have already paid for the materials and labor contained in them, though you may not get paid until a much later date. Even though terms to your customers are net 30 days, you do not necessarily receive your money on that schedule. Obviously there is a potential timing problem because when the money must go out may not be when the money is in. If too much money must go out before it comes in, the company faces a cash flow crisis which can be fatal, despite the fact that the income statement might show a profitable company. This happens all too often.

Instructions on how to calculate cash flow abound in finance textbooks. Avoid aggregating payables under categories that are too broad as shown in most of the examples. The company needs to know exactly what payment is due, to whom, and when. An adequate cash flow system is so simple that it can be set up and maintained on any spreadsheet. However, be advised that it is only as good as the effort that is put into it.

By comparing the weekly totals of *cash in* versus the totals of *cash out,* you will see the weeks in which there are surpluses and shortages. Once you see the situation on paper, you are in a position to begin the real work of cash flow management: collecting receivables and timing cash disbursements for payables in order to maintain a positive cash flow.

Take Receivables Personally

A business transaction with a customer is complete when the customer makes payment, not when the goods are delivered. From your company's perspective, the collection of the receivable calls for an effort of the same intensity that was required to manufacture the product in the first place. Remember that the receivable contains not only the your company's cost, for which it has already paid with its own cash, but also its profit. The small company always has an acute need for the cash stored in a receivable.

A receivable is as good as the creditworthiness of the company to whom the invoice is sent. It's nice to be able to show bankers and investors that people owe you money for products delivered but not nearly as nice as showing that you get paid. A company that is able to collect in a time period reflecting the standard terms of its industry demonstrates that the company is well managed, is valued by its customers, and services a healthy industry. To the jaded and objective eyes of outsiders, an inability to collect receivables can mean only a few things, all bad: (1) you sell to uncreditworthy companies, (2) the customer doesn't think your products are worth paying for, or (3) your industry is financially weak. All finally reflect negatively on your business judgment.

Numerous factors influence how companies pay debts to suppliers. Small companies can be very erratic because of the unpredictability of their own cash flows. Many large companies have a policy of paying promptly to terms. These are good customers who will help you grow. Others, unfortunately, will not. Some large companies have an ingrained corporate culture that vendors are adversaries, and they use their vendors as banks to finance their operations (so do small companies, but usually they really can't help it). Their financial managers consider it good business to stretch out their suppliers because they can get a few more days interest on their money-market accounts. Be wary of doing business with companies like these, and develop adaptive strategies to reduce your risk, e.g., negotiate for them to pay you a large down payment.

Turn your receivables into cash by taking an active role in their collection. If your terms are net 30 days, on the thirty-first day if the check has not arrived in the mail, you should get the invoice number, call the customer, ask for the payables department, get the payables clerk on the line, and ask when you can expect payment. When it comes to collections, the squeaky wheel gets the grease. Collection calls are no fun, but there is truth to the platitude that you can't eat your pride. Act at once! If you have trouble making this call just remember that you made and delivered a product and you are owed the money; it might be your house payment. Nonpaying customers will cause hardship for you and your employees. You and your employees work hard to earn your livings. You are in no position to be a bank for any company.

On the first collection call, be affable but businesslike. Get the full name of the clerk so you know the name. It makes it more personable. Always write down the date, time, and name of the person with whom you speak on all collection calls, as well as highlights of the call. Get a firm commitment for a date of payment. Expect clerks to use the old tricks, i.e., "the check's in the mail" or "Oh, golly, it looks like we lost your invoice." If they say the check's in the mail and it's Monday, tell them that you'll expect it by Friday. On Friday, if the mail comes and it is not there, you should call them back immediately and use your notes to remind them of what they said. If an invoice is missing, say you'll fax another one right away. Then call back to see when it will be paid. If they say that they'll be paying in another "couple of weeks," just say that that is not good enough and ask whom you have to talk to to get it sent earlier. Reiterate that your terms are net 30 and your company and their company have an agreement. You lived up to your side by delivering the goods; they have to live up to their side by making payment.

Each time you have to call back on a collection, you have a right to reduce your affability by two notches. Make it evident that you are displeased and do not intend to play cat and mouse. Payables clerks are human. Most of them are not paid very well and do not like to get hassled over the debts of their company. If they have not paid you, the likelihood is that somebody above them has not released the funds. When you hear them fumbling for an excuse (the best are too well trained to fumble), ask if there is some problem and, if so, to give you the name of their supervisor so perhaps you can get to the bottom of it. You may or may not get the name, but you will get the message across. Most of the time you will get paid.

Occasionally you will be given legitimate reasons that a company is derelict in its payment, for instance, a bona fide cash flow problem.

Good companies communicate this to you before it is necessary to hound them. They will call you and say they have a problem and offer partial payment or a firm date in the future you can plan on. With these companies, if you can afford it, practice the classic Golden Rule. If they make it, they may become good customers and remember your beneficence during tough times.

However, with the customers who are avoiding payment for all the wrong reasons and in all the wrong ways, remember the ungolden rule: Do unto others as they have done unto you. Make a note of that company. Brook no quarter with companies who are either malicious as a matter of policy or who have stupid employees. The next time it orders (if it orders), accept the order with the understanding that the shipment will be COD. Once a few shipments are made COD, then your company can reconsider extending credit. Of course this takes courage, and there is a risk. The company may dangle the carrot of large orders in the future. Don't fall for it. You cannot afford to do business with customers like these. They are worth neither the financial risk nor the mental anguish.

Many management analysts consider the average collection period (also known as days of receivables outstanding) as one of the most important indicators of the quality of overall company management. It takes two easy steps to calculate:

1. Determine sales per day by dividing your annual sales by 360 days. If your sales are fluctuating month to month, then average the sales for three months, then divide by 90. The result of either of these calculations will give you average sales per day. Say your sales have been averaging $120,000 for the past three months, then

$$\frac{\$360,000}{90} = \$4000 \text{ per day}$$

2. Divide the sales per day into the present balance of your accounts receivable. Say your balance sheet shows $210,000 in receivables, then

$$\frac{\$210,000}{\$4000} = 52.5 \text{ days}$$

This is an unacceptably long period. Your average collection period should be kept as close to 30 days as possible and never be allowed to creep over 45 days.

A Revered Institution

Once a large research institution in the Boston area inquired about a pulse generator. A quotation was prepared and sent. A year later, long after the quotation had expired, the institution called back and asked for us to quote it again. We had a much better understanding of the technical risk and our overhead numbers, so the quote went back 20 percent higher than the original. Further, because there was technical risk, it had to be accepted on a best-efforts basis. They ordered the equipment, as per our specification, terms, and conditions.

When it shipped, they still owed us $30,000 on the final installment. When all our project records were analyzed, the numbers showed that we had barely broken even. One, then two months went by, and we still had not been paid. We contacted them, and they said the paperwork had been forwarded to their military customer to justify the cost overrun.

After six months we still had not been paid. Every month their debt was on our receivables aging report. It degraded our financial ratios and made the bank uneasy.

One of our employees had been talking to the contract officer at the institution during this whole time, and the employee was getting a deliberate runaround. Finally, one Friday, the president of the company called the contract officer and said that enough was enough, and asked what the hell was going on. The contract officer lapsed into his litany of excuses that our employee had been listening to for months, about how the revered institution was waiting on their customer for approval, etc. The president of our company reminded him that our contract was with their revered institution, not an armed service, and further said that their lack of payment was causing a hardship for our company because it represented a lot of money, the bank was nervous, we had people to pay, and so on.

The contract officer said he understood, but there was nothing he could do. Our president countered that, in fact, the contract officer did not understand, there was no way he could, and his complacency in the matter was intolerable. He said he was going to hang up and then make a plane reservation, and that he would be at the contract officer's desk on Monday morning. He said that he wanted to deal with the contract officer, or his superior, face-to-face and get the matter resolved. In fact, he planned to stay there until there was a satisfactory result. The contract officer was horrified at a possible face-to-face confrontation. He said that travel should not be necessary and that he would see what could be done. He would call back in two hours.

Faithful to his word, the contract officer called back and said that it appeared something could be done. The payment might get released as early as the first part of the week. He would do all he could to see that it was.

The check arrived by Federal Express before 10 a.m. on the next Tuesday morning.

Develop flexible credit policies appropriate to the customer. Ship on credit only to good credit risks and on a COD basis to bad credit risks. When necessary, use letters of credit. Get credit references from companies with which you are not familiar and check them. Use Dun and Bradstreet credit services. Especially for large orders, do a complete credit check, because you cannot afford a problem with collection. It is easy to want to ship when you have inventory or want to show sales activity; however, this can be very damaging, short-term thinking. An uncollectible sale is worse than no sale at all.

The School of Hard Knocks

In response to our first product release, we received a call from a company that manufactures radio frequency (RF) generators for the thin-film and semiconductor production industry. The engineer was very excited at the possibility of using our device in one of the company's applications. One of our employees had previous experience with this company when she worked elsewhere, and she warned that the company had a terrible payment history.

An order for over $1000 came in two weeks later. We knew this company was a poor credit risk, but we really wanted to book an order, to show there was demand, so we accepted.

Sure enough, we were not paid 45, 60, or even 90 days later. We called numerous times and got everything from the famous "the check's in the mail" ploy to "the whole East Coast is paralyzed by a blizzard." They were skilled at evasion, and we should have known better than to do business with them.

It was the first account we had to turn over for collection. We got back 50 cents on the dollar, almost a year later.

An easy way to help customers compensate you on time is to pay attention to the little details that, if ignored, will give them an excuse to delay payment:

1. Ship the correct product specified on the original purchase order (PO).

2. Ship the correct quantity specified in the PO.

3. Send the invoice for payment the same day as the shipment.

4. Reference the correct PO number in the invoice.

5. Send the invoice to the billing address specified in the PO.

A mistake in any of these will justifiably delay payment. An error on your part means more than losing the opportunity to get righteously indignant with the customer for not paying on time. Much worse than that, it will cost you money. Assume you have a line of credit secured by your receivables. If an invoice for $30,000, against which the bank has advanced you 80 percent, or $24,000, goes unpaid for three months because of an administrative error, and if the interest on your LOC is 12 percent per annum, that equates to $240 in interest per month or $720. $240 was the cost to hold the receivable for the normal net 30 day terms. The other $500 was attributable to sloppy business administration.

The Customer as Banker

A good cash flow strategy is to ask your customer to provide you a down payment and progress payments. This should be policy on high dollar contracts that extend over one month, or your working capital will be dangerously reduced. In exchange, you can agree to verifiable milestones which will lower the risk to the customer of nondelivery.

The customers' purchasing departments may not like these terms because it increases their paperwork and requires them to use their cash, but customers who need what you offer will usually cooperate.

Contracts are very difficult to get financed by a bank, and, in general, banks do not like small businesses because their transactions are too small for the bank to realize any economies of scale. So a small company has little recourse but to request the larger customer to use its cash reserves or its access to banks to help finance the transaction. Projects that span several months, or require large cash outlays for materials and outside services, can exhaust the financial resources of a small company. Do not voluntarily expose your company to a cash flow crisis because you were too proud to ask for progress payments. In fact, you may earn customers' respect because that shows you are professionally managing your finances. If they are dependent on you for a product, your financial well-being is in their interests, too.

The Vendor as Banker

Trade credit is a valuable source of finance and should be carefully cultivated and expanded. Suppliers who will extend you 30-day trade credit will aggregately loan you more working capital than a bank ever will. They are motivated to see you succeed. Unlike the bank, they do not require you to pledge your house as collateral or to submit to the other onerous conditions that are typical of bank lending.

It is good business practice to pay vendors as close to their terms as possible, though for valid cash flow reasons (e.g., you do not have the money) that is not always possible.

If you are going to have trouble paying on time, communicate with the vendor. It is humiliating, but most vendors will respect your honesty and recognize your plight, even though they may not like it. They will be relieved to know that you do intend to pay. Furthermore, when you communicate, they are not as inclined to revert to COD terms.

Plan Disbursements

Being able to control cash out begins with budgeting. Tight budgeting is difficult in a small company when it is engaged in a new product development because it is hard to plan for delays, changes, and other unforeseen costs during development. So it is even more important for the company to exert full control over those major cash outflows that are predictable and fully controllable such as salaries, advertising, and equipment.

To control cash disbursements you must control the amount and timing of purchase orders. In well-managed companies, materials arrive exactly when they are needed, and not a day too soon. The acquisition of materials requires the active management of vendors so that they get materials to you when you need them, not when it is convenient for them. By managing the acquisition process, you can control a large percentage of your cash out.

Protect Cash

The object of cash management is not to hoard cash for its own sake but rather to have enough available to pay current obligations and to accumulate a reserve to insulate the company from unexpected economic perturbations. However, cash inside a small company seems to vanish with rapidity if a deliberate effort is not made to preserve it. The beauty of accounting is that the system is a closed loop. There are only a finite number of places that the money can go. The books of both successful and failing companies balance. If your cash is disappearing, the income statement and balance sheet will show you where.

Check the Income Statement

First, go right to the bottom line and check overall profitability. Are you making money? If not, the losses you show (except for depreciation—a noncash expense) are covered by cash. If you consistently lose money, you will invariably have cash flow problems. A loss once in a while is all right, but consecutive losses quickly get small companies in trouble, because, as a general rule, the *loss has already been paid out as cash before the loss is discovered on the income statement.* For this reason, it is essential to generate an income statement every month and monitor its relationship to the cash flow statement. Too many companies complete an income statement only every three or six months. If they have been operating at a loss for three months, they may find themselves out of cash before they realize that they have been losing money for a long time.

Second, look at salaries. High-tech companies employ expensive people. Is the number of employees appropriately scaled to the sales? In electronics, for instance, a rule of thumb is that there is one employee per $120,000 per annum in sales. So if your sales are $600,000 you should have around 5 to 6 people. This is only a guideline, not a rule. But if you have 10 employees and your sales are $600,000, you should consider whether they are all necessary. Maybe you should have more part-time workers or contract out certain activities.

Third, look at general and administrative expenses. G&A always ends up representing a surprisingly large portion of income. It is usually composed of the most general ledger accounts that may contain relatively small expenses such as office supplies and postage. But because there are so many, they add up to thousands of dollars. Parsimony pays off in G&A expenditures, where it may not in marketing and engineering. Often a cash flow crisis boils down to lacking just a few thousand dollars monthly over a period of time. Many dollars disappear into paper clips, computer paper, and clerical people. Particularly when hiring employees for G&A positions, the question should be asked: Is this position necessary for the business to function or only to make life easier? Recall Maslow's hierarchy. To make life easier may not be a good enough answer.

Fourth, look at development expenses. Development is such a potent cash guzzler that it is treated separately at the end of this chapter.

Check the Balance Sheet

Look at inventory. Cash has a way of turning into bins of materials collecting dust, either in production or, just as often, in desks and work benches in engineering. Is inventory adequate to support foreseeable sales? Of course you want to have the materials on hand necessary to ship products because without shipments there is no cash flow. However, it is wasteful to hold any more inventory than is necessary to support realistic shipments at a moderate growth rate. It is prudent to hold some safety stock for long lead items. However, do not build inventory anticipating that the immediate demand for your product will be so overwhelming that you will not be able to keep up. High-technology products are not Cabbage Patch Kids. In most cases, if a large order is coming, you will have ample time to prepare and plan your inventory levels to support that order. Hold on to cash. If you are short of cash because you have your money tied up in inventory, it is unlikely that your landlord will barter a rent payment for one thousand feet of RG-8 coaxial cable.

Then look at equipment. In the old days of Smokestack USA, equipment was a large item on the balance sheet because it was the means of production for steel, autos, and chemicals. Then balance sheets were supposed to have hefty investments in machinery and equipment and staggering debt to match. That is not as true in many sectors of high technology. Except for companies in process-intensive industries such as semiconductor production and pharmaceuticals, most high-technology companies require comparatively modest investments in equipment. In fact, bankers do not like high-technology companies because they have so little collateral. They do not understand that high-tech companies make their investments in brainpower— their assets are people. Your company does not need to tie up its cash with equipment purchases. To quote the president of a component manufacturer in our town, "Lease everything but the air you breathe." Why? Because it preserves cash. If you have already made equipment purchases, there are many leasing companies that will work a sale-leaseback of your equipment.

Don't be fooled by the tax "benefits" of depreciation. Depreciation rules are generous because equipment becomes obsolete so quickly. Depreciation is phantom money. Depreciation will not help in cash-short times.

The Black Hole of Product Development

In high technology, development can be a black hole that sucks in so much cash that it devours the whole company. Make sure development projects have budgets that are closely tracked for performance. Accountants, entrepreneurs, and the IRS quibble if development expenses should show up on the income statement or go onto the balance sheet and be amortized over the "life of the product." This, of course, makes the assumption that the product will have a life. Amortizing the development expenses may make the income statement look better, but it cannot disguise the cash hemorrhage.

At the onset of a product development, a budget, including worker hours and materials, should be committed to writing and monitored continuously thereafter. The success or failure of a development should be evaluated as much by whether it was accomplished within the budget as by the technical parameters achieved. If a development is running amok, it may be necessary to slow or suspend development, particularly if the company is attempting to develop more than one product at the time.

Off by a Factor of Two

From early in our company's history, we bid special projects on the basis of time and materials to which were added G&A costs and profit. At the beginning of a project, technical people, though mostly salaried, kept time sheets, and each week their hours as well as materials purchased for the support of the project were recorded on a simple spreadsheet.

After several projects, it because painfully apparent that we consistently underestimated worker-hour requirements by a factor of two. If we allocated 100 hours, it actually required 200. Why? Because almost always there were numerous, small, unforeseen glitches in the final stage of the project that required unbudgeted, expensive modifications and testing.

Because everyone was salaried, the higher worker-hours did not directly translate into a high cost for the project nor always represent an opportunity cost because other projects were being pushed out. And most of the time, the special projects were delivered on time.

However, the additional hours came from work completed on nights, weekends, and national holidays. The real cost was exhaustion and poor morale.

Estimating worker-hours to develop something that never existed before is difficult. The president of a company that specialized in developing products for other companies once said that even after 10 years in the business, he thought he was doing well when he estimated labor to within 30 percent! Another reason cash vanishes in new product developments is cited by Richard Foster in *Innovation: The Attacker's Advantage:* "Too many companies develop products empirically. They know things work, but not why they work. They rush through the engineering and then hit some major problem that requires an understanding of the supporting science which they don't have."[2] In other words, these companies do not conduct a rigorous, up-front engineering design to identify potential risk areas. This is endemic in small companies blinded by optimism or pressured by cash flow needs.

Never Plan on Miracles

An accurate cash flow statement enables you to know your bleed rate, that is, the amount per week that you will run short of cash. It is easier to forecast cash out than cash in because you control the former. You can always see a cash crisis coming if you make pessimistic assumptions about collecting. If you have $13,000 in your checking account and another $41,000 in receivables that you will likely collect in the next 30 to 45 days and will have to pay out $59,000 between the current week and week 6, you are heading for a cash crisis. Barring a dramatic and unforeseen windfall, you will be out of cash in six weeks. Plan for the worst.

You have only one option: Lower your costs *immediately,* so the cash hemorrhage slows. Act quickly and decisively so the savings show up soon. Cut every dollar you can without actually stopping the business from being in business. Cancel purchasing of any nonessential items. Stall payments to noncritical vendors. And, yes, if the numbers show it is necessary, look at people. This is all easier to do if you've had a contingency plan all along. Regularly look at the cash flow forecast for a few weeks out and think about what it would look like given a negative scenario. Which vendors will work with you? Which will not? Where are you vulnerable? Be creative. Maybe you have a receivable that you can't hypothecate to the bank because you have hit the limit of your line of credit. Do you know a wealthy individual? If you do and the receivable is one you are certain will get paid, hypothecate it to him. You might pay a higher rate of interest to him than to the bank, but the bank is not an option anyway—you need access to cash.

Hard Times

As the recession deepened and defense cuts accelerated, smaller customers seemed to just vanish. Increasingly our business depended on a few large contracts.

One of the them was to supply a piece of test equipment to a large customer whose customer was another large company. Both were eminent companies in electronics. Payments on this contract were an important component of our cash flow plan for the next six months. An engineer and technician were at work on it full-time.

Though we were privy to little of the companies direct interactions, in the few we were, we detected underlying friction between them. One day a fax came in from our customer: Stop all work on the contract until further notice because they had a contract dispute.

We immediately called for more details and were not encouraged by what we were told. The large companies were at a stalemate, and lawyers might soon be involved. However, the customer was hopeful the contract could be modified to continue work in a few months, though on a lesser scale. A few months?

After a few minutes on a spreadsheet showing cash flow, the financial implications to us were obvious: big cash deficits. We'd be forced to make hard choices.

Within the next few days we terminated an excellent employee and reduced salaries for the remaining staff. Within the next few weeks we increased the deductible on employee health insurance to lower the premium, suspended a consulting contract, reduced our janitorial services, and stopped all discretionary purchases. Finally, we reduced our leased floor space by one half.

Painful, yes. But the cash flow was positive again.

Before a cash crisis is imminent, you should have a plan as to who will get the money first. Establishing the plan will be an exercise in the toughest kind of pragmatism, but it is necessary. From highest to lowest priority, the list might read as follows:

1. Employee withholding taxes. *Never be tempted to use employee's withholding as operating capital for your business. It is unethical and illegal. If the IRS finds out, you can go to jail. The IRS will definitely shut your business down.*

2. Bank payments. Bankers are skittish as part of their job descriptions. Do not give them any excuse to call outstanding loans you might have because the loan agreements you signed with them leave you almost powerless to stop them.

3. Suppliers of materials that are critical to the products you sell. You

cannot risk alienating the suppliers of raw materials to which you can add value and ship.

4. Production equipment leases. You cannot perform value added on raw materials without equipment.

For the remainder of your vendors, use your discretion. Though it may be more embarrassing to stall on a payment to your local supplier, say an office supply company, it will be more damaging to your business if you have trouble with a vendor located out of your geographical area who provides you a key component. You can find another office supply company. A key vendor who provides a product you need to ship your product can strangle you. Prioritize based on survival.

You cannot sell yourself out of a cash flow crisis. Sales activities cost money. Furniture stores can run a full-page ad in the local paper, mark down their merchandise 50 percent to relieve their inventory, and turn it to cash. Car dealers hawk rebate programs. Those are not options for a high-technology company. The buying cycles are too long and that type of impulse buying too rare to relieve the crisis. In fact, it might well be that the prices should be going up. Besides, drastic price reductions will make it difficult to ever raise those prices again where they belong for the company to make a profit. It is much easier to decrease expenses than increase sales.

No matter who or what has to be jettisoned, remember that the company is an entity unto itself. The company must do what is necessary to survive.

9

Pinpointing
the Market

The principal planning mistake companies make is to fail to define with great precision the market they intend to attack. If you can't define who the customer is, how can you invent a product that will satisfy its needs?

WILLIAM DAVIDOW[1]

Many small high-tech companies are small companies because they have a technology but no customers for it. They suffer a common malady in high technology: They are a solution looking for a problem.

Defining a market for new technology is hard. As Peter Drucker concedes, "One cannot do market research for something genuinely new. One cannot do market research for something that is not yet on the market."[2] Despite this, your company's survival is contingent on finding a market in which it can very quickly generate demand and positive cash flow.

You will have a true market only when you can answer a few deceptively simple questions. You must be ruthlessly honest with yourself as you answer them. The answers must be detailed and specific or the questions really have not been answered yet.

Does the Industry Need
Your Technology?

More to the point, does the industry know that it needs your technology? This may seem to be too obvious to require an answer, but it's not.

It's asked too rarely. Many technologists/would-be entrepreneurs, though sticklers for the most meticulous scientific method in gathering data in their laboratory work, answer this question with broad generalities, unsubstantiated assumptions, and hunches.

Note the word *need*. Webster's defines a need as "a condition requiring supply or relief," as denoted in expressions such as animals need food, cars need tires, lasers need lenses, computers need operating systems. Need means absolutely must have, not "might like" or "could be promising." Need implies the system or process, the industry itself, cannot exist without it.

Only industries that already exist have needs. Cars did not need tires in ancient Rome, computers did not need operating systems in the Old West.

Yes, you can create a need where none existed before, but you had better appreciate the scope of the task you are undertaking. Thomas Edison invented the light bulb and then spearheaded the development of entire power distribution systems to enable people to use them. Stories like his are few and far between, and few profit-seeking entrepreneurs would rationally aspire to repeat that scenario. Artificial needs are routinely created in consumer markets, such as demand for CD players and microwave ovens, but artificial needs are rare in industrial business. Creating a new need entails enormous time and cost and the zeal and patience of a fanatical missionary.

Do not panic if the need cannot be completely identified. In early-stage technology it is not unusual to not know if there is a need. You may only suspect there is one. However, the future of the your company hinges foremost on the answer to this question. The best need you can fill is to provide a true competitive advantage to your customers, and usually only the customers can make this assessment because they know their markets better than you ever will.

Grand Prix

Our first piece of marketing literature was riddled with words like *orders of magnitude faster, revolutionary, significantly improved,* and *very high speed.* Our ads were laden with superlatives and photographs of oscilloscope waveforms showing a MOSFET switching almost a thousand volts in a few nanoseconds, truly something worthy of the *Guinness Book of World Records.*

We appeared in the same publications as the leaders in power semiconductors such as International Rectifier and Motorola. It was as if our companies were car lots all lined up on the same street, offering a wide selection to customers. On the other companies' lots, there were inexpensive cars for the teenager, for mom to go shopping in, for that summer vacation, for hauling the kids to soccer practice, and for the business executive looking for an upscale image.

Our lot was different. Amidst all the car lots selling Chevys, Chryslers, Jeeps, Toyotas, Fords, and BMWs, we were there selling Formula 1 race cars.

Who Needs Your Technology?

Markets are an abstraction. What is real are customers in an industry. An industry is composed of companies and the people who work inside them. Can you name the companies in your industry and their locations? Can you name the people inside them that you have talked to and their positions? Products are purchased by people with faces and names. What are their motivations, both in the interests of their companies and in the fulfillment of their own goals?

Missing in Action

DEI's original business plan contained lots of technical detail regarding the MOSFET devices which the company planned to market. Ponderous discussion was given to the shortcomings of conventional technology and how our device was superior in every way. The plan droned on for pages about how inductive terms in ferrous leads inhibit fast switching; how the footprint of the TO-3 package was a remnant of WWII tube technology; how the beryllium oxide (BeO) used as the substrate offered orders-of-magnitude-better thermal dissipation; how we had decoupled the source lead from ground to limit $L \, di/dt$; and, on top of everything else, how our device offered a lower profile and weight.

Markets, the foremost being power conversion, were glibly listed. Noticeably absent from the plan, however, was mention of the name of a single potential customer or major power conversion program which might have an interest.

The customers were absent because we did not yet know who they were.

Who Are Your Competitors?

If an industry exists, then its basic needs are already being met or the industry would not exist at all. These needs may be being met imperfectly, but they are being met. That means there are already other suppliers, your competitors, who have the customer's business. They may be competing against you with a completely different technology from the one you offer, but they are competitors nonetheless. They may not really be competing against you on technology either, but on price or service or reliability. You must know the commercial details as well. How is their product distributed? Have you talked to any of their reps or distributors? Do they have any intellectual property of which you need to be aware?

Can you describe the technology the industry uses now? Do you know how it works, what it looks like, what it costs, how long it lasts, what customers like and dislike about it? (The intent of these questions is not to show how much you don't know, but rather to identify real opportunities.) Unless there is a tremendous dissatisfaction with the suppliers that currently meet the need, you will have difficulty becoming a supplier. The force of habit, an integral part of a "business relationship," is very strong with customers. Your company and your technology represent a change and a risk. You are an unknown. Purchasers will be inclined to buy from companies they already know, with whom they already have an existing history of transactions, even if it is a bad one. This will become increasingly true given the current trend for purchasing departments to reduce their overheads by working with fewer vendors and making longer-term commitments to them in exchange for price concessions, predictable quality, and timely delivery.

Be careful if you cannot identify any competitors. If there are no competitors, it is doubtful that there is a market, or, if so, one that can develop fast enough to sustain your existence. Likewise, if your competitors are all tiny technology boutiques, it is unlikely the market can propel you to sustainable growth.

Does Adoption of Your Technology Require Your Customer to Change Anything?

Ideally, your technology has the same form, fit, and function as the technology it is designed to replace. Why? Because the customer will be reluctant to switch (this topic is treated exhaustively in Michael Porter's *Competitive Advantage*). If your technology is the least bit different from the industry standard, the customer will resist, because your technology will entail the expenditure of time and money for:

- Retraining engineers on how to use it
- Retooling in manufacturing to handle it
- Retraining assembly-line personnel to install it
- Retraining technicians to test it
- Retraining personnel to service it

Furthermore, your technology may make obsolete the existing knowledge base in a company. Will adoption of your technology mean that any of the customer's employees will lose their jobs? Do not forget the paradigm wars from Chapter 2. Technical managers who have risen through the ranks based on their knowledge of the conventional technology will use any excuse you provide them to reject you as a supplier. They may not even be conscious they are doing it and consider their resistance to you to have a rational basis.

An Exception to the Rule

After three years in the market, we got our first true design-in. The customer was a prime to the military, and in order to use the device, it had to be subjected to a battery of rigorous tests, informally called "shake, rattle, and roll."

Because we did not test the device to the level of full military screening, the customer had to search the country coast-to-coast to find an outside contractor willing to perform the testing. The problem with our device was that all the automated test equipment was designed for standard parts. Our part was not standard. It required completely different fixturing, and each still would have to be tested manually, which also meant someone would have to be trained to do the testing. We do not know what the customer paid, but it was no doubt substantial. This company was willing to pay, but many others were not.

Does Your Technology Offer a Performance Advantage?

You will need a performance advantage to attract the attention of companies in the market. You must be able to articulate and demonstrate that advantage to get customers to consider switching.

Just a little better performance, in most cases, will not be good enough. William Davidow treats this topic in a chapter of *Marketing High Technology* entitled "Slightly Better Is Dangerous." The performance must be, in his words, "significantly better in one or more ways that are important to the customer."[3] Large companies can succeed with this "slightly better" strategy; for example, IBM was able to introduce a PC product which was inferior to many offered by more innovative companies. At the time, the market was delighted to have a company with such renown, staying power, and commitment to customer service and gleefully accepted a "me too" product.

However, this strategy will not work as readily for a small company, which leaves it caught in a difficult Catch-22; it must innovate, but not too much. It is well established that successful products are usually only slight improvements over their predecessors, not revolutionary breakthroughs.

Can you quantify how much better your technology is? Can you translate the technical specifications into tangible benefits to the customer? Do not assume customers can or will do this for you. They will not. They are lazy or have more pressing matters. The advantage may not be obvious to them until you quantify and articulate it. Until then, they will not buy. In fact, you have given them the excuse they need not to buy.

Does Your Technology Offer a Cost Advantage?

This is the acid test that determines the viability of your technology. Competent companies, the ones with whom you hope to build your future business, make decisions on the basis of cost relative to performance, not performance alone. (This is treated in more detail in the next chapter.) If you plan to sell a new product to an industry, you must understand its economics, e.g., typical gross margins, markups, percentage of overall system cost your technology represents, possible savings that are represented by your technology, and the value added in the chain from the lowest-level suppliers to the delivery of the finished product.

If your product is priced higher than the competition's, you must be able to demonstrate that the value added to the customer's product or process, gained by using your product, is many times the cost differential, otherwise there is no incentive to change. For example, perhaps your product is more expensive, but it makes a process much more reliable or repeatable; the value you bring is the measured difference in total throughput per unit time using a competitor's product versus using yours. The more this value added can be quantified, the better.

Do not be surprised if your answers to these questions are incomplete. However, if vagueness and uncertainty characterize the answers, that may be the main reason why your company is small and undercapitalized. Good answers are of urgent importance. Without demand, your technology will be only a curiosity, and your company in mortal danger.

10
Marketing High Technology

Staking out uncharted territory is a process of successive approximations. Think about an archer shooting arrows into the mist. The arrow
flies at a distant and indistinct target, a shout comes back, "right of
the target" or "a bit to the left." More arrows are loosed and more
advice comes back until the cry is "bull's-eye." What counts most is
not being right the first time but the pace at which the arrows fly.

GARY HAMEL AND C. K. PRAHALAD[1]

Marketers like to think of themselves as courageous warriors, thus the
popularity of business books with bellicose images in their titles. This
attitude is exemplified by William Davidow in his book *Marketing
High Technology:* "If you have too many nice people in your marketing
department and on your sales force, you are probably headed for trouble....If you plan to win, you should have a fair number of product
crusaders on board. They are easy to spot. They're the ones with fire in
their eyes and blood on their swords."[2] The martial fantasy makes the
mundane work of their jobs more exciting. It also helps motivate them
for the hard work of selling which is frequently humiliating, frustrating, and unproductive. In sales, the melancholy law of averages is
that, as a percentage, you will finally sell to very few of the people
with whom you come in contact.

Though there is something mildly amusing about highly educated
people hanging on every word of ancient writings of obscure oriental
warlords and barbarians, or even more contemporary military strate-
gists such as Napoleon and Rommel, it can be foolish for a small com-

pany to act on these words, because the military metaphor is inappropriate to their circumstances.

The problem with the military metaphor is that readers can start thinking they are something they are not, and assume time, power, and options that they do not possess. Too many textbook descriptions of the market planning process summon up visions of Dwight Eisenhower and the Allied staff planning for D day—scores of generals and their aides hunkered over a map, moving a division here and a division there. That is just not the way it is in a small company. It does not have that degree of control or armies to marshal.

A more useful model for your company is a carnivorous plant like the Venus's flytrap. It knows how to stretch very limited resources. Immobile, the Venus's flytrap is forced to lurk opportunistically in the right place on the probability that something unprotected and digestible will come along. It relies on its natural beauty to lure its prey and its innate intelligence to select a quarry no larger than it can handle. At the same time, it maintains an inconspicuous presence so that it does not attract its own predators.

Products Are Only Bait

By necessity, when it comes to product development, small companies must rely more on trial and error than on market research. Only by entering a product into a market can you have dialogues with customers to learn about what they really want. Truthfully, you cannot always just pick up a telephone and call around and ask "How would you like...?" as is recommended by many marketing pundits. In reality, most potential customers will not take the time to think that hard on your behalf. If your product idea sounds good, of course they will say it sounds good. However, ideas, in the form of nonexistent "vaporware," are epidemic in high technology, and everybody knows it. You will know nothing of real value until you ship a piece of hardware (or software, as the case may be). Customers can give valid feedback only to real things that have size, weight, speed, or other performance parameters, and, equally important, a price and delivery date.

If your technology is truly innovative, you will be confronted by, for lack of a better term, the innovator's paradox. Today much is made about being customer-driven, instead of technology-driven. However, being customer-driven may not be good enough to succeed. Why? Because customers may not really know what is technically possible, so they cannot bridge the gap between what they need and what you can offer. Being more technology-driven, you may have to help customers discover the solutions that reside in your technology in order to sell it.

Gary Hamel and C. K. Prahalad offered a very important observation in a *Harvard Business Review* article entitled, "Corporate Imagination and Expeditionary Marketing." They wrote,

> We believe there are three kinds of companies: those that simply ask customers what they want and end up as perpetual followers; those that succeed—for a time—in pushing customers in directions they do not want to go; and those that lead customers where they want to go before customers know it themselves.[3]

There is a way to do this that minimizes the risk for the company, which the authors call "expeditionary marketing." As they describe it, to learn, you have to react quickly:

> How fast can a company gather insights into the particular configuration of features, price, and performance that will unlock the market, and how quickly can it recalibrate its product offering? Little is learned in the laboratory or in the product-development committee meetings. True learning begins only when a product—imperfect as it may be—is launched.[4]

In the spirit of the above, accept that the first products you offer based on your understanding of a market will probably not be the final product the customer needs. Your product is only a demonstration and proof of capability that convinces the customer that you might be able to satisfy his or her need. Your products may be only approximations of what the "market" ultimately wants. Observed Steven Schnaars in *Megamistakes*, "The ultimate use of the product, its design, the primary customers, and even the structure of the industry are unknown in the beginning, and they often change dramatically as the market evolves."[5]

For a skilled product designer, it takes humility to acknowledge that only a customer can specify a product. This is what it means, in the true sense of the word, to be market-driven. Product development with a customer leading the way is an iterative process. Especially in industrial markets, your product may be part of the customer's new product development process; therefore, both are in a state of flux. Regis McKenna, a Silicon Valley marketing expert, says that "almost all new products are experiments. Few leading edge products are perfectly in tune with the market when they first come out. Instead, they are modified and altered once they meet the market. There's a lot of give and take."[6] McKenna notes that technology-based markets are almost the opposite of consumer markets where companies survey customer needs and then design a product to meet them. "In technology-based industries," he continues, "the product usually comes first. Companies invent things and develop things. Then, they work with the market to see how the product should be used." In other words, these products are only bait.

In the small company you may ship products that, strictly speaking, are still in development, what in larger companies would be considered prototypes. That is acceptable because frequently your customer's products are in a state of development also; both your products will become obsolete together. This does not necessarily mean that your products can be of inferior quality. To be sure, if there is a contract for purchase, it will be accompanied by a specification which must be met. But there will doubtlessly be further improvements and modifications to be made in the future to the product, its documentation, and the test and quality procedures that accompany it.

Give customers the bare minimum they require for the price they are willing to pay. That is more challenging and impressive than compulsively overdesigning a product. Avoid Swiss Army knife products that can do everything okay but nothing particularly well. You cannot afford to incorporate too many features and benefits into a product because you will inevitably waste your time and money. If a new product has a set of three strong technical performance features, most customers are really buying only one or two of them. The performance features will be ranked against other factors such as reliability, price, availability, and company reputation. If you hope to secure the customer's business over the long term, the final product you deliver will reflect the customer's ranking of those factors, not yours.

If your technology is new, the customer may very well have an application with which you have no familiarity or had never thought of. If you are lucky, customers will share with you what their industry really needs and educate you on the economics of their industry, thus pointing you to a genuine business opportunity. Be prepared to be lead into a business you may not have expected to be in.

Time of What?

We introduced a product designed to drive the grids of high-power tubes. We assumed the customers for it would be people responsible for radar upgrades and physicists working with particle accelerators. So we advertised in a couple of microwave and physics publications.

When the leads started coming in, we were surprised to find that few of them were from the customer base we expected. Most of them were from chemists. We had never sold any products to chemists. Naturally, we asked what they were doing.

Without exception they were analytic or physical chemists building time-of-flight mass spectroscopy systems, a technique being used with increasing frequency in biological research to determine the mass of heavy molecules. The chemists had a need for high-fidelity, high-voltage pulses to improve the resolution of ions traveling down a tube to a microchannel plate.

The chemists had led us into an emerging commercial market with growth potential which had never been mentioned in our business plan.

Unfocusing

While we were struggling to sell our high-speed devices, many customers wanted to know if we could build a pulse generator using it. At first we resisted because we wanted to be focused; our focus was selling components. That's how we had defined what the market wanted from us.

But component sales were mediocre and growing slowly, too slowly. Reluctantly, we caved in to customer requests and built an extremely high-speed pulse generator using our device. In addition to speed, it offered pulse width, amplitude, and frequency agility, a set of features rarely found in high-voltage generators.

Soon customers started calling to see if we could offer a pulse generator with all the same features but which switched at slower speeds. This created a real identity crisis because we thought speed was what we were selling.

But it wasn't what customers were buying. So we built several more models of slower generators and made a pleasant discovery—as we became less focused on extremely high speed, our sales were going up.

Advertising Is the Last Thing You Do

When you hear the word *marketing,* the first thing that comes to mind may be advertising, but that is the last thing you should do. The purpose of advertising is to attract customers, but the goal of the marketing plan, of which advertising is a small part, should be to sell to customers. You want to attract a customer only after you have something to sell and know how you will get the customer to buy it.

A technical sale will have one or more exchanges of information. If you attract a customer, will the information be conveyed by an application note? A direct contact by a rep? A phone contact with an application engineer inside your company? Or a visit to the customer site?

If you are going to use a rep sales force, you need to train them. How and where? By written or oral communication? On videotape? By seminar? Your facility or theirs?

You need to determine exactly how a customer's call will be routed from the moment the phone rings. Identify who answers which kinds of questions (price, delivery, technical), who mails literature, who makes follow-up calls to the customer or rep. Any person in your company who will be heard on the phone by a customer, including technical employees, needs to cultivate a friendly, cheerful, and helpful voice. In this sense, high tech is no different from a service business like Disneyland.

Advertising is the easy part of the marketing plan. Humans are innately curious about new things, and we use ads to shop for them. But an advertising-initiated sales lead is, by definition, expensive. The critical task is closing the sale, so it needs to be carefully managed.

Lay the groundwork before you spread the gospel. Until you know exactly how you are going to sell, you are wasting your money if you advertise. More significantly, the amount of money you waste on advertising will be dwarfed by the amount of money lost on sales that never happened.

Spreading the Gospel

Trying to communicate the exciting news of your product to your potential customer base can be like sending radio signals into deep space to find out if there is life in distant galaxies. Responses are few and far between, and a long time coming.

Marketing is the most intuitive and intellectual of the business disciplines. The most vexing technical problem pales by comparison to the seemingly infinite variables at play in the marketing environment. Marketing success is determined more by murky psychological and economic factors than rational and scientific ones. But because marketing is a hodgepodge of science, art, and gambling, the unwary and inexperienced can easily squander lots of money.

Marketing in general, and advertising in particular, is about as scientific as chiropractic medicine, a discipline where one half is true but you never know which half. Nonetheless, marketing professionals are generally better at marketing than nonmarketing professionals.

Marketers spend more time studying markets, and their experiences enable them to develop more refined instincts for what works and what does not, though they may not be able to explain exactly why. Most small companies do not have access to first-class marketers. At best they have a good salesperson on board, but the two are not always synonymous.

Unfortunately, because marketing is a soft science and all of us think we understand why we buy things, we all think we can market well. Not necessarily. Technical people must be especially wary of assuming they market as well as they engineer, because they may not be self-reflective enough to understand their own buying motives, much less those of others. It can be difficult enough for them to objectively assess their designs in terms of costs and benefits to the customer.

To spread your story, avail yourself of every possible avenue of communication, from the cheapest (free) to the most expensive you can afford. The real concern should be to find what is effective, with cost a lesser concern. In actuality, no single means of advertising or promotion offers a complete solution. It helps to understand that your target audience will initially be aloof and indifferent to your message, if, that is, they ever even hear or see it. All technology markets suffer from severe information overload, so you are approaching a tired and jaded listener.

Small companies find themselves in the unenviable position of acting as their own public relations and advertising agency because they lack the funds to avail themselves of professional agencies, assuming any would be interested in the small account that a small company represents. You must proceed on your own because effective marketing is critical to your success. The best technology can fail because of bad marketing, whereas even mediocre technology can succeed with good marketing.

The following guidelines are helpful in your company's marketing efforts:

1. *Try experiments to find the most effective medium or means to communicate to your audience.* You may find that one is vastly superior to others. For example, you may discover that direct mail gets fewer inquiries than magazine advertising but results in more actual buyers. Or you may find that every available dollar should be spent on travel to see customers with demonstration equipment. You will not be aware of what is effective if you do not document it. Whenever potential customers contact you for the first time, ask how they heard about you and what it was about your products that drew their interest. Remember that you have

paid, one way or another, to attract this customer. Your return on this investment begins by getting back some information.

For most companies of any size, advertising is a necessary evil. It is expensive and inefficient. How much and where to advertise are perplexing questions in a small company. Easy, pat answers are not forthcoming. As Regis McKenna bluntly says: "Running more advertisements and mailing out more press releases will not solve today's marketing problems. Customers are already deluged with information....In our society, information has become disposable."[7]

Unfortunately, there is only one way to get a reader's attention with advertising—you buy it with space, repetition, and color. The advertising environment has become very crowded and noisy. Too many publications have too many advertisements. Tons of trade publications are delivered to large and small companies every month, but it is questionable how many receive even a cursory reading. The publications are able to claim large certified readerships because people receive free subscriptions by returning postage-paid postcards. But there is a difference between a reader and a subscriber. And when a modest insertion costs in the thousands of dollars and you have placed an ad, you cannot help but wonder about the real size of the readership and cringe when you observe your own reading habits and those of your colleagues. Many of these publications end up discarded in a trash can or on the bathroom floor, thumbed through at best, within hours after their arrival. What are the odds your message is being seen? Not good. But then again, how many customers are you really looking for?

Established high-tech companies usually spend between 3 to 5 percent of sales on advertising, but that does not mean you should. If you have another way to attract prospects that is cheaper, use it. Too many small companies think they need to advertise to develop corporate image. However, the best way to build corporate image is to be a growing, profitable enterprise.

The Big One

The first two years we advertised intermittently in a publication that serviced the RF (radio frequency) engineering community, a small sliver in the spectrum of electronic engineering. We always got some responses but almost never any orders.

In contrast, we also advertised in a magazine that serviced the power conversion industry. We always received more inquires and orders. Obviously, those ads seemed to be more effective.

However, in the handful of responses to the RF ad was an inquiry from an engineering manager of a company on the East Coast none of us had ever heard of. We sent the standard packet of material.

Within three months we had the largest contract in the company's history.

You are warned again and again by ad salespeople for trade publications not to expect immediate results from your advertising. They know that if you did, you would stop advertising. The impact of advertising is more subtle than that. Advertising brings in customers by very circuitous routes, so circuitous that many times customers do not remember how they found you. Definitely, there is a correlation between advertising and sales, but it is impossible to quantify.

If you do advertise, gear the ad to your product line, target customer base, and financial strength. For example, if you make a component, you will need to advertise to attract prospects for you or your sales representative force to approach. If you make only one component, however, you do not need a half-page ad in full color. If, however, you are building $150,000 R&D laboratory instrumentation systems, you will probably not do justice to your product in a quarter-page black-and-white ad. Scale the ad to the price and complexity of the product.

Do not overlook direct mail. It works if you can target a narrow enough niche to have a high probability that your message will be sent to a quality prospect. Mailing lists can be purchased from magazines at very reasonable rates. Of course most of your mailers will be discarded without being read. That is a fact of life with direct mail. You will do well to get a 1 to 2 percent response rate. Perhaps only a few inquiries will result, but your effort to communicate will have value. Your logo will appear before the customer's eyes. Mail can get you closer to the customer's attention than an ad. Your message will be in customers' hands to receive or not. A trade publication may have a readership of 50,000, and the ad salesperson would have you believe that all 50,000 will see your ad, so the cost per reader is very low with an ad as compared to direct mail. However, few really see an ad in a magazine. There are too many pages. Ads are seen by accident. You may have to advertise numerous times to have your message seen by as many people as a single direct-mail piece. So the direct mail may actually turn out to be less expensive per contact when you factor in the number who do not see the add and the repetitions required to get some attention.

2. *Inside your company, involve more than one person in marketing decisions.* Ask other people's opinions regarding colors, logos, sizes, impressions, names, and any and all topics that people have varying opinions about if they pertain to products or promotion. People have multifarious

perceptions, and they are all valuable. Sony's Akio Morita made the technically brilliant leap behind the Walkman, but it was some of his young engineers who came up with the memorable name. He never liked the name, but the young engineers had a better sense of the market and helped make it a huge success. Morita's real brilliance was in listening. Topics related to marketing should be a source of ongoing dialogue in the company. This dialogue leads to a refinement of the company's message and improved product design. This is as true of industrial products as it is of designer clothing. Customers are attracted to products with performance-oriented names and parameters to match.

Macho MOS

We developed a four-die hybrid power device that was very powerful and expensive. The part number of the device was the DE-375X4/102N30. From the moment the device was first conceived on drafting paper, it was hard to talk about because it was such a clumsy mouthful of meaningless letters and numbers.

One day when people were reviewing a spec sheet, somebody commented that the part really was "macho"—powerful, technically impressive, maybe even a little exhibitionistic. Soon everyone inside the company who talked about the part was referring to it as Macho MOS.

When it came time to announce the product, a spirited discussion broke out among people in the company when it was suggested to formally name the product Macho MOS in advertising and brochures. Objections ran from the name being undignified to it being "politically incorrect." But it was decided to take a risk and publicize the name.

Macho MOS was really too powerful and expensive to ever be a huge success. We sensed that from the beginning. But it was a great silver bullet that proved the company knew how to move lots of power at very high speed. And the engineers and purchasing agents who called us always remembered that part when they needed information, though they might forget the others.

---

3. *Involve professionals outside the company, to whatever degree you can afford them, with special marketing skills in graphics, photography, copy writing, and layout.* Any small, local graphic artist shop has more talent than anyone in your company. They are inexpensive and will do a faster, better job than you possibly can. Impressions are important. Because we are bombarded by advertising, the eyes of the average reader are very discerning. People know what they like and do not like, though they may not be able

to explain why. One reason is that their tastes are more refined than they know. Technically, even the stupidest ads on TV are very well executed. Ad copy or photographs made by amateurs are not as effective as those done by professionals, and amateur work reflects poorly on the company. There is a tendency inside small companies for people to waste time on marketing projects for which they have neither the training nor the ability. No graphics software will compensate for lack of talent.

Logomania

Our first logo was, to be truthful, trite, misleading, and old-fashioned. One of the founders had thrown it together so there would be something to put on the stationery. It was based on a warning sign that is found anywhere in the world where lasers are in operation. It was about as unique as a stop sign. If you opened any laser magazine, you'd see at least fifty other hackneyed variations on it.

When we got our first small injection of outside capital, it seemed like the time to upgrade our image, beginning with the logo which few liked at all anymore. Once the word was out that a new logo was under consideration, all five people employed by the company were trying to design a new logo. No matter what department, in every spare moment, people had pencil, magic marker, or colored pencil in hand, sketching out the future look of the company. Within days everywhere you looked there were logos—on graph paper, green accounting paper, white boards—of all shapes, colors, and styles. None of them were very eye-catching, and nobody liked anybody else's.

Finally, a local graphic artist was called in. We sat him down to make sure he understood what it was we wanted to convey in our logo, emphasizing how special our technology and company was. We showed him the various concepts we had come up with on our own. He politely acknowledged them but showed little enthusiasm for any particular one.

A few days later he returned with several concepts of his own, all of them infinitely superior to any of ours. One stood out above all the rest, and it became our logo.

When he left, we each returned to our desks and dumped our amateurish efforts in the trash and turned our attention to jobs we had the ability to perform.

A few weeks later we got a bill for $500. It was one of the best investments we ever made.

4. *Use any free means to communicate.* All trade publications run free product announcements. These have as good a chance of being read as an advertisement. If there is a particular trade publication you wish to

get in, look at the format of the announcements and imitate it when you write yours. Keep it short and factual. Avoid marketing fluff, i.e., words like *revolutionary, fantastic*, etc. Include key user benefits (so editors can judge if the product will be of interest to their readers), a full specification, and a photo. New product editors receive many more announcements than they can print. Regular, large advertisers receive first priority. It is easier to get new product announcements printed if you simultaneously agree to place some advertising and use the ad salesperson to act on your behalf with the new product editor. Do not be shy about following up the product release with a phone call to the new product editor to see if yours has a chance of being printed. Be appropriately deferential and appreciative of the editor's position of influence. Be prepared to wait longer than you might like. One definite drawback is that it can take three to six months for a product announcement to find its way into print.

Trade publications have a constant appetite for articles, most of which are written by participants in the industry. Writing is time-consuming but requires no cash outlay. If you do not write well, contract a technical writer to edit your piece. These services are inexpensive and increase the odds your piece will get printed. Most publications follow a thematic editorial calendar that is developed months ahead and is available from the publications' sales reps. If you have an idea that is germane to a particular theme, call the editor to introduce yourself to see if there is interest. Editors are interested in articles that are informative, describing a novel solution to an industry problem, not thinly veiled advertisements for products. Your article should have valid technical content. However, it is generally permissible for your product to be mentioned in passing if it is part of the solution. The product thereby gains publicity and credibility. Of equal benefit, your company positions itself as a contributor to the progress of the industry. Needless to say, you have to structure the article in such a way that you provide useful information without revealing proprietary information.

Last, but not least, you can deliver papers at seminars and conferences. Seminars can give you an opportunity to tout your technology, though you might have to disguise it as science. Conferences and seminars are not free, but they can be comparatively low cost if you are speaking to an audience with a good mix of management-level attendees who are in a position to influence buying decisions. You want to choose your audience carefully. It does you no good to pay for travel, hotels, and reprints of your articles to speak to an audience of other sellers like yourself rather than buyers.

One in a Hundred

When the company was only three months old, our technologist was invited to deliver a paper at a power conversion conference. Our paper was the last presentation on the last day of the conference. People were tired and bored, and the crowd had shrunk from a couple of hundred to less than a hundred by the time our speaker took the podium.

When the presentation ended, the crowd gave a polite applause and headed for the exits. In the months that followed, we saw very little business attributable to that conference. It appeared doubtful that the time and expense that went into the presentation were worth the effort.

Over a year later, we were called by a program manager in a large aerospace company. He was very interested in our technology and informed us he was releasing an unusually large order to start evaluating the technology.

As always, we asked how he had heard about us.

Without hesitation he answered that he was at a power conversion conference a year ago and heard our presentation. "I liked what I heard," he said.

Advertising and promotion are only a means to attract customer interest. Do not expect them to sell products. They will sell nothing. It is up to you to make the sale. Remember nothing is ever bought, it is always sold. If your advertising and promotion efforts are effective, they will create an opportunity for a sale by inducing curiosity in a prospective customer. The work has only just begun.

11

Training Technological Salespeople

Companies that succeed in educating customers to what is possible develop both marketers with technological imagination and technologists with marketing imagination.

GARY HAMEL AND C. K. PRAHALAD[1]

The most important activity in your company is selling. Put simply, sales is its life breath—no sales, no cash flow, no business. This inescapable law applies to businesses of the very lowest to the very highest technology.

Unfortunately *salesperson* is a dirty word to many technical professionals. It summons up images of obnoxious and undereducated hucksters in polyester suits and fake gold jewelry. Given this bias, it comes as no surprise that Edward Roberts's research found that the main problem of a majority of the high-tech companies he surveyed was a lack of sales.[2] He also made two other important findings. One is that small high-tech companies have difficulty raising money because their business plans lack detailed sales plans. Another is that companies with sales and marketing departments are consistently more successful than those without them.

Like all stereotypes, this stereotype of a salesperson is no more valid than that of an engineer as a skinny nerd with a plastic pocket protector and pants pulled up to the navel. In fact, far from being a mindless activity, technical selling can be very intellectually satisfying because customers inevitably pose complex and challenging problems. Even the most seemingly trivial technical problem can become significant when it must be solved at or below a certain price to satisfy the customer yet still earn a profit for your company. Many seminars and books about selling, which describe recipes, gimmicks, and manipulative techniques designed to persuade customers to buy from you whether you have what they really need or not, are derived from consumer marketing. But these are all fatal tactics in technical selling because if you fail to solve the customer's problem your company will suffer the repercussions when the customer refuses to pay, insists on additional customer service at your cost, or denounces your company to others in the market niche in which you are trying gain respectability.

High-tech companies make technical sales. Technical sales are made by technical people interacting with other technical people to match a technical problem with a technical solution. Ray Cook, founder and CEO of Raychem, very aptly described the special role the technologist fulfills in sales and marketing, as follows:

> You can't understand the market unless you get your technologists to the customer in a deep and sustained way. Your sales force, the traditional link to the customer, only gets you part of the way. It can open doors and find opportunities, but it can't really solve the customer's problems. And you can't pass the details of what the customer needs through the filter of the salesperson. You can't expect salespeople to have the imagination and expertise to know what can be accomplished through manipulating the technology.
>
> We have technologists at Raychem who are super in the labs. We have salespeople and marketers, most with technical training, who are superb at understanding customer needs. The person who can combine deep knowledge of the technology with deep knowledge of the customer is the rarest person of all—and the most important person in the process of innovation....We have never come up with an important product that hasn't been primarily the work of a technologist. That's because doing something truly important in our field requires knowing all the things that have gone before. You have to have the technology in your bones.[3]

In an early-stage high-tech company, the top technologist must become the top salesperson. The first task in a technical sale is communicating enough credible information to customers to convince them you have the knowledge to solve their problem. Initially, this dialogue is 90 percent technical and only 10 percent commercial in content. It is a very important task because what the customer will ultimately buy is your company's knowledge embodied in a piece of hardware or software. The company must demonstrate first that it has the knowledge. Who is better able to do this than a technologist, maybe the only technologist, in the company?

Many high-tech companies languish because their technologists fail to make the transition from technologist to salesperson when circumstances so dictate. It may be because some technologists have some mistaken notion that selling and intellectual integrity are mutually exclusive, or they may have even purposely pursued a technical profession precisely to avoid ever having to find themselves in the unenviable position of risking the rejection and subservience that a salesperson must live with each and every day (which is why good salespeople, rightfully, are so well compensated). However, it's too late— the technologist in the small high-tech company has already left the isolation and security of a *Fortune* 500 engineering department or university research lab and must quickly discard these erroneous notions, grit her or his teeth, and learn about how to become a more effective salesperson. Both the salesperson's and the company's future literally depend on it. Besides, a pleasant surprise awaits in the transition to salesperson: what the technologist has really become is an educator.

A Bilateral Teaching Process

Technical selling is a bilateral teaching process wherein prospective customers teach you what they need and you teach them what you, your company, and your product can do to satisfy their need. Three excellent books on the "right way" to sell are Robert Miller and Stephen Heiman's *Conceptual Selling* and *Strategic Selling* and Mack Hanan's *Key Account Selling*. The former offer practical and systematic approaches to the entire selling process, and the latter explains and clarifies the preeminent role economics plays in making a sale. These books help you understand why, ultimately, many more nontechnical factors will determine if you make a sale than technical ones. In technical sales, the customer is an organization, rarely a person, thus a matrix of influencers and decision makers collectively participate in the buying decision. Each of these influencers has biases, agendas, and concerns to which you must become sensitive to be effective in selling to them, both individually and collectively. Anyone in your company who will have contact with the customer should study these books, beginning with your key technologist. They teach a professional, consultive style of selling with which any technologist will feel comfortable.

Listen, Then Listen Again

The selling process should begin with the customer doing most of the talking. This is not a ploy to get them to "show their cards," a hack-neyed tactic from the old "we win—you lose" school of business, but, just the opposite, to try to find out exactly what the customer wants in terms of performance and price so you can fashion a "you win—we win" scenario.

Listening intently is not how many high-tech companies, including many large ones, approach the first stage of the sales process. Instead, their salespeople open with a rote recitation of a spec sheet about their product or, in some cases, with an elaborate "dog and pony" show, sometimes replete with overheads or even video, that deluge customers with technical information which may or may not be relevant to their needs. As Miller and Heiman point out, the problem with this approach is that you may find yourself, to use their metaphor, extolling the virtues of using a Ginsu knife to slice a steak to an audience of vegetarians; or, in the context of the high-tech company, touting technical features that are not important and missing the ones that are. In their own words: "Good selling begins not with Show and Tell, but with Getting Information—in other words, with learning. And you cannot learn effectively when you're talking."[4]

It was Peter Drucker who first observed that usually buyers aren't buying what vendors think they're selling. This is especially true in high-technology sales where the product is the diametric opposite of a widely traded commodity, the benefits and value of which are well known and accepted.

In a high-tech transaction, customers may actually purchase a product or service, but what they really seek is a certain outcome. What will be negotiated between you and the customer is a specification, which the customer hopes will enable or cause the outcome. Your real job is to discover exactly what the expectation for the outcome is so that you can ensure that the specification you both arrive at will produce the outcome. The specification is only a list of technical parameters. Certainly it serves as a form of legal protection for you, i.e., if you meet the specification, then the customer must pay you because it is part of an enforceable contract. However, your real objective should be more than to just get paid. You want to satisfy the customer by helping to achieve the expected outcome. You want to get paid not just once, but many times in the future from the customer's follow-on business or the referrals sent your way.

The Prettiest Spectrum

A radar manufacturer down south wanted a solid-state trigger amplifier to drive a magnetron. The company was emphatic that certain aspects of the amplifier waveform had to be a certain way. We weren't really sure why, but our job, as per the spec, was to produce that waveform. So we did.

After we shipped the amplifier, we called to see if they were satisfied with the waveform from it. They said it looked like it was supposed to look from their bench tests, in other words we had met the spec, but there was no excitement in their voices. They said they wouldn't know for sure until they installed it on a working radar. So we waited.

A few weeks later they called and were much more animated. The radar tests had gone well. They were very pleased with the spectrum produced by the magnetron. A spectrum shows the fidelity of an RF signal and translates to improved resolution of the object the radar is tracking.

In fact, one of them said, "That's the prettiest spectrum I ever did see." We thought we were selling a high-voltage pulse, but they were buying a pretty spectrum.

Being a good listener takes discipline. Sometimes technical people fall prey to competing intellectually with their customers, completely losing sight of their primary objective. A unique aspect of true technical sales is that often you are selling to your peers—the salesperson and the customer may have both studied the same technical curriculum. When you buy a house, you do not pretend to know more about building houses than the contractor. However, when one engineer sells to another engineer, or one scientist to another, it is not uncommon that they both, consciously or unconsciously, think they could do the other's job better. In the early stages of the sales process, your questions and your customer's answers are much more important than your answers.

If you are fortunate enough to find yourself in front of a customer, in person or on the phone, be grateful that you have knowledge that might be helpful, and of monetary value, to him or her. Your customer probably does not possess that knowledge or he or she would not be talking to you. Your purpose should be not to show how smart you are, but to discover how you can help and then convince the customer that you can. Never assume that customers are stupid; after all, they turned to you for assistance, did they not? What appears to be a lack of understanding may be, in fact, that the customer is thinking about another related issue about which you are unaware. For instance, customers may foresee a compatibility problem or know from experience that some aspect of the physical environment in which your product will be used and in which it has never operated may cause it to have reliability problems you have never observed before. Besides, even if a customer is ignorant, that is your problem— you need orders to grow, so you must do all you can to educate ignorant customers. A technical interchange between a customer and supplier is not an academic debate. It is no place for knee-jerk specsmanship nor pedantacism. If you win, you'll lose.

The importance of listening cannot be overemphasized. Customers are telling you, quite literally, what the market perceives about your company. The problems for which they seek your solutions are those you have given the market the impression you can solve, and for which customers are willing to pay you. They are presenting you with opportunities.

Learn the Economics of the Customer's Industry

Earlier the statement was made that in the first stage of a technical sale the dialogue is 90 percent technical and only 10 percent commercial in content. However, once the customer is convinced you can technically accomplish an expected outcome (which the customer suspected at the outset or when you were given the opportunity to speak in the first place), the percentages immediately invert; the dialogue becomes 90 percent commercial and only 10 percent technical. Now, it will be your turn to answer questions. The first will be if you can offer not just a technical solution but a *cost-effective technical solution.*

This is especially true when you are speaking with managerial-level personnel. Lower-level technical personnel are judged by their companies on their ability to produce technical results, so their appraisal of you will be based principally on your technology. By contrast, managers are judged by their ability to produce bottom-line financial results. So when the dialogue shifts, the technological salesperson must learn to be as comfortable talking about dollars and cents as about volts, antigens, lumens, or bytes. Why this is so important is perfectly articulated by Mack Hanan:

> Knowledge of how to improve their businesses is the principal element in any sale to key account customers. Nothing, including your physical ironware, is as important for them as that. When you talk about your products, you may think you are discussing tangibles if they have weight, size and shape, texture, color, or aroma. But these are simple bits and pieces of information. They become important only when you can connect them to the reality of the customer's business by showing the financial values they will deliver. In this way of looking at things, only financial values, not products, are tangible.[5]

In other words, you must prove that you can improve their profits by improvements in their productivity, lowering the cost of their products, or by increasing the demand for their products by supplying a distinct advantage over their competitors.

Economic decision makers will focus their questions on your financial strength, quality assurance program, plans to ensure dual sourcing of key components, and even compliance with environmental or civil rights regulations. Your answers to these are as important to the sale as the technical dimensions of your product. If your company is young, customers may forgive incomplete answers, but they will expect answers nonetheless. You should always go into sales meetings with credible answers to nontechnical issues already developed and rehearsed. For example, the customer may ask how you'd handle a large order if you have little space available for manufacturing in your facility. Perhaps you can answer that you already have an arrangement established with another manufacturer (assuming, of course, you do) who has excess capacity to handle such a contingency. Or the customer may ask how you plan to finance the work in process, and you can offer to provide a letter of commitment from a bank. Your answers to these questions will demonstrate that you are serious about your business. More sales are lost for commercial reasons than are ever lost on purely technical grounds.

Your goal should always be to sell the customer on a product that is just adequate to the customer's task, neither more nor less. Too often products are sold with unnecessary bells and whistles, dooming them to failure because they cost too much. As Mack Hanan observes:

> Most products are overengineered. In other words, they are over-costed so that they are overly difficult to sell at high margins or in a manner that can improve customer profit cost-effectively. This is not an argument against quality engineering. It is, instead, an

appeal to permit your key customers to influence the type and amount of quality they need by specifying the profit contribution they expect.[6]

Take care that as the specification takes shape, it expresses what the customer wants, which may not be what you'd prefer to do because, in order to satisfy your own intellectual agenda (i.e., challenge or curiosity), you are biased toward a certain approach, or, equally unproductive, you are looking beyond the specific needs of the customer to the assumed needs of a generic "market."

So What?

DEI's early sales presentations for our component were a series of overhead slides. We figured that, above all else, we had to convince the audience that we knew how to move large numbers of electrons at very high speeds. So the front end of the presentation showed slide after slide of large, technically noteworthy, physically imposing (sort of like something out of the movie *Alien*) pulsed power systems that our engineering staff had designed while employed at a national lab. We recited the Godzilla specifications of each of them; slew rates of 200kV per microsecond, 10 megawatts of peak power, X.XX10 joules of energy.

Most of our audiences had no idea what practical use anyone would have for equipment like that. They would act interested, probably in polite response to our rising tone of excitement, but never once after a presentation did anyone ever ask a single question about a piece of this equipment.

The second half of the presentation focused on the device itself. We showed waveform after waveform, graph after graph, proving it had the fastest speed, best thermal dissipation, lowest weight and profile, narrowest pulse width, most logical mounting configuration of any power MOSFET. The arguments were irrefutable: Our device was a true technical marvel.

After this part of the presentation, we would open the forum to questions. Most frequently asked were: How many could we manufacture per month? What kind of burn-in and reliability testing did we do? Could it be built with a hermetic seal for military applications? What kind of quality assurance did we have? How could we assure them an ongoing supply in the event we went out of business?

Apparently, the fact that we could build systems that, for an instant in time, could consume the entire output of a power plant for a midsize city, did not convince them that such questions were superfluous.

Wishful Thinking

A potential large customer visited our facility. We presented a detailed technical seminar on the state of the art of solid-state power devices. We explained all the conventional technology plus our own, taking great care to be objective and fair toward conventional approaches.

At intervals throughout the presentation, he asked perceptive technical questions. As one after another were answered, it became increasingly evident that our device was perfectly matched to his application; in fact, perhaps it was the only device on the market capable of meeting his requirements. We were elated.

He gave a deep sigh and pushed away from the desk, shaking his head, almost regretful, then said, "You guys give me heartburn. I sure wish you were Motorola."

Be Alert for Techno Macho

Harvard professor Theodore Levitt said, "If you promise the moon, it is reasonable for the customer to expect it."[7] Be warned.

For some scientists and engineers, technical virtuosity becomes a surrogate for political power, sexual prowess, fame, and glory. It is a regressive quality that will be further accentuated if the technologist also happens to be the notorious rugged individualist, antibureaucrat, loner, egomaniac, or renegade frequently found inside small high-tech companies. When the dark side of the entrepreneurial personality combines with an engineer's or scientist's left-brain dominance, the result is a virulent and dangerous case of Techno Macho. Technical salespeople suffering from this syndrome commit their companies to undertake the delivery of products with unobtainable specifications and unrealistic delivery schedules, at prices which ensure that their companies will suffer a financial loss. Indeed, a small company can go bankrupt because of it.

Be watchful for the unmistakable signs of Techno Macho in your selling efforts. A classic symptom is the frequent occurrence of phrases such as "revolutionary," "technically challenging," or "state of the art." At the earliest manifestation, the uninfected members of your company must be prepared to administer a strong dose of business reality. Surprisingly, an emphasis on novelty and innovation can actually be detrimental to a sale because high-level managers are usually risk-aversive; the more you enhance the extreme differences between the technology they have used in the past and the new technology you propose that they use in the future, the more they will sense risk. Be humble.

Disguise your technology as an incremental improvement over what exists. It's much better to make a sale to the customer who then discovers your product really is state of the art rather than for you to say so.

Admittedly, the high-tech business environment provides a fertile breeding ground for Techno Macho. Often hungry, young, pioneering small companies position themselves as innovators to draw the market's attention. This position attracts the customers seeking products at the extremes of technology, where the odds of failure are high. There is a type of customer (see the "Beam-Me-Up Syndrome" in the next chapter) who taunts suppliers by asking for specifications just outside the reach of known technology, the limits of which the supplier is fully cognizant of. Sometimes customers do this because they are on a sacred quest to further the goals of their companies or to prove a point, perhaps already having committed to their managers that they can do it. The net result is that, consciously or unconsciously, they try to get your company's pride entangled in their dire problem.

In these instances, if your company is not cautious, it can sign a contract to deliver a thousand angels dancing on the head of a pin. The customer will expect you to deliver the pin and the thousand angels to boot. After the contract is signed is too late to discover that there are no angels, at least not at a price you can afford. Make a conscious effort to keep your pride out of negotiations. According to Peter Drucker, there can be a tendency in companies for valuable resources to be allocated to the 90 percent of events that produce practically no results. "In fact," he writes, "the most expensive and potentially most productive resources (i.e., highly trained people) will misallocate themselves the worst. For the pressure exerted by the bulk of transactions is fortified by the individual's pride in doing the difficult—whether productive or not."[8]

Steer your customers, as best you are able, toward easy product developments that stretch neither your technical abilities nor your financial resources too far. Avoid products that require arduous or lengthy designs. This may not sound consonant with the image of the swashbuckling, risk-taking entrepreneur, but it is smart.

Practice ruthless objectivity in assessing technical risk. The dilemma for the small company is that many times the only way it can get any business is by tackling projects that no one else will; yet the small company must do everything in its power to avoid these projects. Taking extreme risks should be necessary only during the early stage of the company. As soon as you can gain a foothold in a market, you should deliberately guide the company's technical developments and contractual commitments to easier and safer ground.

Stay Close to the Core Technology

Even a large company has only a few technologies at which it is really expert. An insightful essay on this topic by C. K. Prahalad and Gary Hamel appeared in the *Harvard Business Review* under the title, "The Core Competence of the Corporation." The authors define core competencies as "the collective learning in the organization, especially how to coordinate diverse production skills and integrate multiple streams of technologies."[9] Note the words "production skills" and "technologies," because they are what comprise a technology business. You must possess expert knowledge of the technology, and you must be able to produce it as a cost-effective product as measured by the standards of a market.

Your company may have only one technology at which it is really expert, though it will have a functional grasp of several others. If your company really possesses only one core competency, finding a market niche broad enough to create and support an ongoing business enterprise can pose a challenge.

To secure a market of adequate size to grow your company, you may be tempted to sell products involving higher levels of integration or other technologies with which you have average knowledge but not superior knowledge. This is a strategy fraught with potential problems. Customers will not pay high prices for technologies in which a company is only mediocre, but they will pay higher prices for those at which a company is superior. It is necessary to assess unemotionally where your core competencies reside in order to capitalize on your strengths and avoid overreaching your abilities. Over the long run, customers are never fooled by inferior products.

Knowing your technological capability is only the first step in determining the product options open to your customers. You must also select opportunities appropriately scaled to your financial capabilities, those at a level of technical integration and complexity which you can support with your working capital and complete before you exhaust your cash.

Richard Foster says it succinctly in *Innovation: The Attacker's Advantage*: "Companies fail when their attack depends on expanding their area of expertise."[10] Never underestimate how dangerous this can be, whether you are stretching your core technology, financial resources, or marketing capabilities. Many large, well-managed, and well-financed companies have lost fortunes straying into areas in which they did not belong. Exxon, with all its wealth, never succeeded in office automation. Even the redoubtable Hewlett-Packard, the paragon of market-driven companies, once fell prey to a combination of Techno Macho and overextending its market reach. The HP-01, sold through jewelry stores, was a combination digital wristwatch, stopwatch, and 200-year calendar. It even totalled your long-distance phone calls. Despite a dazzling array of technical features, the HP-01 flopped, though priced at only $750, a real bargain when amortized over three lifetimes.

12
Finding the Right Customers

Customers are the key to any business. Companies are always looking to attract new customers. However, many companies fail to realize which customers they attract is often more important than how many customers they attract.

REGIS MCKENNA[1]

For a small company, a variation on the biblical saying is true: Many customers are called, but few are chosen. Theodore Levitt once wrote that the purpose of a business is to create and keep a customer. The mission of sales and marketing in your company must be to create and keep the right customer because all customers are not created equal. Just as in the famous spaghetti western, potential customers fall into three general categories: the good, the bad, and the ugly. Your company will grow if you focus your efforts on identifying and servicing the good ones and minimizing or avoiding altogether transactions with the others.

Characteristics of the Right Customers

Customers who can help you grow have definite characteristics. Common to all of them is a corporate culture that includes as one of its predominant values what can be best described as a spirit of reciprocity; that is, these customers see business as a balanced, fair, give-and-take process where all parties to a transaction must mutually benefit. Really good customers are few, but a few are all you really need. Most successful small companies conform, on average, to the 80/20 rule—80 percent of their sales and profits are derived from 20 percent of their customers.

The right customers fit this profile:

1. *They have a real need and know it.* These customers are actively searching for an advantage. They have determined that they do not have the resources inside their companies to provide it, so they are looking to both their existing suppliers as well as new ones for assistance. They are open to new ideas and eager to explore fully the alternatives available to them.

2. *They see the value of your contribution and are willing to pay for it.* Of course, good customers will negotiate fair pricing that gives you a decent profit but does not gouge them, and they will have legitimate and enforceable expectations for timely and quality deliveries. That is just good business. But they acknowledge that you play a role in their success that is worth your prices. When they seek a price concession, they are willing to reciprocate with a service or performance concession (in other words, a cost saving) to you.

3. *They treat you as a partner.* These customers share with you the most intimate technical details you may need to know to meet their needs. You have access to all levels and departments in their organization to help you accomplish the required task. These customers also reveal those parts of their business plan, such as new markets they intend to enter and shipping schedules, as well as information about their financial condition, which will affect your business. They will also disclose their future plans so you can guide your R&D efforts and financial plans accordingly.

4. *They make it safe and pleasant to do business with them by having well-managed, professional organizations that live up to the terms of your mutual agreements.* As a small company, you need predictability so you can plan your cash flow. You do not have large resources to fall back on if contracts or payments are delayed. Because your time and resources are scarce, review meetings or transfers of technical information must adhere to a tight schedule so you can maximize your output. They make certain you know their operating policies, such as billing cutoff dates and invoice-processing procedures. Once in a while good customers may ask for an extra service or item not included in a contract because of a special circumstance, but they never abuse this privilege by making this a habit, thereby, in effect, lowering their price and decreasing your profit. You

want companies that are well organized and committed, from the CEO to the mail clerk, especially the purchasing departments that will order from you to the payables departments that will pay you.

Sorting the Wheat from the Chaff

To find good customers, you need to be as diligent at qualifying prospects as you are at qualifying an employee. Do not fall prey to the truism that beggars can't be choosers. You must be. A good customer can make you money, and, likewise, a bad one can put you out of business.

Answer all inquiries professionally, but take only a select few seriously. Many would-be customers are seeking information, not a supplier. Because you represent an innovation, naturally many people are curious about what it is, how you make it, how it works, what it can do for them. Though you must enthusiastically share information about the technology so people can comprehend it, trust it, then use it, most of the time your efforts are wasted. Most prospects are eager to learn but not to buy. Many will be competitors, curiosity seekers, data collectors, academics, or lazy people who want you to perform their design work for them. But once in a while you get lucky and find a very good prospect who is ready, willing, and able to conduct business with your company. You exist to capitalize on those few.

Gain Factor

In the early days the phone would ring every 20 minutes. The callers would be design engineers curious about how we made the devices switch so fast. They loved to talk about arcane issues like the Miller effect, insertion inductance, metal migration, and the like. They were particularly interested in the drive circuits we used, so we would tell them the components they needed to drive our part very fast. Sometimes these conversations would last 20 minutes or more, and then we would send one or more faxes with additional information.

If the caller was from a large company like General Dynamics, Hughes, AT&T, or Westinghouse, we would be excited for rest of the day. Sometimes these callers would mention that they were working on projects that might consume hundreds of thousands of parts. We concluded that if the *big* companies were calling us, we must be onto something *big*.

But we soon noticed that the interest of these callers was not necessarily converting into sales. Moreover, we soon realized that many callers were actually calling to get free applications assistance on how to drive other MOSFET devices faster, not ours. Shortly thereafter we started selling the drivers themselves, and sales increased.

We named our up-and-down emotional responses the "gain factor." A little positive information from a potential customer caused an extreme emotional high, although there was no real basis for it. The inverse was also true: A little negative feedback from a customer caused an extremely pessimistic reaction, likewise with little basis for it.

Over time the gain factor moderated greatly in both directions. We learned that actions speak louder than words, even if the words are listed on the *Fortune* 500.

The quality of your inquiries are more important than the quantity. Of course you need to be polite and businesslike in your dealings with anyone who inquires, but as tactfully as possible you must extract the answers to a few key questions, not necessarily in the order presented below. Don't be bashful about asking them. After all, you are investing your valuable time and resources in responding to their questions. The spirit of reciprocity, remember?

What Is the Caller's Position in the Company?

You want to find out if callers have the authority to buy. Are they managerial level, design engineers, or technicians? If they are design engineers, are they senior or junior? You need to know this because, providing their interest is genuine, you can begin to approximate the time it will really take for your effort to turn into ongoing business. The lower on the corporate totem pole your prospect is, as a general rule, the longer it will take. However, if you are talking with someone who wields some power and influence, like an engineering manager or project manager, the elapsed time from inquiry to a business transaction can be much shorter.

A Tale of Two Companies

Two military airborne power supply manufacturers, both very well known, one located in the Seattle area and the other in Dallas, were interested in our device and invited us to visit to tell our story. The champion of our device inside the Dallas company was a young engineer, only three years out of college. The champion of our device inside the Seattle company was a senior program manager with extensive experience.

We flew to Dallas on an early morning red-eye and were met in the vendor's lobby by the young engineer. He escorted us to a disheveled room for the meeting which was scheduled to begin at 9 a.m. Some people were missing. He apologized and left to go find them. He came back with two older, graying gentlemen whom he introduced, one a senior engineer and the other a program manager. The program manager glanced impatiently at his watch and told us to get started.

The hostility of the older gentlemen was obvious from the beginning. A few slides into our presentation, they interrupted and questioned one of the slides depicting how heat gets out of the device. Then they complained about the thermal capabilities of the substrate. They were skeptical of the speeds, which were shown in photographs of actual oscilloscope waveforms. They were reluctant to tell us anything about their program. In short, they were adversarial the entire length of the meeting to the degree that it was almost comic. They did not care that we had traveled a great distance at a great cost to our fledgling company. When the meeting was over, they were out of the room as hastily as possible. We returned to the airport $2000 poorer, understanding the decline of U.S. competitiveness a little better, but that was not our object. We received no business from them.

In Seattle the atmosphere was altogether different. We were met by a purchasing agent who took us to a conference room. Inside were representatives from purchasing, engineering, production, as well as the program manager and his lead engineer. They gave us a presentation on the scope of their program, where they had successes and where they were short of what they wanted to accomplish. Then they listened to our presentation. Afterward there was a very businesslike discussion in which all parties participated freely. A few months later, we got a nice contract from them.

The difference was more than a few thousand miles. It was the relative positions of our champions inside their companies.

Do They Have Money Now?

In other words, do prospects have a funded project that will lead to near-term purchases? This may seem to be a rude question, but the answer to it will determine the amount of time and effort you can afford to devote to satisfying the inquiry. Customers should be willing to be candid concerning their development schedules, and you should be able to confirm them from more than one source as you get to know others in the company.

If they are working toward something in the distant future, you must be careful because you can make only very modest investments in the future. For example, if they need a proof of principle that requires your time or money, you may not be able to provide it because you will not be paid for it in a period in which you can reasonably recoup your investment. Do not underestimate the risk factor represented by time. The further into the future a business transaction is supposed to occur, the less likely it is to happen. Critical factors such as people, companies, market conditions, and economies change unpredictably over time.

Do They Know What They Need, and Do You Have It?

Customers must be able to articulate what they need and what it must cost so you can determine if you have any solution to offer. If their need is real, customers will be willing to convey all the information you request. It may be necessary to execute a nondisclosure agreement between your companies so the prospect can speak freely, but that, in itself, is a strong indication of a serious inquiry. Don't just dwell on technical details, but also talk about money, e.g., their cost targets and your pricing. Ask if the prospect is interested in visiting your facility or vice versa—a good indication of level of interest because then prospects must invest time or money.

Be careful if you sense a potential customer is withholding information, because in all likelihood the inquiry is not serious. Immediately and politely bring to the customer's attention that she or he is not providing sufficient information. If the customer is serious, more information will be forthcoming. If not, end the dialogue and move on to the next prospect.

If the customer is not able to define the need yet, you may have to help. At the same time, however, you must avoid inadvertently falling into the trap of acting as an unpaid consultant who provides technical direction or conducts free feasibility studies. Express this concern openly and observe the customer's reaction. Working together you may find a way to compensate your company for some of its time and effort. For example, you may be able to agree on a contingency contract that stipulates that if your company determines the feasibility of a solution, you will provide a prototype to see if it fills the customer's needs. In turn, if the solution works, the prospect will agree to test it and to purchase some number of units in a reasonable period.

As expeditiously as possible you want to determine whether the need matches a solution you offer. If so, ask what further action is required from your company to get an order. If you determine there is not a match, so inform the customer, thank him or her for the interest, and stop the dialogue right there.

The Mother of Invention

From an ad in a publication that had otherwise drawn very little interest, we got a visit from a vice president of engineering of an old, midsize company which supplies one of the military services. He needed an innovative piece of equipment and figured that we might be able to help him design it.

Accustomed to keeping secrets, he said very little about his requirements and, during his visit, pretty much let us do the talking, all the while maintaining a reserved demeanor.

Like a fish swimming around a hook, a few weeks later he called again. He said we needed to talk more and returned a week later. This time he began to describe what he needed in more detail. We began to understand, and he asked what we thought it would take to do it. We made a hasty estimate.

A month and a half later, we received an order to commence work. We were surprised, because in the world of government procurement, a month and a half is the life span of a quark. He came out several times during the next few months to check our progress. Toward the end of the project we encountered a technical problem. At once, he came out and stayed, working alongside us nights and on weekends.

During that time, we learned that his company had risked its own money on the development. Already suffering the defense cutbacks and having almost been put out of business by similar cutbacks after World War II, his company was making a last-ditch effort to win a large contract. Their competition for the contract were defense giants like TRW and Raytheon. They needed to win it or face large layoffs of their work force or worse.

Finally, we managed to get a crude, but functional, prototype to work. He left immediately to show his customer. Then for several more months the VP continued to work on the design without our assistance. Necessity is truly the mother of invention. He developed an outstanding product and won the contract.

Our technology helped him succeed in his mission. The reward was a large production order.

Sizing Up Customers

You cannot predict the sizes of the companies that will lead you to growth. Number of employees, annual sales, years in business are really secondary issues. A customer should be measured in terms of its potential to help you grow. Evaluate customers the way a venture capitalist would evaluate you. Key factors include:

- *Market segment.* Is their market segment growing? Do they have a product with a clear competitive advantage so they can take more market share even if the market itself is not growing? Do they already have a record of strong growth in the segment, or is it new to them? Are there references to their products in trade publications? Do you see their advertising?

- *Management.* Does their management give you the impression that they are competent in their functional areas? Do they know their market in every detail? Can they manufacture? Do the lower-level employees with whom you've had contact seem enthusiastic, motivated, and organized? Do they do what they said they'd do when they said they'd do it? Do you get the impression they know what they're doing?

- *Capitalization.* Are they in a financial position to grow? Do they have lots of cash or access to debt or equity markets? Do the areas of the company with which you have contact seem properly resourced? Are the facilities adequate? Do they pay their vendors on time? What does Dun and Bradstreet have to say about them?

Most likely your best opportunities will be with companies larger and more established than your own, not with very young or very small companies. This is said with cognizance that you could risk losing the business of the next Apple Computer when it was still in a garage. The majority of growing businesses in the United States are the small and midsize businesses whose sales range between $10 million and $500 million. Their performance has been so stellar in the past decade that the *Fortune* 500 Goliaths are downsizing and, to use management expert Tom Peters' word, "unglueing" in order to imitate them.

Jim Imai, a business consultant, once said, "Seat of the pants companies can't do business with seat of the pants companies." What he meant is that a struggling small company *probably* will not succeed doing business with other struggling small companies. "Probably" is in italics because your own circumstances force you to allocate your resources on the basis of probabilities. The probabilities are against very fast growth with most very small companies, so you must play the odds mostly with larger enterprises.

Small companies do fit the profile of the ideal customer prospect in one very important characteristic—they are willing to take a risk. They will look at your technology to gain a competitive edge. But they have shortcomings as well. First, it is hard for them to afford purchases because they have little capital. Also, they are not seasoned forecasters and, lacking demonstrable market strength, may be prone to err on the side of optimism, so it is difficult to plan your business around them.

Does this mean you should not do business with small companies? Of course not, only that you should not direct many of your scarce resources toward attracting them.

Small Is Beautiful

One of our first customers was a start-up whose product was a hand-held laser gun to replace conventional radar for police use in identifying speeders on the highways. The product would have real appeal to the police because there were no "fuzz busters" for laser radar, and it is very accurate. It was so fast you were caught before you could hit the brakes.

The forecast was for sales to climb like the space shuttle! Within one year the firm would be using 1000 devices, and 10 times that in three years. It sounded like an exciting story, and we wanted to know more about the project. We were trying to raise capital, and the prospect of an exciting product with our device in it was important to our story. But the prospect was close-mouthed. The whole project was top secret.

We doubted the company would reach its forecast because laser-based systems are twice as expensive as conventional radar. The first two years the companies sales were very modest, true to our expectations. But then the Pennsylvania state police banned conventional radar because they suspected that it caused cancer among their officers who had been using it. The ban received nationwide coverage on TV and in newspapers.

Quickly, the laser start-up grew faster than we did.

The Bad and the Ugly

An ugly customer may cause you grief, but bad customers will cost you money. The line between the two can easily blur because they share certain similarities:

- Technically, in the very areas in which you are trying to contribute, they do not know, or have not really determined, what they want. As a result, they will not be able to help you help them. Yet when they don't succeed at what they didn't really know they wanted to do in the first place, they'll still hold you accountable. (And you are, in a sense, for accepting the order in the first place.)

Big Blues

We contracted with one of the largest electronics companies in the world to design a pulse generator for_____. The reason there is a blank is because the project was so secret that the company could not tell what the pulse generator would be used for.

In the design of a high-power pulse generator, the load into which the pulse will be launched is very critical. Electrical parameters such as inductance and capacitance of the load, the values of which may be irrelevant in other applications, become of paramount importance in pulsed power. Certain pulses cannot be delivered to certain loads.

Because the parameters of the load were secret, we entered the contract on a best-efforts basis with no guarantee of performance. To do otherwise would be equivalent to agreeing to design a car that must go 200 mph for which the customer will supply the wheels, but when you make the delivery, you discover that the wheels are made of concrete.

When we were close to the completion of the generator, two physicists, employed by the customer, visited our facility for testing. We discovered that not only were the wheels made of concrete, they were also square. Yet the customer still expected to go 200 mph because, according to their calculations, it was "theoretically" possible. Of course, although the physicists could mathematically explain on a board the phenomenon of heat, they could not, on a practical level, design even a functional hair dryer or a toaster. They became very belligerent when they realized that what they had specified, and we had delivered, was not well matched to what they needed.

One of our engineers, understanding the magnitude of their error, pointed out that a well-known law of physics, a relatively simple equation, would have shown why what they wanted was impossible. In response, one of the physicists snapped, "You do not understand the problem. Besides, I could solve that equation in my sleep."

Our engineer professionally turned the other cheek and remained silent. Later he said, "Yes, but unfortunately he couldn't solve the equation while he was awake."

- Bad customers are afflicted by various versions of the NIH (not invented here) syndrome. Because they have some expertise in the technical area for which they have turned to you for assistance, they won't really listen to your advice. Though you are ready, willing, and able to help them, they hold latent hostility toward the very fact you even have expertise that can help them. That hostility gets transformed into technical nit-picking and sophistry because unconsciously these customers feel that if they do not understand something, you cannot either. They doom your transaction to a losing situation for both of you.

Alas, Poor Fido

One of the first custom units we built was for a new product being designed by a manufacturer of medical equipment, a leader in the area of in vitro imaging of the human fetus. To extend their product lines, they decided to take their expertise in imaging and try to apply it to shock-wave lithotripsy, a medical procedure wherein kidney stones are broken into small pieces by acoustic waves. Though the imaging technology has similarities to that used in lithotripsy, much higher power levels come to play in lithotripsy. The manufacturer had little experience in this area of electronics and asked us to build a high-power generator under a very aggressive time schedule because the company was racing to the market against several well-heeled, global competitors.

A few days before we shipped, we were contacted by someone closely associated with the project who was aware of the specifications of the equipment we were building. The piece of equipment specified could be, in untrained hands, very lethal. He was concerned about their general lack of knowledge about high-speed power. He said that in laboratory testing, the company was killing a dog a day because the testers had failed to properly focus the beam; rather than dissolve the stone, they were turning an area the circumference of a dime into a gelatinous mass through the dog's torso. Although we were not animal rights activists, this was not a happy thought.

Of greater concern, we learned that they had low-signal digital lines running next to the line transmitting the high-voltage pulse to the transducer. Under the right circumstances, the high-power line, through induction, could confuse the computer running the system and accidentally call for too much power into the transducer and hence the patient. For a canine patient that would be regrettable, for a human, unthinkable.

We contacted the firm to warn its managers about the inherent danger of the system architecture and the lethal power of the pulser they had specified. They did not sound concerned, so when the system was shipped to them, it was covered with orange stickers bearing myriad dire warnings, all with one central message: *Don't use on humans! This could kill them!* We also sent a letter to the project manager saying the same thing.

The project manager called back and snapped, "Don't use on humans? What the hell do you think we're building this for?"

We were starting to wonder ourselves.

- Bad customers are afflicted with the "beam me up" syndrome. This customer is dangerous to you if have any technologists in your company suffering from Techno Macho. In the TV series *Star Trek*, living bodies are transported from one place to another by atomizing them, transferring them in a beam of particles, and reassembling them in their new location. The idea is easy to conceptualize but impossible to achieve. Similarly, a customer manifesting the syndrome will ask you to commit your company and its financial well-being to achieve something on the extreme, ragged edge of technical possibility. Sometimes these customers are ignorant and do not know what they have asked for, but just as often they know very well. They are trying to dupe you into a bad business decision. Their ulterior motive is to *externalize their risk and the expense of failure* by transferring it to your company. Many times in technology, the final result of a highly developmental project is something that has no market value, although human knowledge gets to advance another small step. But the product itself may end up in the trash can. You don't want it to be yours. Customers who want something at the extreme should assume most of the risk and the consequences of failure. Your risk as a small company is the opportunity cost you expend for participating in the development; if nothing comes of your effort, you've lost valuable time and will stay small just that much longer. At least get paid for your time and limit your financial exposure. You are no different from an experienced mountain guide who steers a party to the safest route given their skills because the rope around her or his waist is tied to them. The guide knows that if they fall, the guide falls too. As the expert in your technology you must steer the customer away from risky business. If the customer persists, wish the firm well but walk away.

- The expectation of free technical service support is grossly out of proportion to the actual purchases. Bad customers always want you to travel to meetings, at your expense, to discuss business opportunities that are too small or too remote to warrant your investment.

- Bad customers are intrigued or fascinated by your technology, but even though they do not really need it, they buy it anyway. If they really don't need it, it will not have value for them, so they will constantly bicker about price.

- Bad customers are from the atavistic dog-eat-dog school of U.S. business that has led, in part, to our economic decline. According to this philosophy of business, there are only winners and losers in business relationships. The object is to get all you can from your vendor for nothing and ensure an ultimately short-lived, completely antagonistic relationship.

- The companies of bad customers are poorly organized and administered, and consequently technical information is not transferred efficiently; sign-offs on product acceptance do not occur according to a procedure that ensures payment to terms; development programs lack clear direction so specifications are in a state of constant change for which the vendor is never compensated.

The U.S. Government—A Special Case

The more advanced your technology is, the more likely the ultimate customer, if not direct customer, for your product will be the U.S. government. The government is the largest underwriter of advanced technology development anywhere in the world. In 1992, 21 percent of manufactured electronics went to the DOD. The enormous volume of money that flows through the government each year almost dictates that for any business, the government will be a customer, like it or not.

The government has mandated that a certain percentage of certain programs' procurements must go to small business, but there are definitely drawbacks to doing business directly with the government, especially for contracts over $10,000. It takes a long time to get an order and a long time to get paid. Furthermore, the government has unique contract rights not to be found in any other sector of business, including the right to cancel a contract for virtually no reason, the right to audit your books, and, in many cases, the right to tell you how much profit you are going to make. For this reason, smart companies such as Hewlett-Packard have always limited the type of business it will accept from the government.

The government is not an OEM. The policies of the Federal Acquisition Regulations (FARs), of which you should have a copy if you plan to conduct business with the federal government, cause government buying decisions to be weighted heavily toward price rather than performance or quality. No amount of good service will keep the government coming back to your company again and again.

A further negative aspect of doing business with the government is that the FARs encourage, indeed necessitate, that you add expensive administrative overhead. The government offers no incentive to be efficient. The regulations stipulate that your profit is calculated off your cost. They would rather see you profit 10 percent on $200,000 in bloated costs for a total price of $220,000 than see you profit 100 percent for a total price of $200,000 on $100,000 in cost for the identical project because you were so efficient. This is done in the name of saving taxpayers money! It's for this reason that most large defense contractors have such fat and sluggish bureaucracies. The problem is that government contracts come and go, riding the political whims of the day. When you get a contract, you add staff and facility, but then the government contract goes away. The cost of the staff and facility will remain.

Finding a potential customer inside the government can be difficult because the federal bureaucracy is massive. Sending out letters or getting your name on computerized bidding lists is not much more effective than throwing out a message in a bottle into the open seas. Most times, the government or a prime contractor to the government will find you if you practice the marketing techniques described in Chapter 12. Announcements of pending government procurements are publicized in the *Commerce Business Daily* (CBD), which is available for a modest cost on a subscription basis. But though this would be adamantly denied by government officials, many of the suppliers for these so-called open solicitations have already been selected. If you respond to an announcement in the CBD, the specification in the bid package you receive may have been developed in collaboration with the supplier of choice. In other words, the solicitation is purely a formality, and you will be wasting your time and effort to respond to it.

Small companies are wise to avoid trying to be prime contractors to the government, particularly in defense- or space-related procurements, because those contracts are subject to even more stringent regulations. You are much better off to seek government business indirectly by servicing one of its prime contractors that already has the administrative apparatus in place. Then you can escape some of, though not all, the high cost of doing business with the government. Depending on the size and type of contract, the reporting and documentation requirements can be staggering. You may still need more administrative staff or, at a minimum, additional training of the staff you already have, to comply with government accounting and other requirements.

Be advised that venture funds and investors are rarely interested in companies heavily involved in business with the government because they know that the success of the company will be hostage to the vicissitudes of politics and, by law, will be at best only marginally profitable.

Long-Term Opportunity

We bid on a large piece of test equipment for a highly developmental program to test a semiconductor device. Our effort would be a very small part of a large, well-funded program that was being spearheaded by a joint venture of some of the largest companies in electronics.

Our bid was for a phased development that would extend over the better part of a year. Because the specifications were so difficult, we bid the contract on a cost-plus basis using bare-bones overhead rates so we could get the contract and have the advantage of a predictable revenue stream for those months.

After numerous delays due to paperwork sign-offs, the contract administrator from the joint venture informed us that the military service underwriting the effort had determined that the program offered such a long-term opportunity to all the participants that the profit allowed would be lower than normal.

We complained.

The contract administrator said we were not the only ones. Two *Fortune* 500 companies involved in the effort had also complained.

We said we are not a *Fortune* 500 company.

He said, basically, take it or leave it.

We took it, with the hope that some day we'd be strong enough to leave it.

13

Exporting from Advantage

Increasingly, one's capacity to command both tangible and intangible wealth is determined by the value that the global economy places on one's skills and insights. The ubiquitous and irrepressible law of supply and demand no longer respects national borders. In this new world economy, symbolic analysts hold a dominant position American symbolic analysts are especially advantaged.

ROBERT REICH[1]

Most high-technology businesses eventually become global businesses with 20 percent or more of their total sales coming from export sales or sales of foreign subsidiaries.

The United States maintains a strong competitive advantage in many sectors of technology, rumors of decline notwithstanding. The United States still spends more on R&D than any other industrialized country and, as a result, continues to lead the world in aerospace, imaging, operating systems, software engineering, chip architecture, biotechnology, medical equipment, and communications. Not surprisingly, the rest of the world maintains an insatiable appetite for U.S. technology products. Even the Japanese, with a mercantilist culture that precludes them from buying U.S. technology, send legions of students to the best U.S. universities to acquire our technology indirectly.

Nations take a special interest in science and technology because they are a source of commercial and military advantage. For this reason, in the words of *The Economist*:

...trade is everywhere strongly influenced by government policy of one sort or another: industrial policies (subsidies, regulatory regimes, international collaboration on standards and so on), trade barriers (tariffs, quotas, procurement policies for state-owned industries, etc) and assorted other policies that create or permit "structural impediments" to trade (especially tolerance of restrictive practices). In other words, trade in these industries is anything but "free."[2]

Yet, despite government meddling, science and technology are not easily contained by borders. Ideas freely immigrate and expatriate. The success of the U.S. space program owed a lot to the work performed by the Germans in World War II; in the same way, the Japanese semiconductor industry owes a lot to process technology developed in the Bell labs and Silicon Valley in the 1960s and 1970s. The United States continues to be the beneficiary of the migration of ideas because its open and productive economic system is a magnet for anyone who wishes to attempt to turn an idea into wealth. Hence we see the growing numbers of highly trained immigrants with key positions in U.S. companies and research institutions.

Fortunately, your company is the beneficiary of the U.S. reputation for innovation. And your need to export may be very compelling. By their very nature, the niche markets you serve may be so small in volume that the only way to increase sales is to expand into foreign markets. Likewise, with increased global competition, the only way to protect your U.S. niche may be to dominate the niche worldwide.

Foreign markets can also provide your company a level of portfolio diversity to protect it against domestic economic upheavals. When the U.S. market is down, foreign markets may be up, as many high-tech companies discovered in the late 1980s and early 1990s. Many U.S. companies survived the severe U.S. recession by selling aggressively overseas.

Exporting and the Committed Company

Successful exporting requires patience, determination, and, most important, commitment throughout the organization. Exporting is not quick, easy or cheap, plain facts which would seem to make it less attractive to a small company. Indeed, in the early stages, exporting requires more of your scarcest resources—time and money.

In fact, at first exporting will tax the highest and lowest levels of your organization. Everyone must acquire new knowledge and skills.

Administrative staff must become familiar with export nomenclature, regulations, and procedures. Exporting spontaneously creates additional paperwork in the form of various licenses, export declarations, certificates of origin, or letters of credit. The burden of paperwork is determined by the product, country to which it is destined, and means of financing the transaction. Sales staff will have to become familiar with appropriate contract terms that bind customers, sales agents, and distributors as well as regulatory or cultural issues that may affect the acceptance of products. Engineering may have to modify products to meet local safety standards or tastes of the foreign customers. Financial staff will have to learn about wire transfers, export insurance, and new financial sources and instruments. Shipping may have to take special care in packing or deal with unfamiliar shipping companies that alter their normal procedures. Receivables clerks may find themselves receiving bank drafts issued in a foreign currency and having to get them converted to dollars. The company may have to develop new outside professional support to handle special issues, i.e., in the event of contract disputes, different laws can come to bear with which your regular attorney will not be familiar.

Rarely are the are the benefits immediately obvious because successful exporting takes time. Sometimes you will doubt if the effort and investment required to succeed overseas are worth it. Rest assured, they are. There is a great feeling of satisfaction when you realize that your products are at work around the world. Better yet, exporting can be very profitable. That, in itself, is reward enough.

The EMC Option

There is a way to export and avoid most of the hassles associated with it. You can use the services of a U.S.-based export management company (EMC) or export trading company (ETC). EMCs do not take title to your products but act as commissioned brokers who use their foreign contacts to sell your product and often handle all the bothersome regulatory technicalities of shipping your product. ETCs actually take title to your products then resell overseas.

Although both perform a valuable service, you should think about whether this is a good option for your company. For most high-technology companies, it is not, for several reasons. First, though you get orders, you never develop a market using a U.S.-based intermediary. You will remain too far removed from the customer base. Second, few EMCs or ETCs have the technical staff to do a first-class job of selling your products. Finally, the commissions and discounts the EMCs or ETCs require may well lead either to price escalation that makes your products noncompetitive or to marginal profits for you.

Unless your company is xenophobic, the best option is to learn how to export yourself.

Adopting a Proactive Approach to Exporting

Assume your company will go global and begin preparations as soon as possible. Potential foreign customers will find you before you find them. Every trade publication in the United States has a high percentage of foreign readers who subscribe to keep abreast of the latest developments. If you run an ad or product announcement in one of these U.S. publications, among the responses, either in the lead sheets or on your fax, will be some overseas inquiries. Of course, just as in the domestic market, most of these will be from curiosity seekers rather than genuine prospects. But, once in a while, you'll discover a real sales opportunity. As always, the goal then is for the company to sell a product to the customer, ship as quickly as possible, and get paid; in other words, consummate a smooth business transaction.

Unfortunately, small companies can easily find themselves reacting to an export order in a way that scuttles any chance of a profitable sale because they do not fully understand what is entailed either before or after they accept an order from an overseas customer. As a consequence, when they receive an inquiry, they nonchalantly quote price and delivery, accept the order, and then find the entire organization reacting to one problem after another and the functional departments forced into a piecemeal, crash course on exporting as it pertains to their area of responsibility. The cause of this inept reactive scenario was that the company was in no position to quote price and delivery in the first place because, among other things, it did not know:

- What documentation would be required by the U.S. government or destination countries for the product to ship, if, that is, it could ship at all

- How to establish the customer's creditworthiness

- The appropriate terms and/or instruments to use in order to get paid

- Whether the product conforms to the safety and other standards of the market, which the customer assumes the company knows or it would not have offered a quotation

The net result is that the product does not ship on time, the company does not get paid on time or, in the worst cases, not paid at all. The reactive approach ensures that the export experience will be a bad one for employees involved in the transaction, and the company will likely lose any chance of future sales with that customer.

In contrast, the company adopting a proactive approach knows that before quoting price and delivery or accepting an order, it must study several issues that differ from transactions with domestic customers. Most of the following preparations will have been made before a quotation is ever issued:

1. Specialized functions in the company will receive training in areas they need to understand in order to handle an export transaction.

2. The best customer/countries for export will be qualified.

3. Both U.S. and foreign regulatory and other issues, as they pertain to the products, will be identified.

4. Prices and credit policies will be established.

5. A local agent or distributor will be under contract in countries of interest.

Thus, when the inquiry arrives, as it always does, the company will be ready to quote price and availability, accept the order, expedite the shipment, and get paid.

Two Misconceptions

Two popular misconceptions about exporting must be immediately dispelled. One is that in order to be successful overseas, someone in your company will have to learn a foreign language. In almost every country where there is demand for advanced technology, all the higher-level business managers, engineers, and scientists speak English. So will many payables or receiving clerks. English is now the language of international business in the same way that French became the language of diplomacy. The only language-related point that deserves mention is that anyone from your company who has contact with a foreign customer must try to avoid using any kind of slang in verbal or written exchanges, a task more difficult than it sounds because slang is second nature to most Americans. Your foreign customer may have a limited vocabulary and find the slang totally confusing and meaningless.

Second, rarely will a business deal be queered because of a cultural gaffe, e.g., you do not bow deeply enough in Japan or you use both hands to hand someone a gift in Taiwan. In truth, most foreigners are much more sophisticated and experienced in these matters than average Americans. They understand that the United States, despite its size, is parochial when it comes to the fine points of international business. Though they are not always forgiving, they are very pragmatic. They want your technology, your cultural barbarism notwithstanding. Perhaps the single best advice with regard to business etiquette is to maintain a businesslike demeanor. Many foreigners are uncomfortable with U.S. informality and familiarity, especially early in a business relationship.

Of course, if you have the time and interest to learn a language or study the culture of a particular country, so much the better. There are definite advantages to becoming more worldly and accommodating to other cultures.

However, your success in exporting, just like your success in the domestic market, is determined by the usual factors: a good product that is competitively priced.

Accessing the Export Information Network

When you get ready to export, you'll find lots of help—most of it for free. Every $1 billion in exports creates 25,000 jobs. Every government entity, financial and educational institution, chamber of commerce, and trade association understands the crucial role exporting plays in the U.S. economy. Consequently, a comprehensive network of support services are available to any small business.

The primary point of entry into the export information network is through the Department of Commerce's U.S. & Foreign Commercial Service (US&FCS), with district or branch offices in almost every state. This agency offers numerous seminars and services for new exporters to help make the process as simple and as risk-free as possible. Utilizing such an agency's services is highly recommended because its mission is to help you export, as a sampling of the agency's services attests:

- One-on-one counseling with a trade specialist to help you develop your export plan
- The Agent/Distributor Service (A/DS) to help you locate a foreign agent or distributor

- The World Traders Data Report (WTDR) to help you determine the creditworthiness and business stature of a potential customer or trading partner

- Overseas trade missions to provide you access to influential business and government contacts

- Overseas trade fairs where the United States sponsors a pavilion to give you a base of operations to identify potential customers and competitors

Both the U.S Departments of Commerce and State offer direct contact with their desk officers in Washington, D.C., if you need economic or political information about a particular country. When necessary, these departments can even get you in direct touch with U.S. embassies abroad.

In addition to the U.S. Foreign and Commercial Service, you can receive invaluable assistance from many other organizations:

- The SBA offers a broad range of services, including export training, legal counseling, and financing.

- All major banks have seminars on the various programs available to finance and ensure overseas transactions, how to use letters of credit, and how to obtain or convert foreign currency.

- Shipping companies and freight forwarders will help you determine all the costs associated with getting your product from your facility to the customer and expedite the actual shipment by handling outgoing and incoming customs and even letters of credit on your behalf.

- Local colleges and universities offer credit and noncredit courses on the gamut of export issues. They can help you to develop an overall export marketing plan, to better understand a particular export topic, and to meet other exporters.

- Many chambers of commerce sponsor working groups specifically directed at promoting exports through seminars and networking.

- Many states and regions have official world trade centers or trade associations that provide training and networking to promote exports.

- Many states fund export offices to assist in everything from obtaining working capital financing for an export shipment to sponsoring trade shows in foreign countries to exhibit your products.

Your most important resource may be another company that is experienced in exporting, preferably in your industry. It is unreasonable to impose on the busy staff of any company to teach you the general information you can obtain from the public resources listed above. However, when you need a specific item of information—for example, the name of a supplier particularly good at crating large instruments for overseas air freight or how to best check the credit of a potential customer in India—a more experienced exporter can help and will usually be glad to do so.

All the resources cited above should be utilized to the maximum because they will help accelerate the return on investment in your export effort. But, in the final analysis, there is one thing that none of these services can do for you, and that is sell your product. Only you can create demand. It is useful to recall the scene in the popular movie *Close Encounters of the Third Kind,* in which Richard Dreyfus is being counseled by Francois Truffaut as he prepares to board the alien spacecraft. All you can get from others is their best counsel. Ultimately, your company must make the journey on its own.

Selecting Customers/Countries

The world is a big place. You already know how expensive it is to market in the United States. It is even more expensive to market overseas to customers in any one country, much less many of them. You must be careful not to fragment your marketing effort so much that none of it is effective. Obviously your first priority is to find customers, but the countries in which they are located are as important as the customers themselves because the transfer of technology across national boundaries is highly regulated by governments. In exporting, you deal with two customers, the company and the country in which it resides. Therefore, in this discussion, countries and customers are treated almost synonymously. Usually you'll already be aware of the most likely country candidates because the leading foreign customers and competitors in any technology industry are well represented at trade shows and conferences in the United States.

If your product is patented, two significant criteria in the selection process are: which countries provide adequate protection of intellectual property and in which ones can you afford to file for patents. There are more than 170 patent jurisdictions in the world. The average time it takes to acquire a patent is two to three years, and the average cost is several thousand dollars. If your product is easy to reverse-engineer, there are countries, where piracy is blatantly condoned, to which you will not want to ship under any circumstances.

Other criteria to consider are the actual tariffs charged to land your products in the country, plus whether the country has any nontariff barriers to deter its citizens from importing your products. In export circles the story is legend about a sly nontariff barrier that France used to prevent the onslaught of Japanese-made VCRs. The French didn't levy an onerous tariff, which would have been an obvious affront inviting retaliation. Instead, the French government made all VCRs have to go through customs at a tiny port. The French customs office was open only during limited hours and inadequately staffed so that very few shipments could be processed on any one day.

Excluding Canada, Europe, by far, is the region most receptive to U.S. high-tech exporters with respect to tariffs and other economic barriers to entry. However, Europe abounds with conflicting regulatory standards that vary from country to country. An effort to make them more uniform is underway through the International Organization for Standards (ISO). Information on many of these is available through the American National Standards Institute (ANSI) in New York City. You can also get guidance from your trade association. Regulations you need to explore pertain to safety, labeling, packaging, and quality control.

You also need to appraise the suitability of your product, independent of any regulations, for the country markets of interest. For instance, if your product requires electricity, does it accommodate the country's main voltage or will the customer face the added cost and inconvenience of a transformer? Are the specifications and instruction manuals that accompany your product accurate and descriptive? For instance, unlike Americans, the Japanese are notorious for reading operating manuals from cover to cover. If they discover an inconsistency in the specifications or ambiguity in the instructions, the product will never be removed from the shipping container.

Beauty Is in the Eye of the Beholder

A Japanese distributor with excellent contacts in the laser market was interested in selling one of our specialized high-power switches, which lists for around $1000, a good value given how it performs. When shipped, the switch is first wrapped in bubble pack, then embedded in plastic "peanuts" inside a sturdy cardboard box suitable for air freight.

When the first demonstration unit arrived in Japan, the Japanese distributor opened the cardboard box and immediately faxed to complain that the product was wrapped in bubble pack instead of a finished package. He feared that when he hand-delivered it to the customer, it would not make a good first impression.

We have always shipped our products to U.S. customers with protection of the equipment the foremost packaging consideration. Never had there been any complaints. But in Japan that was not enough. It needed to be attractive also. It made sense when you realized that the Japanese wrap even the cheapest gift items in delicate tissue then place them in artful packages replete with calligraphy and other ornamentation. Impressions are everything.

Exporter Beware

The U.S. government definitely helps you select countries by legislating those to which you may not sell at all or sell only with great effort.

The countries to which technology can and cannot be exported are determined by U.S. foreign policy toward a country at any particular time. Countries come in and out of favor. Most of those that are out of favor, such as Cuba, Kampuchea, and Vietnam, are not prime potential customers for advanced technology anyway. Rightfully, the U.S. government does not make it easy (anymore) to ship advanced technology to countries like Iran and Iraq. The vast majority (80 percent) of exported products are shipped under simple general licenses, especially those bound to advanced industrial countries who have been military allies in the past. However, even being an ally is not always enough if your product has potential military applications.

The logic that governs which products can be exported and which cannot is not always obvious. Some seemingly innocuous machine tools and laptop computers are restricted. So are "data" that can be used in the design, production, and manufacture of certain articles or materials. But that doesn't necessarily mean there is no logic, only that the rationale for most controls, i.e., national security, cannot be openly discussed.

Under no circumstances should a company ignore these regulations. If you intend to export, you need to obtain the Export Administration Regulations (EARs), maintained by the Bureau of Export Administration, from the U.S. Superintendent of Documents. The EARs are also available for examination at all U.S. and FCS offices and many libraries. Though 3 inches thick, the EARs are well organized and readily comprehensible. Familiarize yourself with them. Find your products on the Commerce Control List (Part 799 in the EARs) and find their Export Control Classification Number (ECCN). With the ECCN you can determine the countries to which you can export easily, with some difficulty because validated export licenses are required, or not at all. You can also get an abbreviated reason for the classification, i.e., to prevent nuclear proliferation, biological warfare, etc.

Be aware that not all products are regulated by Bureau of Export Administration. Indeed, other agencies of government control the export of various products as well. For example, arms, ammunition, and implements of war are controlled by the Office of Munitions Control. Narcotics and dangerous drugs are administered by the Drug Enforcement Administration. Nuclear equipment and materials are controlled by the Nuclear Regulatory Commission. There are further controls on ships, natural gas and electricity, tobacco seeds and plants, and endangered fish and wildlife.

The local office of the U.S. Foreign and Commercial Service can guide you through the regulatory maze. However, due to the technical nature of your products, the local office may not have staff with adequate technical background to make a final determination. If you have any doubts that you have identified the proper ECCN, you may query the Bureau of Export Administration for verification by following the procedure described in the EARs. Verification can take one month.

Take the time to find out the regulatory status of your products. Ignorance is no defense. If the regulations are ignored, at best the shipment will be seized in either U.S. or foreign customs. Release of a shipment can take a long time; don't forget that with no delivery, there is no payment. In the worst cases, where the regulations are intentionally violated, officers of the company can be fined, go to jail, or both. Penalties can be equally harsh if shipments are made to intermediary companies operating in neutral countries that ignore the regulations and forward your products to restricted countries. Liechtenstein, for example, is infamous for harboring companies that earn rich profits by obtaining advanced technology on behalf of enemies of the United States. Do not export if you suspect this may be the customer's intention.

Mistaken Assumptions

One of our first sizable device orders was from a company in Germany. It was very welcome because the order arrived in December when domestic orders were slowing due to holidays and we had ample inventory to ship the devices immediately.

We looked through the EARs and were pleasantly surprised to find that the devices could ship G-DEST, which meant no validated license would be required. Thus, without delay, the devices could ship and help make a nice year-end contribution to sales.

Two days after the shipment was picked up by the shipper, we received notification from U.S. customs in Denver that the shipment had been seized. When asked why, the customs agent said he thought the devices might require a validated license. We argued that our reading of the EARs said that the devices could ship under the general license. He asked if that was our opinion or if we had documentation from the Bureau of Export Administration to prove it.

Of course, we didn't. The devices were held in customs for over a month, until an official government letter arrived with an authoritative opinion: The devices were eligible to be shipped under the provisions of a G-DEST.

We were right after all, but it was no consolation. You can't pay the rent with moral victories.

Finding an Overseas Agent or Distributor

To really succeed in an overseas market, you need an ally who lives and operates a business in the market you are trying to penetrate. That ally will be an agent or distributor. Agents or distributors help you get started by loaning you their credibility to compensate for the lack of credibility your company and products will suffer in the eyes of a foreign customer.

You should practice the same due diligence in the selection of a agent or distributor as you do with a business partner. This person is critical to your success. You want to find a specialist in your industry. Agents or distributors will do much more than just sell. They may also:

- Act as a marketing consultant on advertising and product definition

- Help overcome regulatory hurdles

- Assist in collections

- Install or service equipment

- Represent your company at trade shows

- Gather intelligence on competitors

- Advise on shipping and customs

- Monitor political and economic developments that might affect your business, e.g., new regulations and exchange controls

In short, you will depend almost exclusively on their knowledge and judgment on a wide range issues that will greatly impact your success.

Just like your first overseas customer discovered your company through an ad or product announcement in a U.S. publication, so will prospective reps or distributors. However, rarely will you be so lucky as to draw a first-rate agent organization by this means. Usually the best ones already have a full line card, and, unless your product is especially sought after, you represent more risk than reward until you've first proven yourself in the U.S. market.

Be skeptical of inquiries heaping lavish praise on your company and products and requesting you to immediately send 10 sets of brochures, your distributor agreement, and distributor price list. Most of the time, you should ignore companies that send these types of inquiries because they will lack the adequate technical background and right contacts to handle your products. Before you send any business information, fax them requesting the evidence of their technical credentials to sell, support, and service your products. Often you'll find that they deal in a wide variety of commodity goods, none even remotely related to your key markets. They try to find out what you do, then try to find out if there's a market. Many faxes like these originate from hungry trading companies along the Pacific Rim such as Singapore and Taiwan. Once in a while, a customer in their country will route a legitimate inquiry through them to your company, because it is more convenient (i.e., they do not speak much English) to have these trading companies do their exploratory work for them. In these cases, use your judgment; the depth of the technical questions can be a good indication of the seriousness of the inquiry.

A good way to find an able agent or distributor is to talk with other companies in your industry that offer products complementary to yours and that are already established overseas. Ask them if you can use them as a referral or, better yet, provide you a letter of introduction. You can also search in industry buyer's guides and find out who represents successful companies with which you are familiar. Then send a package containing your own letter of introduction, company profile, and technical literature.

If you receive a favorable response, if at all possible, visit the foreign agent or distributor and spend a few days making customer visits with him or her. Foreign agents always appreciate a principal traveling with them to visit customers and help them sell. Not only will you get a chance to make sales, but by observation you can quickly ascertain how well the agents know the market. Quite literally, does the agent know how to drive directly to the customer's facility, or does she or he easily get lost and require maps? If the latter, the agent obviously doesn't visit the customer very often. Do the front-desk personnel seem to know the agent? Does the customer receive him or her warmly? Does the agent know the inside scuttlebutt about ongoing technical developments, management changes, and, most important, the prevailing economics and cost structure in the industry? What's the agent's facility like? Don't expect a lavish office complex; agents must financially control their businesses like you do yours. But do ask if the agent has the equipment to service your products. Does someone answer the phone in the agent's absence?

You want to have a formal, signed agreement in place between your company and the agent/distributor, not just for the legal protection but to spell out the specifics of how the business relationship will work. Negotiating a sales agreement allows you to address all kinds of potential problems concerning logistics and payments. Some countries make it difficult for a principal to fire an agent and even have penalties that require the principal to pay the agent for an inordinate period after the agreement is terminated. However, most agents and distributors will accept a U.S.-drafted agreement. If you are looking at several countries, you may not want to invest in the cost of a lawyer drafting each one. Contact a larger company and ask if they will give you a "sanitized" copy of the agreement they use and than copy it. Make sure that in the event of a dispute, the contract calls for it to be adjudicated in a U.S. jurisdiction.

Be flexible in your business relationship, especially when it comes to money matters. You will not get the best effort from an agent/distributor whom you treat like an arm's-length customer and from whom you extract every last nickel and dime for product literature, demonstration units, and spare parts. Most foreign reps and distributors live in a very competitive environment and work hard for their money. As a result, they know what things cost and whether they are getting a raw deal. Never forget that if they are good, you need them more than they need you.

Setting Export Prices

Small companies that wish to succeed in export markets should price as aggressively as they can afford. To be sure, the cost of a sale of a product to a foreign customer is higher than the sale of the same product to a domestic one. Postage, faxes, travel, administration, and any other costs will be higher. Therefore, the first instinct of many U.S. exporters is to charge a higher price. Indeed, many companies have a domestic price list and a separate export price list that is 10 to 30 percent higher, charging what might be termed an "export premium."

Although this pricing policy may work for larger, established companies, it is not recommended for smaller ones because it can lead to severe price escalation that prices your products right out of the market. Ignore, for the moment, commissions to reps or mark-ups distributors make on your product, and consider the landed price of a $1000 product sold at the domestic price to a domestic customer versus the same product sold directly to a foreign customer with no export premium.

Domestic	Export
$1000 Price	$1000 Price
75 Freight	100 Freight
15 Insurance	25 Insurance
$1090	60 Customs broker
	80 Import tariff
	$1265

Note that at the domestic price, the delivered cost to the overseas customer is already almost 20 percent higher. If you place an export premium on top of this, your price may end up more than 50 percent higher and no longer be competitive.

There is also a further, less obvious risk and direct cost to the customer that can take the price even higher: The customers will pay you in U.S. dollars. Customers will have the cost of purchasing the dollars as well as the risk of the dollar becoming more expensive against their currencies between the time their orders are placed, your deliveries are made, and payments are due. (You should always quote in dollars. For you to quote business in a foreign currency is risky business because you do not have enough volume or expertise to use currency hedges to protect against untoward fluctuations.)

Higher export price lists encourage some customers, usually agencies or state-owned enterprises of foreign governments, to use their buying missions in the United States to obtain your products. This practice is widely used by countries such as Israel and Taiwan. Your agent/distributor will spend the time and effort to convince the customer to buy your product, then the customer will contact its U.S. buying mission to get it the lowest possible price. You may think this is your agent's problem to solve, not yours. But it will become yours when there is an installation or service problem and the agent or distributor checks out the serial number and discovers she or he did not sell the product. The agent will have no obligation to service it. If you must sell to the buying mission, either let it know you only warrant that product in the United States or give your agent/distributor appropriate compensation to support the warranty.

Agent Commissions and Distributor Discounts

Foreign reps and distributors always receive larger commissions and deeper discounts than their domestic counterparts. Most agents will get a minimum of 15 percent, and distributor discounts will range between 20 and 40 percent. But make no mistake, for the services good agents provide, they are entitled to every cent. They perform more services than their domestic counterparts and assume much more risk.

The risk agents assume is using their good name and industry contacts to promote the sales of your products. Regardless of how you feel, your company is relatively unknown. The agent/distributor will have to convince the foreign customer not only of your product's technical performance but of your management, quality, manufacturing capability, and financial strength. As you know from standing in front of your own domestic customers, this is a challenging task.

If you are so fortunate as to obtain ongoing, long-term business, the day may come when you balk at signing a big commission check and ask, "What are they doing to warrant these checks?" Like you, reps and distributors get their payoff when you are successful, not before when you are struggling. The issue will be not what they are doing but what they already did for you in the early days. This is the return on the investment they made in you.

Credit Terms and Conditions

Most countries have different credit terms from the standard net 30 days prevalent in much of U.S industry. In Germany and France, net 60 days is common. In Japan normal terms extend out to 90 days or more. In Italy they seem to be infinity.

It is often tempting to set a policy that no overseas orders will be shipped unless they are under an irrevocable letter of credit (LOC—one of the first acronyms you'll add to your lexicon at any export seminar—an instrument that makes it impossible for the customer not to pay). Although letters of credit do provide 100 percent assurance that you will get paid, they can also delay shipping an order because of the time required for the documents to be prepared. Certain LOCs require your customer to deposit funds with the issuing bank, which can further delay the transaction and needlessly increase the cost of doing business with you. The service fees charged by banks to prepare LOCs are quite expensive in cases where the transactions are relatively small. Admittedly, it is not as easy to check out the credit of a foreign customer, although Dun and Bradstreet has been expanding its international coverage. Your agent or distributor can help you in this matter. In most high-tech transactions with the more advanced countries, particularly in Europe and Japan, the companies with whom you are likely to conduct business are creditworthy. Though your terms say 30 days, you may not see payment for 45 to 60, but you do finally see payment. Whether a letter of credit is really necessary should be decided on a case-by-case basis.

LOCs are necessary when you are conducting business with any third-world country, where the respective foreign government's control of dollar currency reserves held by its banks can make it difficult for even substantial companies to remit a timely payment.

Advertising Abroad

Obviously you advertise only after the preparations for a proactive export program have been completed. Until then, you are wasting your resources.

Advertising abroad is expensive. When you are the purchaser of media in a foreign country, you will remit in their currency. You are then exposed to the risk of currency fluctuations. From the time an insertion order is placed until the tearsheet is sent attached to the invoice after publication, several months can pass, during which the buying power of a dollar vis-à-vis another currency has been in decline. The ad can end up costing more than you budgeted, so you need to proceed with caution.

Small companies cannot afford the services of major international advertising agencies, which usually do not show any interest until an account is in the range of $100,000. Likewise, these international companies will not be familiar with the smaller advertising agencies in the country of interest.

In most cases, the best option is for your company to collaborate with your agent or distributor to identify the best publication in which your ad should appear. Almost every high-tech industry has indigenous trade publications that are narrowly targeted. In addition, there are several pan-Asian and pan-European publications that also serve the needs of a specialized readership. The agent or distributor will have a better sense of which months are optimum for advertising, i.e., to either coincide with major trade shows or avoid issues that experience a lower readership at certain times of year, as is the case in France where factories virtually shut down the entire month of August for summer vacation.

You need to discuss with your agent or distributor how to proceed with the logistics of designing and preparing artwork for the ad. Your agent may be able to provide copies of a publication of choice so you can see if your tastes, conditioned by U.S. standards, are congruent with that of the indigenous market. This is important to find out. If you have ever seen Japanese magazine advertising, for example, the ads appear very cluttered and the color combinations rather garish to the U.S. eye. Even in French and German publications, you will find stylistic differences in print styles, graphics, and colors.

In advertising and promotional pieces, cultural differences must be respected. A German company that manufactures semiconductor equipment once tried an ad in the United States which was a literal translation of an ad which was very effective in Germany. The ad had a few words about the company's products printed over a nice woodcut of an eighteenth-century maiden. The Germans associated the woodcut with a tradition of quality and craftsmanship, but the ad was unproductive in the United States because to a U.S. reader it was too subtle and failed to provide enough useful information. In another instance, a U.S. company sent a corporate brochure to Japan. One of the photos showed a close-up of an engineer's forearm pointing to one of the circuit boards inside a product. His forearm had a tattoo he had acquired during a drunken shore leave in a distant port during his stint in the Navy. The Japanese distributor was aghast, and effectiveness of the brochure diminished because the Japanese associate tattoos with the *yakuza*, their equivalent of the Mafia. Even the presence of a styrofoam cup in a photo can be offensive to the environmentally conscious Europeans. The only way to avoid these problems is to codesign your advertising with your agent or distributor.

If your standard U.S. ad is adequate in the opinion of your agent or distributor, you can have the artwork produced in the United States in conformance with the metric requirements of foreign publications, then have the agent or distributor get a translation of the copy made in his or her country. The copy should be typeset overseas because the typesetting fonts with the characters unique to the language will be readily available. Competent translation services are also available in the United States; however, when dealing with the specialized nomenclature of a technical discipline, sometimes it can be difficult to find a U.S.-based vendor with a sufficient grasp of the technical language to produce a good translation.

Bottom Fishing

In an effort to boost exports, the *U.S. Commercial News* put together a series of issues featuring the products from various geographical areas of the country. This publication has a large circulation, including embassies around the world, and it is moderately priced.

Just looking at the contents, it was doubtful it would be very effective because the mix of products was so diverse that our products were incongruous along with a patented sidewalk chalk for children, a complete log cabin do-it-yourself kit, and similar low-tech items. But to show our support for the Department of Commerce's effort and, hopefully, generate sales, we placed an ad.

A few weeks later a letter arrived with a very colorful stamp from Nigeria. The letter said our company came highly recommended by their contacts in the U.S. embassy. The letter went on to describe that the Federal Ministry of Aviation had been overbilled for a contract in the amount of $82 million. A group of Nigerian officials needed a foreign bank account into which to transfer this sum. In exchange, the Nigerians would remit $24.6 million as payment for the use of our account. We were invited to send blank letterhead, with officers' signatures and our account number at the bank. They'd perform the courtesy of filling out the blanks and then make a wire transfer of the funds to the bank. We were also cordially invited to personally visit the parties involved.

Though we could have used $24 million (still could), we never responded because it sounded too good to be true—plus, of course, it was clearly illegal. Over the next few weeks, we received over a dozen similar letters, one of them even from a prince! (In fairness to the U.S. government, it issued a public warning as soon as it got wind of the scam.)

Finally, months later, we heard on the radio that a U.S. businessman had responded to a similar letter and traveled to Nigeria. He had been held at gunpoint and had to pay a sizable ransom to leave. Apparently he didn't hear the government's warning or ignored it. He must have needed the money even worse than we did.

Financing Exports

As usual, there is a dearth of capital available for small companies trying to export, but the situation is improving as the government and major financial institutions face the realities of global competition and the critical role small businesses must play to improve the balance of trade. Even the Exim Bank has come down off its lofty pedestal recently to offer some financing to small business.

The SBA offers the Export Revolving Line of Credit (ERLC) program, which provides guaranteed loans of up to $750,000. However, according to *Export Today* magazine, in the first 10 months of fiscal 1992, the SBA made 500 loans worth $174.35 million to U.S. exporting companies, an insignificant amount when the Commerce Department estimates that 130,000 companies are vying for these funds.[3] The program has grown considerably in recent years, so, provided Congress continues to bless it, access should open to a larger number of companies.

Banks are leery of export financing because they know there is little recourse if a foreign customer doesn't pay. For this reason, many banks are unwilling to finance the receivable of a foreign customer. In the cases where banks are willing to loan, in most cases the transaction will include irrevocable letters of credit.

Almost half the states now also provide export financing assistance through loan and insurance programs. The insurance programs are especially effective because they enable banks to expand their export lending by reducing the risk.

Finding sources of export financing takes as much time as finding overseas customers. Start as soon as you can to explore your options. You'll want to know them because the availability and type of financing effects the price and terms of your quotations to overseas customers.

If you are successful at exporting, the government offers favorable tax treatment for export earnings through Foreign Sales Corporations (FSCs) and Shared Foreign Sales Corporations (SFSCs), the details of which you can learn from major international banks and accounting firms. These begin to make financial sense as soon as your export sales approach $200,000. Needless to say, seeking tax advantages is a high-class problem that deserves to be at the bottom of your proactive exporting plan.

Spend most of your time and effort to get the business first. You can always find a way to finance it because exporting is as important to your country as it is to your company. Truly, as grandiose as it sounds, your success is in the national interest.

14

Managing the Unmanageable

From immigrants and outcasts, street toughs and science wonks, nerds and boffins, the bearded and beer-bellied, the tacky and uptight, and sometimes weird, the born again and born yesterday...from the coarse fanaticism and desperation, ambition and hunger, genius and sweat of the outsider, the downtrodden, the banished, and the bullied come most of the progress in the world...."

GEORGE GILDER[1]

Managing in a small undercapitalized company is like being a paramedic administering emergency triage to victims at the site of a plane crash. You do not worry about minor lacerations and broken bones. Your attention is riveted on the basics: heart beat, breathing, stopping major hemorrhaging. Good management is a challenge under the best of circumstances. Many small companies do not exist under the best of circumstances because the necessary conditions to nurture good management—time, money, and expertise—are, to one degree or another, absent. So management must focus on the most pressing issues, and, of necessity, the secondary ones languish.

Recognize that there are no quick and easy cookbook recipes to make management easy. Outsiders, perceiving that some area of management is overlooked, may think that your company is not well managed. Sometimes this is true, but, just as often, it is not. The company may be managed very well, given its circumstances. To successfully manage a small company requires modes of thinking and behavior that only vaguely resemble the conventional nostrums about how to plan, organize, direct, and control. Control, or lack thereof, is the very essence of the problem. The small company is not in control. It is easily victimized by severe supply-demand imbalances where there is either insufficient staffing for the business level or, vice versa, too much. The planning horizon is too short because management rarely has an order backlog to provide it with enough visibility to plan its cash and staffing needs with certainty. Hence management's success depends as much on agility, tenacity, and resourcefulness as on vision and leadership.

Viewed from the outside, a small company appears to be a relatively simple business to manage. Certainly the corporate structure is minimal, and there are few employees, customers, vendors, products, facilities, investors, machines, or materials to manage. However, small-company management is made complex because of the large amount of output that must be generated per small unit of input. The biblical multiplication of the loaves and the fishes is impossible to replicate in a business environment, yet, for an undercapitalized small company, that is the equivalent of the task at hand.

In the spirit of Maslow's hierarchy, management focus must move in a logical, protean succession—from getting a product financed, to engineering the product, to marketing the product, to ramping up for production. At any one time, due to capital limitations, some aspect critical to the business's success will be emphasized, while, in turn, others are deemphasized. Your company may pay little or no attention to important but secondary matters such as pension plans, employee policy manuals, insurance exposures, and minor legal issues. Each secondary issue may carry the risk of turning out to be problematic, but you must run the risk that it will not. You literally may not have the time or money to worry about secondary issues.

Living Dangerously

Our lawyer charges over $100 per hour. We have not been either a conventional or a lucrative client for him. He is a visible and upstanding member of the community who served on the local school board. Though by no means an expert on all the laws relating to securities, patents and trademarks, trade secrets, product liability, etc., he knows where to find that information and never pretends to know what he doesn't.

He worries about us because of the unorthodox ways in which we are apt to go about things, depending on our financial situation at the time, and because he has only a slight understanding of our business.

Trying to be quasi-businesslike, we like to have him review employee agreements, contracts, nondisclosures, the minutes of corporate meetings, and other such routine business matters. It seems the more he learns about us, the more concerned he becomes, which is okay, because that is what he is paid for.

Shortly after we received a small investment, he wrote a letter that read in part:

"I recognize that much of what an entrepreneurship organization does is determined by the circumstances in which it is operating. I also recognize that you can only afford a limited amount of legal and technical advice. Now that you have a fairly substantial, funded capital, it is important that your corporate structure be kept in the best order possible so that your entity can ultimately support further public scrutiny (if you go to larger offerings) or be attractive to a possible buy out by some larger enterprise." He further advised "...judicious use of legal input."

His valid concerns, listed dutifully, included potential state securities violations with how the founders issued stock to themselves, their partnership arrangement, the presence of a foreign investor, and even a new trademark he noticed on our stationery. Some of his concerns were self-serving in that as a legal professional he would be derelict in his duty not to bring them to our attention, and he would also be able to increase his billings.

Over two years have passed since his letter, and most of the issues he raised still have not been resolved. Yet life and business go on.

I know someday, when something goes wrong, he will say, "I told you so." Then we'll finally be a lucrative client.

Monitor the Dark Side

If there is a management problem in a your company, you may not have to look very long or hard to find it. The odds are high that you are the source of the problem. The psyches of both the entrepreneur and technologist have definite characteristics that make them predisposed toward poor management. If the entrepreneur and technologist are one and the same person, the odds are even higher.

According to Robert Bendit, "Some of the very qualities which make a man able to start a new enterprise are likely to cause distress in those attempting to work with him. Stubbornness to the point of bull-headedness, independence, sullenness, argumentativeness, peevishness, periods of elation and depression, anxiety and insecurity—all go into making up his total behavior."[2] Indeed, a psychologist writing for the *Harvard Business Review*, went so far as to attribute a very dark side to entrepreneurship. "Many entrepreneurs are misfits who need to create their own environment," he observed.[3] Needless to say, these misfits are not inclined to interact optimally with other people. "People who are overly concerned about being in control," he said, "also have little tolerance for subordinates who think for themselves."

As if being an entrepreneur were not handicap enough, being a technologist is an additional handicap. Hodges Goldson, writing for a professional association on the problems of management, counseled: "Remain aware of the psychological profile of technically oriented people in general. That is, they are typically characterized by high intelligence, social reserve (at times bordering on detachment and aloofness), seriousness, and tendencies to become overly wrapped up in their own thoughts, ideas, and projects."[4]

Listen unto Others
as You Would Have Them
Listen unto You

Megalomania is not just a matter of poor management "style." It can be lethal. Not surprisingly, when John Argenti researched his book *Corporate Collapse: The Causes and Symptoms,* he discovered that the single foremost cause of business failure is bad management.[5] Of course, saying a company failed because of bad management is like saying a runner lost a race because he did not run fast enough, both uninformative tautologies at best. Argenti delved beneath this facile generalization to identify six, discrete structural defects in management. Three are worthy of special attention given the psychological profile of the entrepreneur/technologist.

The first defect Argenti called "one-man rule." He points to a mind-set or way of doing things. He is not singling out the sole proprietor of the small business or head of a small management team. Certainly many small company decisions are made by one person, as many should and must be. What Argenti is referring to is more onerous. He means "chief executives who dominate their colleagues rather than lead them, who make decisions in spite of their hostility or reticence, who allow no discussion, will hear no advice." These are egomaniacal and autocratic individuals who are found in both large and small companies. He astutely observes that autocrats are not always overbearing, pugnacious, type A personalities who bully people. Many are "relatively retiring people who impose their will by superior knowledge." The latter are very commonplace in high technology. *The problem is that they may well be knowledgeable, but typically in a narrow technical area, not in every technical area and certainly not in critical business areas.* Most technology products bring several special areas of expertise to bear in a design. Similarly any business decision brings several areas of business expertise to bear in the decision. A brilliant electrical engineer is not likely to also be a brilliant mechanical engineer and is even less likely to be a brilliant financial manager as well.

One-person rule is only a single component in the larger matrix of failure. It is not, of itself, a sufficient condition for failure. There are plenty of pompous asses and scoundrels who are quite successful. Everyone knows a few. However, the odds of failure are much greater for autocrats because the business environment is very complex, particularly in high technology, and leaders are in dire need of critical control and feedback mechanisms to keep them on course. The major source of these moderating, balancing influences must be other people inside the organization.

Autocracy breeds disloyalty and indifference. Repressed employees tend to withhold information and their best efforts. The autocrat is inclined to ignore the accountant who says the cash balance is getting dangerously low, the technician who says there is a design flaw that exposes the company to costly field failures, the sales manager who says the price is out of line with the economics of the industry, the production manager who says the engineering design is too difficult to build. The tragedy is that, when these companies eventually fail, autocrats take down not only themselves but all those who were ready and able to help them.

It is important to be aware of these characteristics of the entrepreneur and technologist in case you are one or the other or both. They are antithetical to the ideal behavior of the humanistic, egalitarian, modern manager. Never forget that your success is measured by the output of others within the organization.

Invest in Management First

A successful company is a group effort. There are no exceptions. The role played by management "stars" in corporate settings is greatly exaggerated by the business press because it is much easier to explain the performance of a complex organization by reducing it to the heroic efforts of a single individual.

Not surprisingly, Argenti cited an "unbalanced top team" as another management-related cause of failure. His conclusion is corroborated by Roberts' statistics in *Entrepreneurship and High Technology.* Not surprisingly, Roberts found that the broader were the management skills represented by the founding teams of the companies he studied, the more likely these companies were to grow profitably and succeed.[6] In the modern business environment there is too much specialized knowledge for a single individual to possess, and every bit of it you can marshal increases your odds for success.

It goes without saying that all technical disciplines are becoming increasingly specialized. So are the business disciplines. But, concurrently, the breadth of knowledge required inside each is expanding. Consider the know-how encompassed in a business specialty:

Sales and marketing—channels of distribution, contract law, promotion, negotiation, pricing, order entry, forecasting, sales management, market research

Finance—financial and cost accounting, banking, investment, tax law, cash-flow management, budgeting, receivable and payables management

Purchasing—contract law, vendor management, receiving, inventory management, negotiation, purchase order administration, incoming QA

Production—manufacturing QA, assembly, testing, training, master scheduling, equipment maintenance, safety

Personnel—recruiting and hiring, benefits management, law (state, federal, local), training, negotiation

Export—licensing, regulations, customs, foreign currencies, political risk, distribution, finance

Management information systems—computer technology, software, programming, telecommunications

The object of this list is to illustrate the array of know-how that is resident in a balanced, well-managed high-tech company, and all this knowledge is as important as the technology itself. Some technologists have a tendency to trivialize the expertise required of various business functions, but, in each of these areas, the company will be more vulnerable to failure than for technical reasons. Technologists who do not see the value of this expertise generally never develop companies of much value.

If developing a product that will generate sales and cash is a small company's first priority, its second should be, as soon as reasonably possible, to divert investment from technology development to bringing on management professionals, especially in the areas of finance and marketing. And, of course, as soon as possible other functional experts should follow. All will be necessary.

Always give priority to spending money on people over nonpeople expenses, unless those nonpeople expenses generate immediate income, such as a piece of equipment you need to manufacture your product. Managerial synergy generates increased output.

Selecting management employees for a small high-tech company is not easy. Only certain types of people function well in a fast-changing, underresourced environment. Many people who have fantasized about the invigorating challenges of working in an entrepreneurial company find the reality more trying than challenging. The tough aspects of working in a small company should be discussed openly in job interviews. This does not just mean talking about the financial uncertainties, but the day-to-day drudgery and long hours a job may entail. For example, a sales professional from a larger company may find he will have to do his job with no administrative support. He will personally address, stuff, and stamp envelopes with product information going out to leads. Or an engineer will solder her own boards, or an accountant do her own bookkeeping, or a purchasing manager write the actual purchase orders.

It is useful to have one key manager with experience in a larger midsize or *Fortune* 500 company. This manager often can offer a broader management perspective and migrate useful administrative procedures and organizational structures to the company. By introducing the original entrepreneurs to proven business practices, the manager helps relieve them of the arduous, and usually unproductive, efforts they are inclined to expend to invent innovative business structures with the same vigor they invent technology but without a commensurate level of expertise.

The Role of Outsiders

The limitations of your company's management can be compensated for by a constellation of mentors to whom you listen carefully. The individuals who comprise a constellation can vary by the type of decision that needs to be made. For example, a financial decision might involve a couple of people inside the company such as your controller and purchasing manager, your outside accountant, a banker, and another businessperson. At least one person inside the informal constellation should be someone who will think the opposite of how you are leaning on the decision. You always want to listen carefully to contrarians. Good decisions are often hybrid compromises, not either/or logic gates.

A board of directors is the conventional business structure used to ensure that a company stays on track. An active board of directors is a natural check to one-person rule. But a board can be harmful to a business if it is a pretense and does not have serving on it individuals who understand the critical areas of your business. In fact, Argenti cites a "nonparticipating board of directors" as another management cause of business failure. A board of directors provides an active, experienced, and diverse advisory group to help guide the CEO and compensate for her or his weaknesses. Most small companies do not have a board of directors, or, if they do, too frequently it consists of wives, relatives, friends, fellow parishioners, and Rotarians, you name it. Boards of directors composed of yes-people and dolts are useless. Too often such a board acts as a mechanism to siphon money off the company in the form of directors' fees, or to subsidize family vacations (e.g., the husband and wife "directors" go to Hawaii for corporate planning) and makes no real contribution.

No one person should exert complete control over decision making in a company. No key decisions should be made without ample consultation with others who will be affected by the decision or who are in a position, due to knowledge and experience, to contribute toward a better decision. It is worthwhile to reflect periodically on how your decisions are being shaped. You should be able to recall the specific opinions of others, as well as their voices and facial expressions when they offered them to you. If you cannot, then you were not really listening.

The best defense against egomania is to develop habits and procedures in the company which make it difficult, even impossible, not to listen. For instance, make it a policy that no new product development can be undertaken without a formal meeting where the views of every department that will be involved in the product are presented. Obligate the departments to speak to the merits of the proposed product and the drawbacks as well.

Every company needs its loyal opposition to escape "groupthink," a term coined by Yale psychology professor Irving Janis. Janis describes *groupthink* as "a mode of thinking that people engage in whey they are deeply involved in a cohesive in-group, when the members, striving for unanimity, override their motivation to realistically appraise alternative courses of action." David Dreman, an investment adviser, cited Janis in a book about stock market investing. Dreman said, "The more cohesive the decision-making group and the more they respect and are attuned to each other's thinking, the greater the danger that independent assessment will be abandoned and will be replaced instead by concurrence seeking tendencies. Poor decisions are frequently the result."[7] The small company should take heed because its camaraderie and close working conditions make it naturally prone to this mode of behavior.

Division of Labor

Because many small-company managers find themselves relatively isolated from other managerial professionals, they easily fall into the habit of sharing managerial dilemmas with employees who are not, by temperament or experience, qualified to participate in a decision. This may appear to fly in the face of popular concepts such as "empowering" the employee, but it does not.

Democracy is a wonderful political philosophy, but its application must be limited in a business setting, especially in a small company. This is not to advocate autocracy, as has been properly condemned above. However, a few business issues are amenable to management by democratic consensus; most are not. Democracy can be too time-consuming and inefficient for a small company. When there are many issues to decide, it can also be distracting.

Employees should be competent to perform the job they have been assigned and be given the authority and resources, as available, to assume an appropriate degree of responsibility for achieving the desired results. But remember that your company is much like a B-25 on a bombing run into Europe during World War II. The plane has a mission to accomplish, but it is running low on fuel and is already damaged from antiaircraft fire. Each member of the crew may be a good buddy down on the ground, but they are highly trained specialists with particular responsibilities and authority when the airplane is in the air. Someone must fly the plane. Someone must navigate. Someone must identify targets. Someone must be on alert for enemy interceptors. Someone must load bombs. In the thick of battle, each function is absolutely critical, and none more so than another. The navigator must be paying attention to his compass and flight charts, not telling the pilot how to handle the rudder, nor the bombardier second-guessing if the navigator is properly reading the compass.

A clear division of labor insulates employees from the ambiguity and uncertainty natural to small companies. If information circulates too freely due to the close physical confines of a small company, employees can be diverted on all kinds of unproductive, imaginary tangents. The emotional stress can make everyone prone to second-guessing everyone else. One means of discouraging second-guessing is to avoid sharing too much information or providing forums that will lead people to second-guess. Too much open discussion of a specific situation in a company can open a Pandora's box that results in bad decisions and bad morale. For example, there is no purpose in discussing with all the employees how to manage a contract dispute that is causing delay of a payment. If they are unfamiliar with the history of the transaction that led to the dispute, the salient legal issues, and the financial status of the company, it is unlikely that they can contribute toward any resolution. Or, as another example, it may not be useful to discuss the pricing structure of a product with employees other than those who have specific knowledge of the market or who have given considerable thought to the matter. A technician who tests a product and has a deep understanding of its operation does not necessarily have the insight from which to calculate its value to a customer.

Forget Perfection—Strive for Constant Incremental Improvement

Your goal should be to do things better, not to do things perfectly. Perfection is out of the question in a small company because the resources are not available for perfection to be any more than an aspiration. In a small company, perfectionists are doomed to an unhappy life, and they can doom everyone around them to unhappy lives too.

Though it seems a contradiction in terms, a rejection of perfection does not necessarily lead to complacency. Alfred North Whitehead, the great mathematician and philosopher, said the purpose of human reason is first to enable us to live and then to enable us to live better. A desire to do things better is a positive force. It expresses itself as a vague dissatisfaction with the status quo and an urge to change things. Within the limits of its resources, the company should strive to incrementally improve every facet of its business each time an opportunity presents itself. Goals that reflect a philosophy of incremental improvement might state that

- The next product will have a more finished front panel.
- The next written quotation will be better composed and more professional in appearance.
- The next manual will be more informative and complete.
- The next ad will communicate more effectively about the company or product.

- The next sales presentation will be more organized and structured to elicit customer input.
- The next cash flow will be more accurate.
- The next product will be designed faster.
- The next vendor will be more reliable or better priced.

And so on. Obviously there is no end to the list. This point cannot be emphasized enough with respect to product development. Perfect products have a way of never being completed so they can be sold. Perfection can become a rationalization for incessant and expensive changes. Though perfection is never really achieved, the steady progress that does get made becomes obvious to everyone inside and outside the company. That is a worthy achievement in itself.

Protecting Intellectual Property

Your business exists because you know something everybody else does not—yet. It may be a technique, process, architecture, topology, whatever, and for the moment, it is unique to you. And it is probably your sole competitive advantage. Definitely you need to take reasonable and appropriate precautions to protect it. A well-written, practical guide to intellectual property matters, entitled *Protecting Engineering Ideas and Inventions* by Ramon Foltz and Thomas Penn, identifies the issues you need to address.

At a bare minimum, every managerial and technical employee should work under the terms of an employee agreement that incorporates enforceable language with respect to trade secrets and noncompetition. This agreement, which is relatively inexpensive, should be drafted by an attorney familiar with intellectual property matters.

Patents are expensive and time-consuming to obtain, but they play a strategic role in most high-technology businesses. For this reason, you must become familiar with them by reading David Pressman's book *Patent It Yourself!* or another like it—but don't try to patent anything on your own. Patents are too important to be left to amateurs. Patent law is arcane, and its language, especially as used to structure the claims, has very precise and special denotations. You should retain an experienced attorney familiar with the field of your company's inventions. Only an attorney with a deep understanding of the field can fashion a strong patent position for you. However, you can provide critical assistance and perhaps accelerate the process if not lower your fees by understanding the general terms of patent law and by being able to fully articulate the novelty and usefulness of your inventions.

The best intellectual property protection you can provide your products is to become so well entrenched with your customers because of your performance, price, and service that a competitor with an identical product will have a difficult time getting a foot in the door. However, rarely are small companies that well positioned, so patents can provide an important, though temporary, barrier to competition until they do. Patents also help your public relations efforts. The public at large is impressed by them because they think patents are ipso facto money-making secrets that have received the government's seal of approval. Bankers and investors may perceive them as intangible assets with enormous future value. Ironically, a patent somehow legitimizes the technology even though it may not even work or have any demand.

Patents guarantee nothing. As Alan Tripp observes in his book *Millions from the Mind:* "Seventeen years exclusivity—great! Provided, that is, that someone doesn't come along and pay the $1500 fee required for a reexamination of your patent, saying it was granted improperly. Provided somebody doesn't sue you, saying your patent partly infringes a prior patent of theirs. Provided someone doesn't go ahead and make a product like yours and tell you to go fly a kite."[8] This is most likely to occur if you have a product with enormous demand that attracts the attention of large competitors. If you do, and a large enterprise offers to license your company's technology, you should give it serious consideration. There is always a chance that if you refuse, the other firm may copy your technology anyway. Understand that a patent is only as good as its enforcement. Government has no watchdog agency that supervises industry and steps in to prosecute infringers. This role falls to the holder of the patent.

Unfortunately, if you are undercapitalized, you are in a poor position to enforce a patent. When you see an organization infringe your patent, you sue them. The average cost to litigate an infringement is over $250,000. Some large companies now make patent infringement suits a profit center. Semiconductor chip makers Intel and Texas Instruments are well known for this. TI has accumulated hundreds of millions of dollars in settlements. Keep in mind, however, that these companies have a strong inducement to protect this technology because of the enormous investment they have made—chip development can easily cost $10 million, and the fab to make them over $250 million. These are high stakes. You must ask yourself if your stakes are as high. You will pay many of the legal fees up front because few attorneys will take a small company's work on a contingency basis. If you rebuff the overture of a larger company for a license, then all you may get is legal expenses for years while the opposing attorneys use a plenitude of legal ploys to stall the resolution. You could be broke or dead by the time you win, if you win.

However, if you are aiming at a niche market, patents can give a virtual monopoly against competitors. A small power supply manufacturer that services the thin-film industry has created a powerful barrier to entry against potential competitors by getting a patent on a conventional aspect of switch-mode power supply design when used in sputtering applications. Their niche is so small and the competitors so weak that no one challenges the patent though it is based on widely used circuits and dubious assumptions about plasma physics. But by clever use of this patent, the company has managed to protect a $15 million business by informing customers they intend to sue any challenger for patent infringement and thereby interrupt the challenger's ability to deliver product. However obnoxious this might seem, it is a smart, effective, and legal business strategy.

Approximately 30 years ago Gordon Gould filed the patent on the laser. His patent was ignored, and a whole industry bloomed despite it. Then, in 1979, a company called Patlex, whose CEO is a former astronaut, was formed specifically to sue the companies which violated Gould's patent and force the violators to obtain a license. As of today, over 100 companies have been licensed and many millions of dollars in royalties paid to Patlex.[9]

If you are lucky, your proprietary know-how will not be too important so the world will not be motivated to copy it. If it is, you can plan on it. For every Gould story, there are hundreds who cannot afford the litigation. It is in the economic interest of the larger society for technology to proliferate so prices come down, thus making it more accessible and growing the economy. For this to occur, there must be competition. The plodding and expensive patent process is well designed to ensure that this happens.

Focus on Basics

The aspiration of a small company is to grow into a larger, financially successful enterprise. What it aspires to become is personified in the successful midsize companies such as Millipore and Thermo Electron. These companies were the subject of a provocative book by Donald Clifford and Richard Cavanagh entitled *The Winning Performance: How*

America's Midsize Growth Companies Succeed. They listed six key management traits of these companies:

1. They instill a strong sense of mission and shared values—and work constantly to reinforce a deeply ingrained sense of beliefs.
2. They pay relentless attention to business fundamentals.
3. They treat bureaucracy as an archenemy.
4. They encourage experimentation.
5. They think like their customers and work hard on behalf of them.
6. They count on people and put development and motivation of their people at the top of their list of priorities.[10]

It is noteworthy that their management systems are simple and aimed, first and foremost, at financial results. These successful companies tend to focus on smooth and efficient operations to squeeze out the highest possible return. As a result, these companies are able to generate "margin dollars that can be used to develop new products, to support expansion, and to build organizational strength." This simple formula is worthy of emulation.

Confucius on Leadership

In China, around 500 B.C., Confucius wrote the *Analects,* containing the passage below, which describes the attributes of leadership more insightfully than all the volumes written by management experts on the topic since.

Nine things there are of which the superior man should be mindful:

- To be clear in vision
- Quick in hearing
- Genial in expression
- Respectful in demeanor
- True in world
- Serious in duty
- Inquiring in doubt
- Firmly self-controlled in anger
- Just and fair when the way to success opens out before him

Translated by William Jennings.[11]

15

Cashing Out

There is a tide in the affairs of men
Which, taken at the flood, leads on to fortune....

WILLIAM SHAKESPEARE
Julius Caesar

For most entrepreneurs, the time comes to cash out. In preparation for this eventuality, your long-term strategy should be to build the company itself into your highest-value-added product.

The reasons for wanting to cash out vary. For some, the real goal of building a company in the first place is to sell it to gain personal wealth and independence. Maybe they desire to pursue other business interests, travel, or retire. Maybe they do not desire to grow into managers of larger enterprises. Or maybe the business outgrows their management capabilities because they are like good field officers who are only at their best in the heat of combat and are ill-suited to the mundane activities of a peacetime army. Or, finally, some will foresee an untoward change coming, such as a formidable competitor or new technology, and have the sense to get out before the company has little value.

Whatever the reasons, the time finally comes to transfer the business to someone else in exchange for cash or cash equivalents. To succeed in building so much real value into a company that someone desires to own is, in itself, a notable achievement. Even more notable is to turn the buyer's desire into a reality by consummating a sale, giving you the option to be paid income for what you did (creating an ongoing, productive asset), as opposed to income for what you do (selling your time).

Much of this chapter is devoted to how a business is actually valued in preparation for a sale because it is important for you to understand how the decisions you make now, due to the tremendous power of the multiplier effect, will increase or decrease the value of your company in the future.

Myth and Reality

The best-known method of cashing out is to go public, that is, by selling stock on one of the stock exchanges, but that is because going public is so widely publicized, not because it is typical. For most owners and shareholders of high-tech companies, dreams of going public are like young boys' dreams of being professional football players: The fact is that many are called, but very few are chosen. Going public is reserved for an elite group of companies. In any one year, about 10 percent of the average venture capitalist's portfolio goes public. Even in a record year for initial public offerings (IPOs) such as 1992, the number of companies that go public is measured in the low hundreds. Obviously, fortunes will continue to be made through the magic of the stock market. If you were so fortunate as to hold a single share of Microsoft stock valued at $1 in 1981, it would be worth approximately $1500 today.

But the odds that your fortune will be made through the stock market are slim. The companies that go public have no missing ingredients, especially capital. VentureOne, a California-based venture capital company, conducted a study that found that on average companies raised approximately $21 million in private capital before they went public on Wall Street.[1] The process of going public is lengthy, grueling, and very expensive. Even a small $10 million offering can cost $100,000 in accounting fees, $150,000 in legal fees, and $100,000 in printing costs, in addition to as much as $1.5 million (15 percent of the offering) to the underwriter. Then, even if your company makes the passage from privately held to publicly traded, if you are an insider or major shareholder, your stock is subject to numerous restrictions that determine when and how you can convert your stock holdings into cash. The stock may be selling at an all-time high, but you are prohibited from liquidating your position to profit from it.

Very likely your fortune will be made through the more prosaic method used by most other owners and stockholders of closely held high-tech companies: to be acquired by a larger company or a group of private investors. Make no mistake, this method can be quicker, less risky, and much more lucrative.

What Buyers Are Buying

Large enterprises know that it is easier to acquire an ongoing enterprise than to start a new one. From your own experience, you should understand, as they do, that no large enterprise will match either your dedication to success or low overhead when it comes to product and market development. They know they can buy the innovations for which small companies are celebrated for a fraction of the amount it would cost them to undertake the equivalent effort within their own organizations.

As you engage in dialogues with potential buyers, you will not know exactly why they are buying. It may not be in their interest for you to know, although, within the limits of the law, you should try to find out by talking with their vendors, former employees, competitors, or consultants. Among the reasons may be:

- Access to complementary products to expand their sales

- Access to your distribution network for their products

- Access to your markets to leverage their technology

- An increase in income (increased earnings per share)

- Access to technical or management talent

- Increased utilization of their manufacturing capacity

Because you may not know their motives, you will not know what your business is really worth to them. Always remember that the buyer will value the business in light of what it believes it can make of it, not necessarily what you have made of it. A large, well-financed enterprise can find markets and applications beyond those you ever imagined. In the 1970s Bill Gates bought a computer operating system for $100,000 from a small company called Seattle Computer Products. The product he purchased was called Quick and Dirty Operating System, known by its acronym as QDOS. Gates turned QDOS into MS-DOS, then convinced IBM to use it in its first line of personal computers.[2] The rest, as they say, is history.

Becoming a Target for Acquisition

In order to have your company become a candidate for an acquisition, you must develop four selling features. First, the company must no longer be dependent on you. (In fact, you want to convey the impression to a potential buyer that the company would be worth more without you, for reasons explained shortly.) The arts and entertainment business has lots of one-person shows, but the artistry of a Picasso dies with him; likewise, a high-tech company's vision and/or technology can depart with the founders, and its value along with them. So you must recruit and nurture a talented and independent management and engineering team that will continue, in your absence, to innovate and compete effectively.

Second, you must have tangible products that incorporate sought-after knowledge. This knowledge must reside in documentation, drawings, circuits, formulae, and apparatus. Your trade secrets must be embodied and reproducible. They must be packageable, manufacturable, and serviceable. There really is no market for brilliant ideas, only brilliant products.

Third, you need an established customer base with demonstrated and continuing demand for your products. This is best evidenced by a strong sales history and a growing order backlog.

Fourth, you need to have total understanding of the financial details of your company. From the first pages of this book an emphasis has been placed on the paramount importance of accurate financial information. It is critical not only in operating a business but also in selling it. Once the decision to sell is made, you will begin to make financial changes to enhance the company's value in preparation for the buyer's valuation. With a total grasp of the financial details, you'll be much more effective protecting this value when it is challenged by the buyer and the buyer's agents, as it surely will be.

Timing and the Multiplier Effect

The buyer is purchasing a stream of expected future earnings. Therefore, in order to get top dollar, you want to cash out when your sales and profits are trending upward, not at the top, and certainly not when they are trending down. Because of the multiplier effect, timing is everything.

The multiplier effect is simply the product of a multiple, usually between 1 and 10 and based in large measure on future expectations, times your company's earnings. As you will discover later in this chapter, although businesses are valued based on lots of historical numbers and rational financial analysis, the final price will reflect a largely subjective, optimistic or pessimistic, view of what is likely to happen to your company and industry in the future. The trends the buyer sees will place either a premium or discount on the expected earnings.

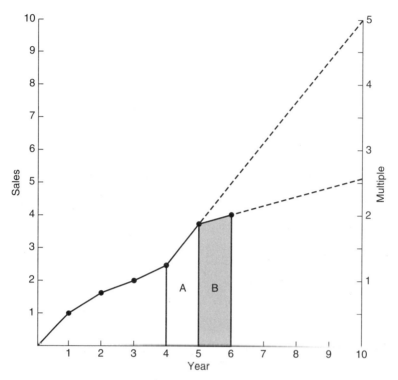

Figure 15-1. The multiplier effect is the product of a multiple times your company's earnings. This graph shows the relative impact of the multiplier effect on High Technology Inc.

This point is illustrated in Figure 15-1, showing the relative impact of multiple-based valuations made of the hypothetical HTI (High Technology Inc. from Chapter 7) during period A versus period B. The solid lines represent actual sales history, and the dotted lines are the extrapolations of future sales that will be made by a potential buyer. The multiples on the right axis reflect the relative weight a buyer will tend to give the higher earnings that result from the higher sales; these are only a gauge, not absolute values, but they are realistic and serve to show the critical importance of timing. The buyer's eyes will follow the solid actual sales into the dotted trend lines just like yours do because the buyer is buying future expectations, not the reality of the present. Of course, other historic and forecast industry and economic data will be gathered to confirm the probability of the dotted line, but the final multiple will primarily reflect a best guess of the future. The important lesson to derive from the illustration is that the price HTI sells at will be 25 to 50 percent higher because it is sold in period A rather than period B.

Selling a business takes time, usually a year or more. In view of this and the powerful influence of the multiplier effect, you should start preparations as early as possible to orchestrate the selling process so that the valuation of your business results in the highest attainable price.

Shifting Gears to Maximize Value

Typically, profits (earnings) shown on the income statement of a privately held company are understated in order to minimize the company's income taxes. All kinds of owner's compensation and perquisites for key managers such as cars, condos in Cancun for annual meetings, lawn mowers, home computers, airplanes, and other nonessential items are buried in the financial statements.

However, what worked well to reduce the IRS tax exposure works against you when its time to sell the business. The two most important elements in the valuation of a company are cash flow and real profits. You must weigh whether the modest pleasures of consumption today are worth far greater pleasures in the future. Once you have decided to sell, you must begin to restore the earnings that have been siphoned off back into the income statement and balance sheet because, due to the multiplier effect, $1 not spent today may be worth $10 only a year or two later. More to the point, a "company" Chevy today may cost you a Rolls-Royce on sale day.

Of course, the buyer will expect you to say the company is worth more than it appears to on paper. However, you won't be able to get away with a conspiratorial wink for your clever tax strategies at valuation time because it will be to the buyer's advantage that you showed the lowest possible profits—you will have inadvertently saved the buyer many thousands, perhaps millions, of dollars in payments to you. Indeed, the buyer will use your own tax returns to diminish the value of your company.

Establishing Value

Accurately valuing a closely held company is a complex process that requires expert advice. The term *closely held* encompasses most small corporations, partnerships, proprietorships, and even joint ventures.

As applied to a corporation, closely held means simply that there are relatively few shareholders and little, if any, trading in the stock occurs, so it is difficult to establish an objective fair market value. In the case of a large publicly traded enterprise like Microsoft, a crude valuation can be established on a given day by multiplying the outstanding shares by the price of the stock on the NASDAQ. The price of the stock reflects a large number of willing and informed buyers and sellers.

In contrast, the valuation of a privately held business boils down to the opinions of a few lawyers, accountants, and merger and acquisition (M&A) specialists, working in conjunction with the buyer and seller. The valuation is a calculated number that both sides use internally for their own purposes, e.g., to explore financing schemes or to determine an acceptable range of prices.

The techniques used to make a valuation vary depending on the purpose for which the valuation will be used. A valuation used to establish the replacement value of a business's assets for a hazard insurance policy differs from that which will be used by the IRS to determine estate taxes in probate or, for that matter, to buy out a shareholder or to spin off part of a company. Similarly, the valuation of a company for purposes of a bankruptcy liquidation is different from that of a going concern. The process described here is specifically designed for the purpose of establishing the value of a going enterprise in preparation for a sale.

The buyer will conduct a formal, detailed valuation of your business with the assistance of contracted or, if the buyer's company is large, staff professionals. You should conduct your own valuation as well. It should be no less rigorous and professionally documented. You will need the information from it to counterbalance the effects of the fear/greed factor that will come to play in the negotiations. Most of the time, for obvious reasons, the buyer will arrive at a valuation that is lower than yours. Your own valuation provides you hard evidence, at your fingertips, to prove value and maintain a psychological advantage in the seller-buyer interchange.

The Fear/Greed Factor

The fear/greed factor shapes all transactions. It will yours, too. For both sides, the sale represents potential opportunities and pitfalls, profits and losses, dreams and delusions.

The buyer dreams you have an asset that will grow money like a lawn grows grass. But she or he also fears that you are a liar and a trickster: You've concealed that there's a catastrophic lawsuit pending because of a personal injury to someone using the product or because the manufacturing process pollutes the environment; a new technology will be announced the day after the contract is signed that makes the products obsolete; the equipment is on the verge of falling apart; the inventory is worthless; your patents are unenforceable; an asteroid will hit the factory and destroy all the wealth-producing assets, especially the engineering talent, inside of it.

As the seller, you dream that the buyer will deliver a huge volume of cash, at least an oil tanker full, that will allow you to pay cash for a vacation home in Hawaii, a yacht (a big one) in Greece, etc., plus still leave many millions so you can live in conspicuous opulence and never have to work again. But you also fear that the buyer is inept or devious. The buyer will run the company into the ground and destroy your handiwork; six months after the sale is made, the check won't arrive in the mail; the contract for sale will have invisible print that allows the contract to be voided because of a clever legal subterfuge; the company is worth billions because the buyer knows something you don't so you're selling too soon and too cheap; the day after you get the big down payment check the asteroid will hit you.

To be sure, the established rituals of negotiation and participation of legal and financial professionals serve to dampen the extreme forms in which these emotions can express themselves, often to the degree that they kill the deal. Behind every interchange between the seller and buyer, the fear/greed factor is at work. It will be evident in the types of information both sides request (the buyer wants to see the BMW lease to make sure you get to pay for the rest of it), the contract stipulations (the buyer suspects you are still critical to the operation and wants you on-site for at least two more years), and financial terms (you want a large down payment when the deal is closed because you don't think the company will continue to perform financially without you).

Regardless of how many professionals fill supporting roles, the sale finally gets down to the decisions of two individuals—you and the buyer. You have to get the fear/greed factor under control and create some trust so you can structure a deal. If you are conscious of how it is influencing the negotiating process, it can work to your advantage—you'll be much more effective because you won't take the process too personally, even though it is.

Purging the Numbers

Aspects of the valuation will be tedious and, at times, even painful because every aspect of the business is subject to the closest possible scrutiny. The value, or lack thereof, of various assets will be challenged. Your management performance may be questioned. Therefore, throughout the process you must try to maintain your objectivity, not an easy task when you have worked hard to build a business and are on the verge of surrendering ownership.

When the balance sheet and income statements are examined by the buyer or agents, their supposition will be that the balance sheet is overstated and the income statement is understated. As such, they will dig into the numbers to prove their suspicions, then start making adjustments that lower the company's value. You should do the same, but begin months, even years earlier, before the buyer and agents ever see the statements, so that by the time they do, there is no basis for major adjustments. You will have already made them in order to increase your earnings and the multiplier effect. Some of the actions you take may actually reduce your earnings and equity in the short term but return many times in the long term; you will rob buyers of arguments to take the valuation even lower. Assume the buyer will be exacting and shrewd, so you won't be able to hide any waste or mismanagement. Apply the stringent logic of the buyer to your own numbers and adjust accordingly.

Items in the Balance Sheet

The following are items in the balance sheet:

Receivables—Slightly late accounts will be checked to see if they are likely to be paid. Very late ones will be written off, reducing your equity and reducing earnings on the income statement because what you showed as sales was not a completed sale. The receivables must be as current as possible when the valuation is made.

Inventory—Both finished assemblies and materials in support of bills of material for slow selling or dead products should be written off. If you can, sell them as scrap.

Unamortized development costs—These are only an asset if the product resulting from the development is selling so the expense can be amortized over the life of the product. If not, these should be written off.

Real estate—If you own a building, it will be separated and assessed at fair market value. However, the buyer probably will not be interested in paying a premium on it because his or her interest is in buying a technology company, not a real estate investment. Be prepared to separate it from the sale and, perhaps, offer to lease it to the buyer.

Equipment—A large investment in equipment does not necessarily enhance the value of a high-tech company. Buyers may be more interested in your company's people, processes, and products. They can get equipment anywhere at rock bottom prices at liquidation sales. Slow down capital purchases as you near the sale.

Items in the Income Statement

The following are some items in the income statement:

Officers' salaries—The buyer is well aware that you will be inclined to reward yourself with a generous (above-market) salary if you have labored to create a going concern. But a larger buyer will replace you with professional managers, whom they can pay less. Be ready to show what you or other principals were paid.

Sales—Buyers will examine your customer list. They will want to know if a disproportionate percentage of sales comes from only a few customers. If so, buyers will want to know more details about the present status of these, and probably they will communicate directly with them. A narrower customer base means higher risk. Buyers will look at gross trends over the years, asking for explanations of vacillations that are not economy dependent.

They will also check to find out whether there are any extraordinary items artificially inflating the sales figures, e.g., you sell off old equipment or a product line to another company and receive a one-time boost in income.

Items Related to Cash Flow

Cash flow will be as important to your buyer as it is to you. By examining the historic cash flow your company has been able to generate, then adding the additional cash flow the buyer expects to generate (buyers naturally assume they will get more out of businesses than owners have been able to—and sometimes they do), the buyer will estimate whether the cash can support his or her growth plans or will require more cash. Also, the buyer can see what cash will be available to structure an earn-out on your equity.

The existing annualized cash flow available to the buyer will be calculated as explained below:

Year-end pretax profit		$
Add:	Depreciation	+$
	Amortization	+$
	Excess salary	+$
	Other excesses	+$
	Interest and principal	+$
	Adjusted cash flow	$
Deduct:	Income tax on adjusted cash profit	-$
	Adjusted after-tax profit	$
Add:	Decrease in working capital	+$
	Sale of long-term assets	+$
Deduct:	Purchases of long-term assets	-$
	Increase in working capital	-$
	Net cash flow	$

The buyer will start with the year-end net profit you show on the income statement. Depreciation and amortization will be added back in, just as they are in your monthly cash flow statements, because they represent noncash expenses. (These were really paid in cash earlier when the assets were purchased and appear on your income statement as monthly expenses simply to conform with approved accrual accounting methods, which are intended to match revenues to expenses.) The salary excess, simply the difference between the salaries you pay yourself or other managers versus what the buyer would pay his or her managers is added back in. Excesses in other accounts discovered in the income statements will also be added back in. Finally, interest and principal payments will be added back in because the buyer will likely arrange her or his own financing. All these items are added to determine the adjusted pretax cash flow.

Nonfinancial Items

Though the issues below are not quantifiable, they are just as important to a potential buyer.

Litigation—You will have to disclose whether you have any pending or anticipated litigation such as patent infringement, nonperformance on a contract, or disputes with former employees. The final purchase contract will include a clause that you have made a full disclosure or otherwise the deal is void.

Patents and copyrights—The scope, strength, and term remaining for all intellectual property will be checked.

Employee agreements—To ensure that key managers or technical personnel are bound to the company, the buyer will need to see their employee agreements. The buyer will want an adequate level of innovation to ensure a steady stream of earnings. The buyer will also want to know that it will not be easy, if the employee does not like the change of ownership, to leave and go to work for a competitor.

How to Make Your Own Baseline Valuation

Once all the factors have been duly considered and weighed, they are reduced to a mathematical approximation of value. The actual method used will not be as simple as the oft-heard rules of thumb that your company's value is 1 times annual gross sales or the company's annual net profit times the average price earnings multiple of similar companies on the New York Stock Exchange (as if they really were similar).

In real practice, professional appraisers avail themselves of various combinations of discounted cash flow methods, book value, and earnings. The exact combination is determined by the size and age of a company and its industry.

Derivations of the six-step method presented here, in which several methods are combined into one, are widely used in the valuation of privately held companies. It is easy to put on a spreadsheet and, assuming you have good financial information, it will give you a solid rough-order-of-magnitude estimate of your company's value. You should make a periodic informal valuation of your company whether or not you intend to sell it. Even if selling is a distant goal, by understanding how the valuation is made, you will become more cognizant of how to create value.

Below, each of the six steps is explained, and then a simplified example follows that will clarify how to apply the method to your company.

Step 1. Calculate the adjusted after-tax profit each year for the company by taking the pretax net profit from the income statement and adding to it any excess salaries, perqs, and extravagances. Then apply the appropriate tax rate and deduct taxes from the profit. Enter this number on this line: (1) _____.

Step 2. Calculate net equity (assets minus liabilities) based on fair market value of the assets. The balance sheet will not necessarily show the real market value because it is based on historic costs and reflects your depreciation methods, which may or may not reflect real market value. For example, if you own a building, the balance sheet may show an inflated reduction in value because of tax depreciation when, in fact, the property has been appreciating because of increased demand for your location. Or you may have taken accelerated depreciation on some equipment that has more liquidation value than shown. Enter this number here: (2) _____.

Step 3. The net equity is the capital the company owns. This capital could be invested passively in any number of other investments that do not require the risks and headaches of capitalizing an operating, high-tech company. So you calculate a reasonable rate of return on a more conservative investment, say the one year T-bill rate plus 5 percent. Multiply this rate times the net equity from step 2 and enter the result here: (3) _____.

Step 4. Now the annual active operating income, the component of profits that result from a company being a going enterprise, is calculated by subtracting the figure from step 3 from the figure in step 2. Enter the result here: (4) _____.

Step 5. This is the most important step. The value of the stream of active operating income is calculated by adding two multiples: (a) the capitalization rate multiple, based on the near-term past, and, (b) the expected earnings multiple. The cap rate multiple is arrived at by applying a standard investment formula, which is expressed as

$$V = \frac{I}{R}$$

where V is the value of the investment
I is the active operating income
R is the capitalization rate

The capitalization rate is nothing more than the annualized rate of return an investor expects on a comparable investment, based on past performance and the assumption the past will be similar to the future. Typically the past three to five years of earnings are averaged. In the case of a high-tech company whose earnings can fluctuate, an investor would expect, at the very worst, a fairly high rate of return, say 20 to

25 percent. Usually, the capitalization rate is converted to its recipro-
cal and expressed as a multiple of earnings, e.g., $1/.20 = 5$, $1/.25 = 4$.
Therefore, if a company generates \$500,000 annually in active operat-
ing income and the investor expects a return of 20 percent, then the
value of the stream of incomes (ignoring discounted cash flows) is 5
times \$500,000, or \$2.5 million. Note that as the percentage goes up,
the multiple goes down, hence so does the value.

However, in the case of a company showing strong growth like HTI's
in the graph earlier in this chapter, where there is a reasonable expectation of increased earnings, an additional expected earnings multiple is
added to the cap rate multiple to arrive at a combined multiple. As
shown in the graph, the premium multiple ranges between 1 and 5. If
the earnings are growing over 25 percent per year, the premium multiple chosen could fall between 2 and 5. If earnings are growing less than
25 percent, the multiple will fall between 1 and 2. The number chosen is
based mainly on a subjective element—hope, conjecture, instinct, gut
feel, call it what you will.

Once you arrive at a combined multiple by adding the two, multiply it
by line (4). Enter this number here: (5) _____.

Step 6. To arrive at an approximate valuation, simply add the net tangible assets shown from step 2 to the value of the active operating
income shown in step 5 and enter it here: (6) _____.

As shown in the graph, High Technology, Inc. (HTI) has achieved
solid sales growth and financial performance as you can see from
highlights of its financial statements. To keep the example straightfor-
ward, the debt component of HTI's capitalization will be ignored.

	Year				
	1	2	3	4	5
Sales	\$1,000,000	\$1,750,000	\$2,000,000	\$2,400,000	\$3,750,000
EBT	100,000	175,000	200,000	240,000	375,000
Equity	200,000	350,000	400,000	480,000	750,000

Because of HTI's robust growth, only the last three years are used
to calculate average profit. The financial statements indicate that the
increased sales are due to the first phases of a solid, long-term contract
with some OEMs, not from selling off a major product line to another
company. Also, profits were approximately 5 percent higher than

shown because of excesses—a board of directors meeting in Cancun, some BMWs, a condo in Vail to entertain customers, a few expensive life insurance policies, etc.—that must be added back in. So the adjusted pretax income (assuming no interest) would be [(200,000 + 240,000 + 375,000) × 1.05]/3 or an average of $285,000 (rounded) per year. Figure that taxes would be 26 percent, so adjusted income would be $285,000 × 0.74 = $211,000 (rounded). This amount is recorded on line 1.

HTI's most recent balance sheet (year 5) shows a net equity of $750,000. Assume this reflects appropriate adjustments to show the fair market value of assets and enter this amount on line 2.

Figure that 10 percent is a fair passive rate of return on HTI's equity. That is what HTI could earn on the capital by putting it in a conservative mutual fund with little risk and no work, so take 10 percent of $750,000 and enter this number ($75,000) on line 3.

HTI's active operating income is $211,000 less $75,000. Enter the result—$136,000—on line 4.

To complete step 5, assume that 20 percent is the target cap rate, which translates to a 5 multiple. As shown on the graph, the growth prospects look good for a high-premium multiple. Research indicates the industry is forecast to be robust for at least a few more years. A multiple of 5 may be a little high, but certainly it's over 3, so say 4. The combined multiple then is 5 plus 4, which equals 9. Multiply 9 by the figure on line 4. Enter the result, $1,224,000, on line 5.

So one good estimate of HTI's base value is $750,000, its net equity, plus $1,224,000, the value of future income streams; enter this new figure—$1,974,000—on line 6.

Obviously, in this example, several important variables such as the passive interest rate, the cap rate multiple, and the expected earnings multiple have a profound effect on the value. When using this method, you can make only educated guesses that approximate how a much more involved professional appraisal is made.

However, if you follow this method, you will understand the multiplier effect—its dynamic dependence on timing and earnings. You will also be better able to help your professional selling team help you.

Making the Deal

The actual selling price is established by negotiation between you and the buyer and some combination of your respective agents. The buyer will focus on the records of the past and the risks of the future. You will focus on the achievements of the past and the opportunities of the future. Of course, the buyer believes in the future as well, or he or she would not be buying. Never forget this.

In establishing price, expect many factors to come into play that have nothing to do with the valuation. A significant factor is the financial structure of the deal, specifically, the methods used to give you your payoff. Very rarely does a transaction take place where the buyer hands you and the other shareholders a big check and you walk away. To some extent, the larger the check you receive at the time the deal is closed, the lower the price will be.

There are several reasons for this. Sophisticated buyers understand the present value of money. They will resist separating themselves from large sums of their own cash and will want to pay you with future depreciated dollars. They may also want to reduce their real cost by taking advantage of tax laws to treat as much of the transaction as possible as normal business expenses. Consequently, your deal may consist of some amount of money for the purchase of assets, some for a consulting contract, and still more for a noncompete agreement. Your payments may come indirectly from annuities or zero-coupon bonds, or there may be a royalty arrangement that allows the buyer to treat your payments as expenses and for you to treat them as capital gains. Assume the deal will not consist of a large, one-time wire transfer to your Swiss bank account.

Why to Use Professionals

The sale of your business is a momentous event. A persistent message throughout this book has been the importance of seeking outside assistance with specialized business activities that fall outside the scope of your expertise. For most readers of this book, nothing will fall more outside their expertise than the sale of their business. No matter how savvy you fashion yourself to be as a business person, you and your management will not be competent to negotiate and close this type of transaction. Neither will your company's lawyer and accountant. The sale will have enormous financial and legal implications for you, perhaps larger than any other single event in your life, so it is time to get the best professional assistance you can afford.

Remember that you'll likely be acquired by a larger company. If so, you may be sitting across the table from people who buy and sell between three and five companies per year. They are pros. You may sell a company once every 10 years or even once in a lifetime, so you are no match. Your selling team must include a mergers and acquisition (M&A) specialist, tax accountant, and lawyer. You need them all because there are times, as the buyer is duly diligent, that your pride can get compromised if you are too close to the effort, which can be detrimental to the deal. You definitely need to be involved and make the key decisions, but in a negotiation that takes months, different personalities and talents come to play at different intervals.

You can find M&A specialists from a number of directories such as *The Directory of M&A Intermediaries* (Venture Economics, New York). All the major accounting firms also have experts in this area.

M&A specialists will use an auction approach to selling your business. They know that talking with only one buyer may shorten or simplify the selling process, but also you may not end up with the highest possible price. They try to create a multiple bidding process with more than one serious potential buyer. Also, they will screen out flakes, curiosity seekers, and competitors who can waste your valuable time or take negative advantage of the pending sale to gain access to important information about your company.

If you do not use a lawyer referred by an M&A specialist or accounting firm, call around and find one experienced in selling businesses. You want a final contract that is binding, gives you swift recourse if the buyer fails to pay you, and protects you from letting the buyer run the company into the ground before you are paid off.

When everything is said and done, the professionals may cost you 10 to 15 percent of the deal, but their skills will generate a return far in excess of the costs to you. They know how to get top dollar and how to help you keep it. Use them. You want to play to your strengths and have the wisdom to use professionals to shore up your weaknesses. When it comes time to sell your company, you'll have worked too hard to leave money on the table.

The Final Act

When it comes time to cash out, you have only one last sale to make, one last transaction to complete. The financial and selling skills that have been developed through the arduous years of creating the enterprise must shine brightly one last time. The manner in which you lead the negotiations will have greater impact on your future than any technology you ever conceived. It's your finest moment as a technical entrepreneur, the culmination of all your efforts. Enjoy it. You made it across the high-tech high wire. You're home free.

Epilogue:
Are We Rich Yet?

> Companies that have risen to global leadership over the past 20 years
> invariably began with ambitions that were out of all proportion to
> their resources and capabilities. But they created an obsession with
> winning at all levels of the organization and then sustained that
> obsession over the 10- to 20-year quest for global leadership.
>
> GARY HAMEL AND C. K. PRAHALAD[1]

The answer is no, not yet. It took us six years to reach annual sales of
over $1 million, which meant we were short of forecast from our origi-
nal business plan by a factor of five. Today our prospects remain very
bright, but we do not expect to be featured on the cover of *Fortune* any
time soon.

We started DEI with many missing ingredients, which had to be
obvious from the anecdotes. Undercapitalization was a nagging problem; however, we were largely responsible for our capital plight.
Certainly, the impact of DEI's missing ingredients were further compounded by the effects of a precipitous decline in electronics caused by
defense cutbacks as well as a deep and protracted general recession.

The problems we encountered were foreshadowed in the original
business plan. It is enlightening to take a look back with the cold objectivity that comes with time.

From the beginning, the plan was unfocused in that it called for the
company to operate with two product groups, systems and components, serving multiple markets. Regis McKenna described DEI accurately when he wrote, "I've encountered many start-up companies that

focus on getting orders rather than on developing markets. They go after and get business in diverse and often unrelated markets, taxing their already limited resources."[2] A venture capitalist tried to warn us about this, but we had many counter-examples of success stories from electronics such as Hewlett-Packard and Motorola, to refute his arguments. Of course, our argument was groundless because companies like those became multiproduct, multimarket firms over a long period; they did not start that way.

However, if you are pioneering a new technology, focus is a two-edged sword. If you focus on the wrong opportunity, you increase risk rather than reduce it. If we had focused on some military applications that looked promising in the first two years of the company, we would have gone out of business. However, because we were not intimate with any particular market, it was easy to be infatuated by many. One looked as good as another.

In conformance to averages, like so many high-tech companies, we were too technology-driven (and still are, though less so). Our plan was riddled with techno babble, an unmistakable symptom. A short sampling of representative phraseology will suffice to make the point: "1 nanosecond switching times," "slew rates > 300 kilovolts per microsecond," "low inductance," "electro magnetic symmetry," "stripline technology," "deionization time after turn-off," "plasma shutter," and "alumina substrate." To evaluate the plan required the reader to be an electrical engineer with a deep background in the arcana of pulsed power electronics, a specialty of which literally 99 percent of the electrical engineering community is completely ignorant. Emphasis was given to dazzling specifications, breathtaking speeds, and ungodly power levels, all of which were intended to demonstrate an awe-inspiring control over the behavior of electrons through the ingenious manipulation of the laws of physics.

What was noticeably absent were concrete details as to the specific markets that needed our technology. In Edward Roberts' words, we proved that we could "do it better than anyone else" but forgot "to demonstrate that anyone wants it."[3] Complex markets were summarized by a sweeping generality that included "a broad range of industrial, medical, and military applications, including sonar, radar, telecommunications, lasers, particle accelerators, cancer treatment equipment, and nuclear instruments." Events would prove us partially right and partially wrong. The most erroneous words were "a broad range." As it turned out, the range was very narrow for the extremely high-speed, high-power technology, which was our manifest reason for existence.

The plan contained several assumptions that proved to be untrue, though they had an authoritative ring when written down. A major assumption was in the marketing section where we stated our technology "has numerous commercial applications." This really was a hypothesis, not a fact, and should have been posed as a question: "Does the know-how...have numerous commercial applications?" In reality, commercial applications for this technology were few and far between. Almost all were military applications, which should come as no surprise, because defense demand consumed almost 40 percent of U.S. electronics at the time.

The original plan made scant mention of the names of potential customers or competitors because we did not really know who they were. As competitors for our components, we named International Rectifier and Motorola because they were major manufacturers of MOSFETs. However, in this we truly flattered ourselves, because few of their products were vulnerable to replacement by ours. The entire DE Series product line would amount to fewer than 6 pages of one of their 3-inch-thick product catalogs.

The marketing plan for systems was treated like an afterthought. We outlined the specifications for two pulse generators that could be used in linear accelerators and lasers. Again, not a single customer name was mentioned. Ironically, it turned out that the products proposed for lasers, a growing industry at the time, were not fast enough. One of the products described proved to be useful in accelerators, but in very low volumes. We included electronic testing as an application for our technology but did not say exactly what would be tested. Ironically, this application did occur, but in testing a semiconductor product of which we had scant knowledge.

When it came to sales and distribution, the plan was equally vague. Mention was made of reps and distributors for the MOSFET. However, as we spent more time in the market with the device, it became obvious that the engineering support required for the sale made it almost impossible for the average rep to sell. Furthermore, the long market gestation inherent in a pioneering technology did not generate a fast enough payback for most reps. To make the sale even more difficult, we were reluctant to reveal information that would make the DE Series MOSFET easier to sell because it would diffuse information we considered proprietary to systems we planned to manufacture. This was self-defeating because you cannot sell a pioneering technology without an extensive effort to educate the customer base, sharing everything you know. Every bit of information you are able to provide feeds the imagination of the customer, and it is the customer's imagination that will create the product that drives demand for your product.

With regard to pricing, the plan commented that the "unique features of the DE Series will command premium prices." To an extent this was true, but what we failed to point out was that a high price for the device would also restrict its potential acceptance. We confidently speculated what we could get the price down to in volume at a contract assembly house. The number was off by at least a factor of two because we did not have hands-on experience with the various processing steps required to make the devices, the cost of the equipment, or the cost of materials. We were very much like the architect who designs a beautiful house and who knows it is buildable but has little idea of either what it will actually cost or the practical problems the carpenter, plumbers, or electricians might encounter in trying to build it.

The plan mentioned markets, such as power conversion, which were completely outside the ken of the company's expertise in pulsed power electronics. In reality, some segments of power conversion could benefit from the technology, but not for the reasons we touted. Power conversion could not utilize the device's speed, which we believed was the key selling feature. Theoretically, it was true that fast switching would reduce circuit losses and make switch-mode power supply designs more efficient. However, having little experience in switch-mode design, we did not know that the supporting electronics, such as diodes and magnetics, did not exist to support power transistors at these speeds.

The plan spelled out a clever R&D strategy that called for DEI to use government contracts to subsidize the development of our standard products for wider commercial and medical applications. The problem with this strategy, as we came to discover, was that the government agencies, such as the DOD or DOE, rarely had requirements for products with any commercial potential.

How, you might ask, did we find ourselves so far off the mark? It was easy. We lacked direct experience in most of the markets we targeted, which is evident when you look at the biographies of the founders. Actually, had we been familiar with the defense market, we would have seen that defense was headed for a freefall. Quiet cutbacks actually began in 1987, the same year the company was started. To our credit, we noted military use of the DE Series could be as high as 50 to 60 percent of sales. This was not far off, but it turned out to be more like 75 to 80 percent, an important difference when the drastic defense cuts began to occur.

The statement was made that the founders had "considerable experience in high technology product engineering, sales and marketing, and administration." This was true on its face, but our experience was not optimum for the markets that were to be addressed. High technology is hardly a homogeneous market. The number of niches is enormous.

Though it seems glaringly obvious now, our plan showed no recognition that we lacked market knowledge. On the contrary, the plan assumed the existing management team had the marketing savvy to develop the company to a point where its next key management requirements would be for a financial officer and manufacturing manager. This was a gross oversight. What the company really needed, from its first day, were seasoned sales and marketing professionals from the markets to which our products were directed. This lack of understanding led us to make investments in technology development rather than in market development. Too often marketing expenses were treated like they were discretionary rather than absolutely necessary. But we discovered it is counterproductive to feed the engineering costs of new product developments by starving the efforts to sell the existing products.

Finally, and most importantly, we underestimated the amount of time required to gain acceptance in a market. It is a slow process. There is little that can be done to hurry the process, and it is easy to waste resources trying.

These are some of the many reasons that we did not get to $5 million in sales in five years. To be sure, given the number of missing ingredients in our organization, it might seem a miracle that we exist at all.

But, in our defense, we also did many things right. First and foremost, we learned fast. As we learned, we began to make the adjustments in every facet of the company, from the way we interacted with customers to how we structured the financial transactions with them. Much of what we learned is presented in this book.

We were, and remain, a pioneering technology company. Our technical staff has managed to develop an array of exciting, high-power technology applications in extremely short time frames and on ridiculously small budgets. Few larger companies could boast such a high degree of engineering productivity. True, the ultimate monetary potential of the technology remains to be seen, but it already serves in diverse applications and locations throughout the world in radar, semiconductor testing, and electro-optics. We are following some of our large defense customers as they migrate from military applications to commercial ones. These customers intend to apply the same technology used in target acquisition and isotope separation to collision avoidance systems in automobiles and new lithography systems to enable sub-sub-micron geometries in future generations of super-high-density memory chips. And, using the marketing lessons of Venus's flytraps, we're finding new customers who are looking for an advantage because they are competing for their lives in rough-and-tumble industrial markets such as induction heating, thin-film processing, and communications, all far removed from our original customer base in the pristine labs conducting Cold War research. To adapt to the new high-tech business environment, our technologists are learning to fret as much about cost as they did performance.

The founding team lacked some business skills, but finance and administration were not among them. From the very beginning, we tightly controlled cash. We knew where it was going and when it was coming in. We always knew what our inventory was with a high degree of accuracy. We tried, not always successfully, to avoid fixed costs unless we could see that the cash would be there to support them. Projects were tracked to see whether they were coming in on budget. If one was over budget because of unforeseen technical problems, we made cuts elsewhere or delayed expenditures. We assiduously maintained accurate, up-to-date financial statements so that a banker or potential investor could always trust the business side of the company, even though the technology side might remain a mystery.

Despite recessions and federal cutbacks, the company is growing and profitable. There's money in the bank and always a small order backlog that will carry us for a few months. But we are hardly complacent. We are still up on the high wire, where business conditions change quickly. And there's no escaping the paradigm wars.

Although we have yet to generate fast growth and big returns, those remain our aspirations. Slowly we are making the investments to fill in our missing ingredients. Soichiro Honda once said, "I don't think anyone can make a prediction about his own destiny." Neither, really, can a company. We used to spend lots of time trying, but we don't as much anymore. We are optimistic about the future, but above all else we are pragmatists who are determined to survive in the present.

Things take time. A high-technology business is a long throw of the dice that tumbles through the years. As long as you're in the game, you have a chance. That's the thrill of it.

Notes

Chapter 1

1. Robert Reich, *The Work of Nations* (New York: Vintage Books, 1992), p. 85.
2. Edward Roberts, *Entrepreneurs in High Technology: Lessons from MIT and Beyond* (New York: Oxford University Press, 1991), p. 141.
3. Gerald Gunderson, *The Wealth Creators: The Entrepreneurial History of the United States* (New York: Penguin Books, 1989), p. 179.

Chapter 2

1. Michael Porter, *Competitive Advantage: Creating and Sustaining Superior Performance* (New York: Free Press, 1985), p. 165.
2. David Birch, "Live Fast, Die Young," *Inc.*, August 1988, p. 24.
3. Peter Drucker, *Innovation and Entrepreneurship: Practices and Principles* (New York: Harper and Row, 1985), p. 125.
4. Thomas Kuhn, *The Structure of Scientific Revolutions* (Chicago: University of Chicago Press, 1962), p. 4.
5. Ibid., p. 7.
6. Ibid., p. 64.
7. "Gene Dreams Deferred," *U.S. News and World Report,* September 24, 1990, p. 68.
8. George Guilder, *Microcosm: The Quantum Revolution in Economics and Technology* (New York: Simon and Schuster, 1989), p. 106.
9. John Diebold, *The Innovators: The Discoveries, Inventions, and Breakthroughs of Our Time* (New York: Truman Tally, 1990), p. 88.
10. Kenichi Ohmae, *The Mind of the Strategist: Business Planning for Competitive Advantage* (New York: Penguin Books, 1983), pp. 201–202.
11. Charles Ferguson, "Computers and the Coming of the U.S. Keiretsu," *Harvard Business Review,* July–August 1990, p. 57.
12. Paul Solman and Thomas Friedman, *Life and Death on the Corporate Battlefield:*

How Companies Win, Lose, Survive (New York: Simon and Schuster, 1982), pp. 97 98.

13. Steven Schnaars, *Megamistakes: Forecasting and the Myth of Rapid Technological Change* (New York: The Free Press, 1989), pp. 129, 135, 137.

14. Andy Kessler, "Textbook," *Upside,* November 1990, p. 67.

Chapter 3

1. Orivis Collins and David Moore with Darab Unwalla, *The Enterprising Man* (East Lansing, Mich.: Michigan State University Press, 1964), pp. 242–243.

2. "Speedier Drugs," *The Economist,* December 7, 1991, p. 18.

3. "Reinventing America," *Business Week,* 1992 Bonus Issue, p. 185.

4. Birch, "Live Fast," p. 23.

Chapter 4

1. David Scheff, "Don Valentine Interview Part Two," *Upside,* June 1990, p. 72.

2. Roberts, *Entrepreneurs,* p. 200.

3. Gunderson, *Wealth Creators,* p. 176.

4. Ibid., p. 177.

5. Arthur Lipper, *Venture's Financing and Investing in Private Companies* (Chicago: Probus Publishing Company, 1988), p. 83.

6. Stanley Rich and David Gumpert, *Business Plans That Win $$$: Lessons from the MIT Enterprise Forum* (New York: Harper and Row, 1985), pp. 19–20.

7. Birch, "Live Fast," p. 24.

8. "Venture Capital in the '90s: What's Hot and What's Not," *Upside,* September 1991, p. 101; "VC Consolidation," *Upside,* August/September 1990, p. 12; Robert Stavers, James D. Atwell, Brian Goncher, "Venture Capital Analysis: Not as Bad as You Think," *Upside,* November 1991, pp. 115–121; "Even Hotshot Startups Are Feeling the Chill," *Business Week,* December 2, 1991, p. 136.

9. "The Capital Formation Drought," *Upside,* October 1990, p. 42.

10. Drucker, *Innovation,* p. 29.

Chapter 5

1. Charles Handy, *The Age of Unreason* (Boston: Harvard Business School Press, 1989), p. 55.

2. Abraham Maslow, *Motivation and Personality* (New York: Harper and Row, 1954), pp. 80–106.
3. "Emerging Entrepreneur," *Inc.,* December 1992, p. 95.
4. Regis McKenna, *The Regis Touch: New Marketing Strategies for Uncertain Times* (Reading, Mass.: Addison Wesley, 1985), p. 27.
5. William Davidow, *Marketing High Technology* (New York: The Free Press, 1986), p. 141.
6. Peter Drucker, *Managing for Results* (New York: Harper and Row, 1964), p. 11.

Chapter 6

1. "Reinventing America," p. 185.
2. John Argenti, *Corporate Collapse: The Causes and Symptoms* (New York: Wiley, 1976). The observations in this chapter are derived primarily from Chapters 7 and 8.

Chapter 7

1. Harold Geneen, *Managing* (Garden City, N.Y.: Doubleday, 1984), p. 37.
2. Richard White, *The Entrepreneur's Manual: Business Start-ups, Spin-offs, and Innovative Management* (Radnor, Penn.: Chilton, 1977), p. 36.
3. Theodore Levitt, *The Marketing Imagination* (New York: The Free Press, 1983), p. 115.
4. *The Best of Inc.: Guide to Business Strategy* (New York: Prentice Hall, 1988), p. 29.

Chapter 8

1. Drucker, *Innovation,* p. 194.
2. Richard Foster, *Innovation: The Attacker's Advantage* (New York: Summit Books, 1986), p. 105.

Chapter 9

1. Davidow, *Marketing High Technology,* p. 138.
2. Drucker, *Innovation,* p. 191.
3. Davidow, *Marketing High Technology,* p. 38.

Chapter 10

1. Gary Hamel and C. K. Prahalad, "Corporate Imagination and Expeditionary Marketing," *Harvard Business Review,* July–August 1991, p. 87.
2. Davidow, *Marketing High Technology,* p. 152
3. Hamel and Prahalad, "Corporate Imagination," p. 85.
4. Ibid., p. 87.
5. Schnaars, *Megamistakes,* p. 172.
6. McKenna, *Regis Touch,* p. 48.
7. Ibid., p. 8.

Chapter 11

1. Hamel and Prahalad, "Corporate Imagination," p. 87.
2. Roberts, *Entrepreneurs,* p. 182.
3. William Taylor, "The Business of Innovation: An Interview with Paul Cook," *Harvard Business Review,* March–April 1990, p. 104.
4. Robert Miller and Stephen Heiman, *Conceptual Selling* (New York: Warner Books, 1987), p. 67.
5. Mack Hanan, *Key Account Selling* (New York: AMACOM, 1989), p. 11.
6. Ibid., p. 73.
7. Levitt, *Marketing Imagination,* p. 117.
8. Drucker, *Managing for Results,* p. 10.
9. Gary Hamel and C. K. Prahalad, "The Core Competence of the Corporation," *Harvard Business Review,* May–June 1990, p. 82.
10. Foster, *Innovation: The Attacker's Advantage,* p. 191.

Chapter 12

1. McKenna, *Regis Touch,* p. 77.

Chapter 13

1. Reich, *Work of Nations,* p. 244.
2. "Selective Realism," *The Economist,* January 9, 1993, p. 59.
3. "Washington Watch," *Export Today,* November/December 1992, p. 8.

Chapter 14

1. George Guilder, *Microcosm: The Quantum Revolution in Economics and Technology* (New York: Simon and Schuster, 1989), pp. 113–114.

2. Robert Bendit, "Working with the Entrepreneur," in *Entrepreneurship and Venture Management,* ed. C. Burnback and J. Mancuso (Englewood Cliffs, N.J.: Prentice Hall, 1987), p. 398.

3. Manfred F.R. Kets de Vries, "The Dark Side of Entrepreneurship," *Harvard Business Review,* November–December 1985, p. 162.

4. Hodges Golson, "The Technically-Oriented Personality in Management," *IEEE Transactions on Engineering Management,* vol. EM-32, no. 1, February 1985, p. 35.

5. Argenti, *Corporate Collapse,* p. 123.

6. Roberts, *Entrepreneurs,* pp. 180–182.

7. David Dreman, *The New Contrarian Investment Strategy* (New York: Random House, 1980), pp. 261–262.

8. Alan Tripp, *Millions from the Mind* (New York: AMACOM, 1992), p. 57.

9. Erik Larson, "Patent Pending," *Inc.,* March 1989, p. 105.

10. Donald Clifford Jr. and Richard Cavanagh, *The Winning Performance: How America's Midsize Growth Companies Succeed* (New York: Bantam Books, 1985), p. 89.

11. "The Confucian Analects," in *Classics in Chinese Philosophy,* ed. W. Baskin (Totowa, N.J.: Littlefield, Adams and Company, 1974), p. 25.

Chapter 15

1. David T. Gleba, "Garage to Wallstreet," *Upside,* August 1992.

2. "Microsoft's Web of Fear," *The Economist,* January 9, 1993, p. 58.

Epilogue

1. Gary Hamel and C. K. Prahalad, "Strategic Intent," *Harvard Business Review,* May–June 1989, p. 64.

2. McKenna, *Regis Touch,* p. 45.

3. Roberts, *Entrepreneurs,* p. 199.

Bibliography

Baskin, W. *Classics in Chinese Philosophy.* Totowa, N.J.: Littlefield, Adams and Company, 1974.

Baumback, C., and Mancuso, J. *Entrepreneurship and Venture Management.* Englewood Cliffs, N.J.: Prentice Hall, 1987.

Blackman, Irving. *The Valuation of Privately Held Businesses: State-of-the-Art Techniques for Buyers, Sellers, and Their Advisors.* Chicago: Probus Publishing Company, 1986.

Clifford, D., Jr., and Cavanagh, R. *The Winning Performance: How America's Midsize Growth Companies Succeed.* New York: Bantam Books, 1985.

Davidow, William. *Marketing High Technology.* New York: The Free Press, 1986.

Diebold, John. *The Innovators: The Discoveries, Inventions, and Breakthroughs of Our Time.* New York: Truman Telley Books, 1990.

Dreman, David. *The New Contrarian Investment Strategy.* New York: Random House, 1980.

Drucker, Peter. *Managing for Results.* New York: Harper and Row, 1964.

Drucker, Peter. *Innovation and Entrepreneurship: Practice and Principles.* New York: Harper and Row, 1985.

Foltz, R., and Penn, T. *Protecting Engineering Ideas and Inventions,* 3d ed. Cleveland: Penn Institute, 1989.

Foster, Richard. *Innovation: The Attacker's Advantage.* New York: Summit Books, 1986.

Geneen, Harold. *Managing.* Garden City, N.Y.: Doubleday, 1984.

Guilder, George. *Microcosm: The Quantum Revolution in Economics and Technology.* New York: Simon & Schuster, 1989.

Gunderson, Gerald. *The Wealth Creators: The Entrepreneurial History of the United States.* New York: Penguin Books, 1989.

Hanan, Mack. *Key Account Selling.* New York: AMACOM, 1989.

INC. Magazine Editorial Staff. *The Best of Inc.: Guide to Business Strategy.* New York: Prentice Hall, 1988.

Johnson, H., and Kaplan, R. *Relevance Lost: The Rise and Fall of Management Accounting.* Boston: Harvard Business School Press, 1987.

Kuhn, Thomas. *The Structure of Scientific Revolutions.* Chicago: University of Chicago Press, 1962.

Levitt, Theodore. *The Marketing Imagination.* New York: The Free Press, 1983.

Lewis, Jordan. *Partnerships for Profit: Structuring and Managing Strategic Alliances.* New York: The Free Press, 1990.

Lindsey, Jennifer. *Joint Ventures & Corporate Partnerships.* Chicago: Probus Publishing Company, 1989.

Lipper, Arthur. *Venture's Financing and Investing in Private Companies: A Guide to Understanding Entrepreneurs and Their Relationships with Investors, Lenders and Advisors.* Chicago: Probus Publishing Company, 1988.

Malone, Michael. *Going Public: MIPS Computer and the Entrepreneurial Dream.* New York: Harper Collins, 1991.

McKenna, Regis. *The Regis Touch: New Marketing Strategies for Uncertain Times.* Reading, Mass.: Addison Wesley, 1985.

Miller, Donald. *The Meaningful Interpretation of Financial Statements: The Cause and Effect Ratio Approach.* New York: AMA, 1966.

Miller, R., and Heiman, S. *Strategic Selling.* New York: Warner Books, 1985.

Miller, R. and Heiman, S. *Conceptual Selling.* New York: Warner Books, 1987.

Milling, Bryan. *Cash Flow Problem Solver.* Radnor, Penn.: Chilton, 1981.

Ohmae, Kenichi. *The Mind of the Strategist: Business Planning for Competitive Advantage.* New York: Penguin Books, 1984.

Peters, Tom. *Liberation Management: Necessary Disorganization for the Nanosecond Nineties.* New York: Alfred A. Knopf, 1992.

Porter, Michael. *Competitive Advantage: Creating and Sustaining Superior Performance.* New York: The Free Press, 1985.

Reich, Robert. *The Work of Nations.* New York: Vintage Books, 1991.

Rich, S. and Gumpert, D. *Business Plans that Win $$$: Lessons from the MIT Enterprise Forum.* New York: Harper & Row, 1985.

Roberts, Edward. *Entrepreneurs in High Technology: Lessons from MIT and Beyond.* New York: Oxford University Press, 1991.

Schnaars, Steven. *Megamistakes: Forecasting and the Myth of Rapid Technological Change.* New York: The Free Press, 1989.

Solman, P., and Friedman, T. *Life and Death on the Corporate Battlefield: How Companies Win, Lose, Survive.* NY: Simon & Schuster, 1982.

Tripp, Alan R. *Millions from the Mind: How to Turn Your Invention or Someone Else's into a Fortune.* New York: AMACOM, 1992.

White, Richard, Jr., *The Entrepreneur's Manual: Business Start-ups, Spin-offs, and Innovative Management.* Radnor, Penn.: Chilton, 1977.

Index

About the Author

David Adamson is president of Directed Energy, Inc., a manufacturer of modulator electronics for lasers, radar, and semiconductor test equipment that earns $1 million in annual sales. He cofounded this company in 1987, and has also been involved in two software company start-ups. A frequent speaker on high technology and international trade, Mr. Adamson has written for *Managing Technology Today* and publishes *Growth Notes*, a monthly management newsletter. Appointed by the Secretary of Commerce, Mr. Adamson was a member of the U.S. District Export Council.